The Public Garden

Architecture International Rotterdam
NAi Publishers

The Enclosure and Disclosure of the Public Garden

CONTENTS

INTRODUCTION

Breeze of AIR, Innovative concepts for urban gardens in Rotterdam ANNE-MIE DEVOLDER 9

THE CHALLENGE

The Enclosed Garden ADRIAAN VAN DER STAAY 19

Hortus Conclusus: the law of the garden ERIK DE JONG 29

Weak Boundaries IVAN NIO 38

Four Shades of Green ERIC LUITEN & FRANK DE JOSSELIN DE JONG 44

DESIGNERS' PROPOSALS

The Lijnbaan gardens HARGREAVES ASSOCIATES 52

Central Station area ATELIER QUADRAT 58

The inner garden of Boijmans Van Beuningen Museum CHARLES CORREA 66

Rooftop of Las Palmas KAZUYO SEJIMA & RYUE NISHIZAWA – SANAA 72

Arboretum Trompenburg WEST 8 80

Hofplein viaduct – Agniesebuurt GROSS.MAX. 88

Valkeniersweide KAMEL LOUAFI 96

Spinoza park PIET OUDOLF 104

Museum Park – Het Park GEORGES DESCOMBES 112

ARTISTS' PROJECTS

360° Oasis TERESITA FERNÁNDEZ 122

Placebo: Compass Room ANTHONY DUNNE & FIONA RABY 124

Afwerkplaats voor kleine wagens DENNIS ADAMS 126

Iride MAURA BIAVA 128

Onder-tussen II ZEGER REYERS 130

Untitled (Travel Agency) CRISTINA IGLESIAS 132

I never promised you a rose garden MICHAEL ELMGREEN & INGAR DRAGSET 134

Two Trees III CILDO MEIRELES 136

AFTERTHOUGHTS

Nature, Art and the City TANJA ELSTGEEST 141

Park, Garden, Rotterdam MARC TREIB 146

Afterthoughts from Istanbul TURGUT CANSEVER 152

Urban Parks in Europe: topology and geometry, economics and aesthetics KEN WORPOLE 156

The Urban Garden as Public Space IVAN NIO 161

Prelude to a new understanding of garden design ERIK DE JONG 167

AIR - A BRIEF CHRONOLOGY 170

PERSONALIA 172

CREDITS 174

6

The Public Garden

The Public Garden

Introduction

1. The seventeenth-century French expression 'se jardiner' means something like 'to get a breath of fresh air'.
2. This event took place from April 28 to July 1, 2001, at various locations in Rotterdam as part of the 'Rotterdam is many cities' programme in the context of Rotterdam 2001, Cultural Capital of Europe. This text was written in February 2002.
3. This essay appeared in *De ontwerpopgaven, vernieuwende concepten voor stadstuinen in Rotterdam*, AIR Foundation, October 2000. See also 'De tuin als dialoog met de natuur', the opening lecture given by Adriaan van de Staay at the start of the event, published in *OASE*, no. 56 (2001).
4. In late 1999 a working party commissioned by the board of the AIR Foundation and chaired by Anne-Mie Devolder, the Foundation's director, prepared the initial memorandum for the seventh edition of AIR. Those taking part were Paul Achterberg, landscape architect (Atelier Quadrat); Henk Hartzema, urban designer (West 8 landscape architects); Erik de Jong, architectural historian (Vrije Universiteit, Amsterdam), Piet de Jonge, curator of modern art (Boijmans Van Beuningen Museum); Eric Luiten, landscape architect (Academy of Architecture, Amsterdam); and Christian Zalm, landscape architect (Urban Planning and Public Housing Department, Rotterdam).
The programme of the event was directed by the Breeze of AIR advisory committee for programming. Chaired by Anne-Mie Devolder, this otherwise consisted of Joost van Hezewijk, landscape architect and visual artist (visual arts adviser to the Government Buildings Agency, Government Architect's office); Frank de Josselin de Jong, landscape architect (H+N+S Landschapsarchitecten); Eric Luiten, landscape architect (Academy of Architecture, Amsterdam); Nadia Mabrouk (director, Euromed Foundation); Ivan Nio, sociologist (urban researcher, Amsterdam); and Erik de Jong, architectural historian (Vrije Universiteit, Amsterdam).
5. See *De ontwerpopgaven*, AIR Foundation, 'Vraagstellingen en thema's' (unpublished).
6. See Luiten and de Josselin de Jong in this publication, p. 44 onwards.
7. The basis for this was the municipal memorandum *De Recreatieve stad* (The Recreational City) of 1999, in which these policy resolutions were explained. In the preliminary study *Tuin-Park-Bos-Landschap* (Garden-Park-Wood-Landscape) by Eric Luiten for the 'Rotterdam Spatial Plan 2010', an (urban) garden was defined as follows: a very definitely bounded green space that can be completely or partially closed off, without express anchoring in the urbanistic sense, established with a single function or theme and changeable over time, with a cultivated, well-tended, intensively managed character and weekly maintenance schedules (trimming and sweeping); the experience of symbolic, manipulated nature or group utilization of serviceable nature is the main priority; its publicness is generally subject to certain conditions based on responsibilities that are contracted out; its use depends on the season; its users are members and interested parties who wish to take an active part, or visiting strollers.
The memorandum *Ruimtelijk Plan Rotterdam 2010* (Rotterdam Spatial Plan 2010) was published in 2000. This introduced a new typology for Rotterdam's green space that met the wishes for a better use and differentiation of that space. The plan proposes that in the future four clear categories be used: city gardens, city parks, city woods (and pools) and finally city landscapes. This typology covers the range of desirable green urban spaces and gives pointers for the apportionment or reapportionment of financial, programmatic and managerial resources at city level.

ANNE-MIE DEVOLDER

Breeze of AIR
Innovative concepts for urban gardens in Rotterdam

A breeze refreshes. Relaxing in gardens and parks allows one forget the busy, suffocating and raucous life of the city for a moment.[1]

Under the title Breeze of AIR, the AIR Foundation (Architecture International Rotterdam) organized an interdisciplinary event on the subject of the public garden.[2] Designers examined whether urban green space can be made more distinctive, more expressive and more accessible by introducing the typology of the hortus conclusus, the enclosed garden. Artists explored the concept of the hortus conclusus for the modern city. Through research, design, debate and publications, Breeze of AIR has generated new visions of urban development in which public gardens can play a key role.

Hortus Conclusus

The essay 'Hortus Conclusus', written by Adriaan van der Staay,[3] formed the inspiration for the theme of Breeze of AIR. In it, van der Staay approaches the issues he raises from a cultural-historical perspective. The reintroduction of the hortus conclusus resumes a long tradition of enclosed gardens in the Netherlands, even as they are gradually disappearing from the cityscape. Whether updating the hortus conclusus type might also offer solutions for the associated problems of design, management, maintenance and use of urban green space, became a leading premiss for the research, design and debate of Breeze of AIR.[4] This spawned a number of sociological observations on the introduction of the enclosed garden in a contemporary urban context.[5] Several dilemmas were deemed relevant for investigation within the framework of the event. Five were identified: the significance and use of the garden (between seeing and using); semi-public status (between privatization and urbanization); new forms of management (between government and private parties); the garden between nature and culture; and the garden as part of a network as against its place-making capacities. This analysis expanded both the number and variety of design sites for a public city garden.

Urban green space

In Rotterdam the surface area devoted to public green space has increased enormously in recent decades. During the post-World War II reconstruction, planners made inventories of the perceived need for greenery in the daily living environment of the modern city-dweller, which was then translated primarily into quantitative objectives. Rotterdam now boasts the most green space per capita of all the large cities in the Randstad area. Yet the qualitative development of all that greenery has largely been neglected, with the result that Rotterdam is not regarded as a green city. Whereas creating an urban park was once an expression of high culture, since the 1960s and 70s the planning of urban green space has become part of the spatial articulation of a growing city.[6] These days green space is planned as a noise buffer, a ground cover for a filled waste dump or for land with highly contaminated soil, or as compensation for urban sprawl. Save for the woodlands of Kralingse Bos, Het Park and Zuiderpark, the greater part of Rotterdam's green space must be rated as a uniform entity that lends the city neither sufficient opportunity for expression nor quality as a place to live in or visit. In short, the quality, accessibility, attractiveness and distinctiveness of Rotterdam's urban green space must be improved and better differentiated.[7]

[fig. 1]
Working visit by Go Kuwata and Kazujo Sejima to Las Palmas, 31 August 2000

[fig. 2]
Working visit by Adriaan Geuze (right) to Arboretum Trompenburg, 13 September 2000

[fig. 3]
Working visit by Kamel Louafi to Valkeniersweide, 28 September 2000

[fig. 4]
Working visit by Piet Oudolf to the Spinoza park, 2 October 2000

[fig. 5]
George Hargreaves talking with residents and wardens of Lijnbaanhoven, 9 October 2000

Garden design

The making of gardens is one of the most important historical mainstays of landscape architecture. Until the beginning of the twentieth century, garden design was also one of the most prominent forms of cultural production. Many private gardens were open to the public. Examples in Rotterdam include Het Park and nearby Park Schoonoord, the Erasmus University garden and Arboretum Trompenburg.

As regards Dutch garden design, the garden was an essential part of the city from a historical perspective, yet in modern urban planning it could not count on continuity as a cultural given. The bombed-out centre of Rotterdam was rebuilt according to modernist principles in which the intimate space of the garden no longer figured. Moreover, two complementary movements have emerged in the last several decades. On the one hand the ownership, layout and maintenance of a private garden has largely been stripped of its elitist character. On the other, the private garden laid out entirely in accordance with an architectural design has become an exception. Contemporary garden design is now pursued in the service of companies wishing to see their corporate identity underscored by a beautifully conceived garden.[8] These private gardens, which function as semi-public areas, can do much to boost public space in the city.

Interestingly, the current reappraisal of garden culture seems to be proceeding in concert with an increasing dynamic in the city itself. As the city gets more hectic, crowded and noisy, so there seems to be more of a need for urban oases offering peace, quiet and contemplation.

Sites and designers

So as to seriously launch a debate about innovative forms of design, management and use of urban green space and precipitate a change in the way we think about it, nine sites were selected for Breeze of AIR as the focus for the event and a design brief was drawn up.[9] The idea was to actively boost the quality of public green space through a number of interventions spread across the city. In selecting the sites, the diversity informing the addressed issues was met by differentiation as to the type of design brief, the client, the location in the city, the catalytic function and the exemplary role for urban areas elsewhere in the Netherlands. The use of the garden, the degree of semi-public status, the various forms of management, the different relationships between nature and culture, and the garden as place-maker were determining factors when selecting the sites.

The selection of designers was based on the idea that the event should include both Eastern and Western garden traditions. The choice went to designers from these traditions with an 'inquiring design approach' to programmatic and conceptual innovation. To get the designs realized was not the foremost criterion for Breeze of AIR.

Taking the art of garden design as a stepping-off point, we selected five differing types of space in the city: a museum courtyard, existing public gardens, a roof garden, an arboretum and an old historic garden.

For the courtyard of the Boijmans Van Beuningen Museum the design brief was to develop 'a sublime museum garden for garden art'. This was assigned to the Indian architect Charles Correa.

For the design brief aimed at expressing the tug-of-war between public and private, between reconstruction and innovation and the differences in use, the site chosen was Lijnbaanhoven, a pair of courtyard gardens at the Lijnbaan shopping precinct. The American designer George Hargreaves was given the task of designing

8. See, among others, the garden of the VSB bank in Utrecht and that of the headquarters of Interpolis in Tilburg, both designed by West 8.
9. In association with municipal departments of the City of Rotterdam (the Urban Planning and Public Works departments, and the Rotterdam City Development Corporation), sub-municipalities and residents' organizations.
10. 'Erasmus made this step in his *Convivium Religiosum*, establishing a spiritual foundation for a tradition of inner gardens, which is today regarded internationally as a specifically Dutch contribution to garden history. In English it is termed the Erasmian Garden. This is a type of enclosed garden where one can briefly withdraw from a hostile world, from wars and the lack of inner harmony, there to focus on the better things in life. The Erasmian Garden comprises elements mentioned as essential to the hortus conclusus: safety (the surrounding walls), shelter (a loggia) and intimacy (the restricted access). Peace and quiet is another precondition, while water is present in the form of a central fountain. Erasmus even thought to include an aviary, while inspiring expressions of culture are present in the form of a library with a reading room and educational murals.'
11. See Luiten and de Josselin de Jong in this publication, p. 44 onwards.
12. Study commissioned by the AIR Foundation, unpublished. See Ivan Nio, *Lijnbaanhoven – de stedelijke openbaarheid van Pocket Parks*, 2000; Ivan Nio, *Valkeniersweide – de heterogenisering van een tuindorp*, 2000; Ivan Nio, *Spinozapark – van de wijkgedachte naar een uitsortering van een tuindorp*, 2000.

[fig. 6]
Working visit by Eelco Hooftman and Bridget Baines to Agniesebuurt, 13 October 2000

[fig. 7]
Paul Achterberg (left) and Roy Bijhouwer are briefed at the Central Station site, 7 November 2000

[fig. 8]
Working visit by Georges Descombes to Museum Park, 17 November 2000

[fig. 9]
Adriaan van der Staay's opening lecture at the launch of Breeze of AIR, 11 October 2000 in Rotterdam

a city garden for visitors, residents and urban nomads in increasingly hectic surroundings.

For the rooftop of Las Palmas, which in a few decades will lie amidst high-rise buildings with a view of the Rotterdam skyline, the Japanese architects Kazuyo Sejima and Ryue Nishizawa were asked to design a roof garden open to the public that would invite contemplation yet also respond to the uniqueness of the site.
For Arboretum Trompenburg the Dutch landscape firm of West 8 was invited to design an 'Erasmian Garden' for the twenty-first century.[10]

Georges Descombes, from Switzerland, was assigned the task of articulating a historic garden of the Erasmus University as an enclosed garden.

For the last two sites the brief also focused on accessibility, reachability and a more logical connection between garden fragments and the various spheres in the surrounding areas.

Two of the nine sites were in the post-war residential districts to the south of the city centre: Valkeniersweide in Tuindorp Vreewijk and the Spinoza park, in the centre of the post-war residential district of Lombardijen. The brief for Algerian-born Kamel Louafi encompassed a design for 'the garden of the four corners of the world' in Valkeniersweide. This green adjunct to Zuiderpark, marked by multi-faceted and intensive use, functions as a sort of open-air international living room for the city.

The brief for Dutch designer Piet Oudolf was to strip the largely undefined green space of the Spinoza park in this tree-studded neighbourhood back to its essence: a small, precious and unique garden that could be appropriated, maintained and managed by the local residents.

Two other sites were about future large-scale urban transformations: the Central Station area and the railway viaduct of the Hofplein line in Agniesebuurt, a neighbourhood marked by a heterogeneous population and a harsh, concrete environment. The brief for the designers of Gross.Max. from Scotland was to design on or adjacent to the Hofplein viaduct a community garden as an injection for the neighbourhood, and to transform the viaduct into a defining promenade leading away from the city.

The brief for the Dutch firm of Atelier Quadrat called for an inquiry into the agenda of the semi-public space for travellers, visitors and city residents in and around Central Station, and into the role within that agenda of public urban gardens as places to spend time.

A survey of the changing use and significance of the landscapes, woods, parks and urban gardens of Rotterdam provided the historical framework for the design briefs.[11] For three sites in particular – Lijnbaanhoven, Valkeniersweide and Spinoza park – sociological research into the use and perception of the spaces gave a framework for the design.[12]

Private, semi-public and public

In examining the significance of the garden for the city, Breeze of AIR distinguished between various public urban domains.

The garden in the public domain of the city, amidst privatization and urbanization, was the focus for the garden designs for three inner-city areas, Lijnbaanhoven, Museum Park-Het Park and the Central Station area. A key theme here was to insert the gardens into the fabric of Rotterdam city centre. The sites are at crucial places where the attractions of lingering there and the ambience can be enhanced by high-grade design. The designers examined whether the garden could conceptually create

[fig. 10]
Exhibition advertised on a Rotterdam tram

[fig. 11]
Dennis Adams's installation at the exhibition with Atelier Quadrat's presentation in the background

[fig. 12]
Presentation of work by Gross.Max. with that of work by Maura Biava in the background

[fig. 13]
Opening of the exhibition; left to right, Bartomeu Mari, Adriaan van der Staay, Anne-Mie Devolder and councillor Els Kuijper, 28 April 2001

[fig. 14]
Exhibition foyer during the opening

a specific place which, thanks to its seclusion and green character, could distinguish itself from the recently reprofiled parks, squares and shopping streets in the area. Can the garden reinforce the cohesion of public open space, or should the garden in a city like Rotterdam strengthen the fragments and places instead?

The public space in the city centre is undergoing a process of privatization, driven particularly by a sense of a lack of safety. In this light the central-city garden has an ambiguity of meaning. On the one hand, urban gardens can lend legitimacy to the privatization of public spaces. On the other, they can be deployed in the interests of civic culture to *urbanize* the collective domains, for example at Lijnbaanhoven and in and around the new Central Station. To what extent does the garden provide urbanistic leverage in preserving by means of programming, design and management the public status of outdoor space? In this respect the public urban garden makes clear-cut demands of commissioning bodies and managers.

The second theme concentrated on the garden in the semi-public domain of the city – between collection and image. Here the courtyard garden of the Boijmans Van Beuningen Museum, the rooftop of the Las Palmas warehouse and the new extension to Arboretum Trompenburg were the subject of discussion. Urban gardens that are open to the public are no longer a task reserved for government. Which other parties are prepared to act as client and manager? Does the garden also offer opportunities for third parties to strengthen their involvement with the city? The three plans investigated the garden as confirmation of a specific public institution, a unique landmark building, a historical location, a particular resonance or as an extension of a social status or role. To what extent can the urban garden function as a design laboratory, as a reservoir of images, as an exhibition? Urban institutions in the twenty-first century can figure as the new proprietors of open, green space in the city. Is the city garden an adequate means to enhance urban identity and orientation? Which spatial resources, materials and stylistic considerations does this involve?

The third theme focused on the garden in the multicultural domain of the city – between avoidance and encounter. The sites relevant here were the Hofplein viaduct in Agniesebuurt, Valkeniersweide in Vreewijk and the Spinoza park in Lombardijen. These design sites are in districts where gradual but significant changes in the traditional demographics of the population have taken place. They have become heterogeneous urban areas, which has altered the use and meaning of their public space. The introduction of the garden in these three distinct areas occurred against diverse spatial backdrops: from reducing an excess of public space with new boundaries, to dual land use. One question for the discussion is the significance and surplus value of gardens in relation to parks or squares. In what regard do 'traditional' public spaces lend themselves to an application of the garden concept, whether in nineteenth-century or post-war districts? In sociological terms the garden has a relationship with specific lifestyles and use forms. Renewal of the hortus conclusus can therefore be tied in with developments in the use of leisure time in multicultural Rotterdam, with the many different takes on nature expressed in the various plantings.

The three design briefs are situated in the field of tension between looking and using. How can the designs, in their programming, layout and management, take account of the increasing heterogeneity of these districts? Public spaces in heterogeneous urban areas should provide city-dwellers with the opportunity not just to meet but also to avoid one another. To what extent do the gardens reinforce the possibilities of appropriation, identification and involvement for the different residents? When does self-management of the garden become an option? To what extent is the

13. The subject of the 2001 Clusius Lectures given by Charles Correa and Erik de Jong accorded well with the theme of Breeze of AIR. De Jong's lecture had previously been published by the Clusius Foundation, Leiden.
14. Parallel with the main exhibition in Witte de With, almost all Rotterdam galleries opted for the theme of *hortus ludi*, the playground. This resulted in a welter of projects by 50 artists in the gallery and in Rotterdam's weekend leisure gardens *(volkstuinen)*.
15. See Treib, p. 146; Worpole, p. 156, and Cansever, p. 152 in this publication.

[fig. 15]
Breeze of AIR magazine and an invitation in Arabic

[fig. 16]
The first telecast by Breeze-TV

[fig. 17]
Breeze-TV, Kazuyo Sejima, Ryue Nishizawa and a project assistant on the roof of Las Palmas

[fig. 18]
Breeze-TV, Charles Correa in Boijmans Van Beuningen Museum

city prepared to invest in high-maintenance gardens, and which other parties (residents' associations) are prepared to take part?

Art and criticism as a means to reinterpretation

The interdisciplinary and international character of the event and the AIR Foundation's collaboration with the Witte de With centre for contemporary art, the Clusius Foundation and the Rotterdam galleries, made for an exceedingly broad approach to the theme of the hortus conclusus, giving rise to syntheses and new ways of thinking about the enclosed garden as a typology and idea for the contemporary city.[13] Witte de With invited an international group of eight artists to create work inspired by the Erasmian idea of the hortus conclusus, an idea that is meaningful for contemporary society and specifically for Rotterdam. The humanist Erasmus saw the enclosed garden as a place for discovering the inner self, for contemplation. Unlike the designers, the artists were asked for an autonomous, free interpretation of the theme. The work was to be executed in the public realm with a link to the gallery spaces of Witte de With.

The invited artists were Maura Biava (the Netherlands/Italy), Anthony Dunne & Fiona Raby (UK), Elmgreen & Dragset (Denmark), Zeger Reyers (the Netherlands), Teresita Fernández (USA), Cristina Iglesias (Spain), Dennis Adams (USA) and Cildo Meireles (Brazil).

The contributions of designers, artists, poets, scientists and critics generated a dialogue about the cultural significance of urban gardens for the contemporary city. The interdisciplinary formula also made it easy for other cultural institutions to join the project from their own field of operation.[14]

It was deemed important to get an independent reading of the city and the designs from various cultures. Three visiting critics, the American landscape architecture historian Marc Treib, the British sociologist Ken Worpole and the Turkish urban designer Turgut Cansever, were invited to address themselves to Rotterdam's public space and give critical comment on the design studies and the artists' proposals.[15]

Programme and public

There are various ways of interpreting the fact that Rotterdam is perceived as an insufficiently green, brick city. There is enough green space, but its quality is often so poor that it is scarcely perceivable as green, being concealed or difficult to access. This oft-repeated observation about the perception of urban green space provides a first-rate opportunity to delve more deeply into that space and offer the public a broad spectrum of information and experiences. Which is why the Breeze of AIR/*Hortus Conclusus* exhibition, where the garden designs were presented alongside the art installations, was the centrepiece of a whole range of public activities, such as city walking tours, poetry, storytelling and open-garden days. In so doing, Breeze of AIR addressed both the general and the professional public.

The Breeze of AIR magazine, printed in a large edition and distributed at the start of the event, showed many facets of Rotterdam's green space using photo essays, descriptions of walks, interviews with users and managers, documentation of the design sites and a guide to the garden architecture weekends. In the *Open AIR* outdoor programme, poets from Iran, Suriname, Belgium and the Netherlands read the best of their garden poems. The Egyptian storyteller Sherine El Ansary recited stories from *1001 Nights* and Italo Calvino's *Invisible Cities*.

The closing event was the symposium. There, the designers debated with policymakers, managers, scholars and interest groups about the role and significance of the urban garden for our modern-day city, using the design proposals as case studies.

[fig. 19]
Weekends of Garden Design, 12-13 May, 9-10 June In Ms Dagnelie's garden in Kralingen

[fig. 20]
Reunion of participating garden owners at the 'design weekend' in the Arboretum, 11 June

[fig. 21]
Open AIR storytelling and poetry, 23, 24 and 25 May in Arboretum Trompenburg; the speaker is Rien Vroegindewij

[fig. 22]
Open AIR storytelling and poetry, 23, 24, 25 May in Arboretum Trompenburg; Sherine El Ansary unfolds a tale

[fig. 23]
Visiting critics. Left to right: Turgut Cansever, Tjeu Strous, Ken Worpole, Erik de Jong and Marc Treib

The results and deliberations of the designers and artists were explicated and confronted with the ideas and experiences of the visiting critics and others. This facilitated the exchange of ideas and forming of opinions about trends in the use, design and management of public urban green space. The recommendations this brought forth were articulated by Adriaan van der Staay, Ivan Nio and Erik de Jong, in the provinces of cultural politics and public governance, sociology and architectural history respectively.[16]

The results

The symposium brought about a consensus regarding the need for more funding to be made available for the layout and maintenance of gardens and parks. There was also agreement that rules relating to their use and maintenance needed establishing. An important recommendation was that the government and other parties should act as a commissioning body for these special green spaces. It was recommended that the design and layout should be viewed literally as a form of garden art; the government would invest in this just as it does in public art or promote a policy similar to that pertaining to country estates, subsidizing the management of private gardens in return for the owners opening them to the public.

The symposium also witnessed a call for firmly installing the urban garden on the cultural agenda with institutional backing. Opinions varied on the form this should take – a special green-space inspectorate might well have a levelling effect. In the tradition of the old system of *stadsbouwmeesters* or city architects, former Government Architect Wytze Patijn argued that Rotterdam should appoint a *groenmeester*: an expert designer responsible for an effective policy of high-quality green spaces in the city.[17]

With unobtrusive work in the urban realm and autonomous installations in the Witte de With exhibition spaces around the notion of the hortus conclusus, the artists raised cultural-critical issues with regard to nature, art and the city, by which they sought not so much to reach conclusions as to stimulate the public to reconsider, or take a fresh look at, the public space in their city.[18]

The designs for nine different locations presented during Breeze of AIR variously explored and raised for discussion the relationship between spatial form and the contemporary significance of the boundary.[19] These designs for urban gardens have elicited new forms for urban culture and use of leisure time. The hortus conclusus typology has proved a fertile spatial concept that can attain concrete results. For example, it is striking that glass houses were proposed for four sites, as a tropical hothouse, a meeting place, or as a series of transparent spaces with a view. The hortus conclusus was also developed as an island, a pocket park and a traditional walled garden.

The designers' various approaches to the enclosed garden typology raised essential issues: one pertained to the form and significance of the boundary as enclosure, another to the transitional zone between the public and private domains as an area of exchange for public domains of differing spheres and degrees of activity. The boundaries or transitions between culture and nature and between high and low culture were also explored. Finally, much thought was given to the transforming of undefined space into meaningful spaces for the city.

As for involving users and local residents in the ideas on the new urban garden, a few of the designs responded to the usages of people with different demographic identities and lifestyles. The application in some of the designs of theming and programming in juxtaposition with flexibility and simultaneous use by different groups,

---

16. See van der Staay, p. 19; Nio, p. 161, and de Jong, p. 167 in this publication.
17. See Dolf Broekhuizen, 'Revival van het stadspark', *Items*, 2001, no. 4, p. 64 onwards.
18. See van der Staay, p. 19 and Elstgeest, p. 141 in this publication.
19. See Nio, p. 38 in this publication.
20. AIR explores architectural issues of the European city, with Rotterdam and its surrounding area acting as a case study. AIR serves as an independent laboratory for urbanistic and architectural issues. Linking local topics with international themes, it engages policymakers, managers, government bodies and residents in innovative perspectives on issues of spatial development. The plans developed are not aimed at realization, rather they approach design-directed research and presentation of results through lectures, debates, exhibitions and publications. Within the scope offered by the event, briefs for concrete sites are assigned to national and international architects and urban designers.
For an overview of the AIR events up to 2002, see 'AIR - A Brief Chronology', p. 170.
21. The 'Erasmian Garden' (West 8), the 'garden of the four corners of the world' (Louafi), and the Lijnbaan gardens (Hargreaves).

[fig. 24]
Kamel Louafi, lecture given on 14 December 2000

[fig. 25]
Paul Achterberg, lecture given on 11 January 2001

[fig. 26]
Eelco Hooftman, lecture given on 15 March 2001

[fig. 27]
Charles Correa, Clusius Lecture, 1 June 2001

[fig. 28]
George Hargreaves, closing symposium, 15-16 June

was a direct response to the heterogeneous make-up of the Rotterdam population.

Attractively laid out and well-tended urban gardens strengthen the sense of involvement by local residents in their daily living environment. To be attached in some way to an urban garden implies constant maintenance and management for which someone or some group must feel responsible. With the exception of Louafi and Hargreaves, the designers did not propose direct solutions for problems of management and upkeep, but they did tap into new potentials and opportunities.

In conclusion

Breeze of AIR slots into the AIR tradition of addressing current spatial issues in the European city, more specifically, improving the quality of public space and the role of gardens within it.[20] The research and design pursued by Breeze of AIR succeeded in charting certain spatial and social 'conditions' in greater detail. More insight was gained into the dynamic and resilience of one type of place within the changing urban field. By making the enclosed garden a topical issue for the contemporary city, Breeze of AIR fuelled the discourse on the attractiveness and variety of public green space in the urban environment and how we perceive it.

The enclosed garden, and with it the policy category of 'urban garden', has been given a contemporary connotation for Rotterdam, and its introduction into the cityscape accelerated at three sites so as to test its viability.[21]

For landscape architecture, which in the Netherlands mainly concerns itself with multi-sectoral and complex planning and layout issues, Breeze of AIR focused attention on the design of the urban garden and facilitated an international exchange of knowledge and experience.

Alongside the policy-related, professional and social reflections on urban green space, the programme of Breeze of AIR provided numerous opportunities to explore along experimental lines the phenomenon of the urban garden as an inseparable component of urban culture, and to experience activities and interventions in urban green space.

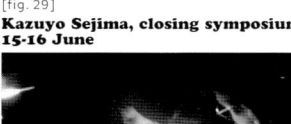
[fig. 29]
Kazuyo Sejima, closing symposium 15-16 June

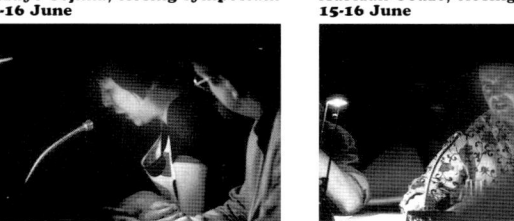
[fig. 30]
Adriaan Geuze, closing symposium 15-16 June

[fig. 31]
Georges Descombes, closing symposium 15-16 June

[fig. 32]
Piet Oudolf, closing symposium 15-16 June

[fig. 33]
Impression of the symposium

16

The Public Garden

The Public Garden
The Challenge

[1] Adriaan van der Staay, *Hortus Conclusus, Amsterdamse Boekengids interdisciplinair*, no. 20, Amsterdam University Press, December 1999.
[2] Adriaan van der Staay, 'De tuin als dialoog met de natuur', *OASE, tijdschrift voor architectuur* (2001) no. 56.

ADRIAAN VAN DER STAAY

The Enclosed Garden

This essay is divided into three sections, the same number of phases as in the development of my contributions to the Breeze of AIR event, dedicated to the hortus conclusus. The first section is in effect the article published in an Amsterdam journal[1] in 1999 that proved to be the impetus for holding the event. The second section is a précis of the lecture I gave at the opening of Breeze of AIR. It includes an investigation into whether the garden is a component of culture rather than just a collection of flora and fauna at a given place and time, and refers to the importance of having a conception of nature when designing a garden. In other words, is the culture of a certain era, along with its insights and values, reflected in the garden and vice versa?[2] The third section consists of a succinctly formulated series of questions arising from the results of the project. It examines the place of the garden in contemporary culture. If it is true that the garden is a reflection of the insights and values of our culture, which of these does the garden actually mirror?

Although a critical view of contemporary culture implicitly resonates in these questions, I do not pretend to provide specific answers. The future is always a blank page, on which contemporaries will formulate their own answers to this and many others questions as they desire. To each his own enclosed garden.

Hortus conclusus

Terminologically speaking, the enclosed garden or *hortus conclusus* could almost be called a tautology. Etymologically, the words garden, hortus, orchard, garden, court and park all refer to 'girding' with a fence, hedge, wall or embankment. In the Western world, the notion of a partitioned space has always been associated with the term 'garden'. It is widely accepted that the first garden to appeal to the Western imagination was the walled garden of a Persian king who, according to the Greeks, devoted a great deal of time to it. The Greek word for the Persian for 'garden', *paradeisos,* gave a name to the most desirable garden of them all: paradise. But in the Proto-Germanic tradition, garden or orchard also suggests enclosure. The garden is a piece of nature that is isolated from untamed, unsullied nature.

Here is not the place to outline the history of the Western garden, which does not exclusively derive from the enclosed garden. Two comments will suffice. In the first place, the term 'garden' was confronted with actual transitions to untamed or unsullied nature early on in its history, whereby the emphasis on enclosure lost some of its meaning. Take, for example, the division of the Roman garden into three parts: the inner garden, the outer garden and the orchard [fig. 1]. During the Renaissance there was the transition from the formal garden to the hunting forest *(bosco)* [fig. 2]. And all too familiar is the perspectival breakthrough of the French garden, beyond its boundaries, to the landscape and the horizon [fig. 3]. In addition, there is the idealized conception of the eighteenth-century English garden, in which the landscape, deliberately disguising every distinction between inner and outer garden, reached as far as the house in the form of a park [fig. 4]. The most recent stage of this development is the modernistic blurring of the term 'garden' into an indeterminate greenness, a kind of nature without interior or exterior, at any locus and in every shape and size. The garden is thus gradually losing its characteristic seclusion, and garden, park and landscape are becoming mutually interchangeable [fig. 5].

In the second place, the opposite also pertains: the amalgamation and more precise

[fig. 1]
La Casa del Relievo di Telefo, Herculaneum

Inner garden, outer garden and orchard

[fig. 2]
Villa d'Este, Tivoli
Etching by Étienne Du Perac

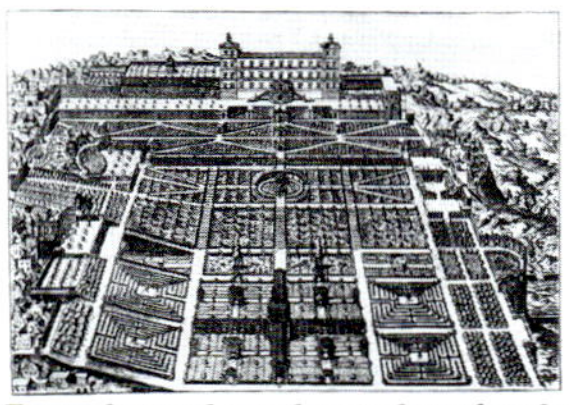

From formal garden to hunting forest

[fig. 3]
André Le Nôtre, Vaux-le-Vicomte
Etching by Israel Silvestre

The perspectival breakthrough

[fig. 4]
View from the house, in *The Red Book for Armely* (1810)

The park reaches as far as the house

[fig. 5]
Bijlmermeer, Amsterdam

Garden, park and landscape are interchangeable

definition of the garden, or a part of it, into a specifically detached microcosm where people can experience nature intensively; not only in the midst of nature and the landscape, but also within the cultivated surroundings of park and city. In this 'concentrated' garden with its paradisaical effect, one finds a number of elements that are scarce in the world outside: safety, shelter, privacy for contact with intimates, peace and quiet are present, but also selected aspects of nature, such as water, rocks, special plants and animals. This garden is still connected with the cosmos, the sun, the moon, the stars and the seasons. It is sometimes also related to the erotic – that nature in the very heart of humankind – which requires privacy. This small Garden of Eden is found in every great culture, also beyond the occidental tradition, and has all manner of appellations, including 'hortus conclusus'.

It is no coincidence that the Netherlands has a significant, though little known or recognized, tradition of secluded and enclosed gardens. Since the fifteenth century, the Netherlandish tradition of the *Devotio Moderna* has placed a marked emphasis on the inner life and introspection. It is an easy step from individual meditation to the sociable intimacy of the hortus conclusus. Erasmus made this step in his *Convivium Religiosum*,[3] establishing a spiritual foundation for a tradition of inner gardens, which is today regarded internationally as a specifically Dutch contribution to garden history. In English it is termed the Erasmian Garden.[4] This is a type of enclosed garden where one can briefly withdraw from a hostile world, from wars and the lack of inner harmony, there to focus on the better things in life. The Erasmian Garden comprises elements mentioned as essential to the hortus conclusus: safety (the surrounding walls), shelter (a loggia) and intimacy (the restricted access). Peace and quiet is another precondition, while water is present in the form of a central fountain. Erasmus even thought to include an aviary, while inspiring expressions of culture are present in the form of a library with a reading room and educational murals. The remnants of such an Erasmian Garden can be found in Leiden in the reconstruction of the sixteenth-century garden of Clusius (Hortus Clusianus), though certain important elements have now disappeared, including the didactic *ambulacrum*, which might be considered the first museum in the Netherlands.[5]

Because the hortus conclusus emphatically responded to a more widely felt need for privacy among the citizens of the Netherlands, one finds this intimate type of garden in a whole variety of forms: in the little courtyards of almshouses or other charitable foundations or in the rear gardens of city mansions; but also in the semi-public form of, say, the Begijnhof in Amsterdam, even for today's tourists a counterpoint to the hectic metropolitan environment. The enclosed garden could be considered a form of resistance to an already overly exteriorized culture [fig. 6].[6]

It would be incorrect, even ludicrous, to think that the enclosed garden is an exclusively European cultural form. Even within Europe itself it is possible to find remnants of traditions other than the hortus conclusus. To this very day, the Moorish courtyard gardens [fig. 7], for example in Granada, reveal another, exotic tradition, namely that of the patio, with peace and quiet, water and salutary foliage. However, one might argue that even this Moorish garden is nothing more than a variant of the occidental tradition, being derived from the fusion of the Roman garden with the Persian *chahar-bagh* or quadripartite water garden, and both these belong within the ambit of occidental culture [fig. 8].

The most autonomous, non-Western tradition of enclosed gardens is discovered in classical Chinese culture. Beyond China, the most important variants can be found in Japan and Korea. The Japanese hortus conclusus in particular proved to have a powerful appeal for garden designers and the Chinese tradition has proved to be a com-

[3] Lucy Schlüter, *Niet alleen, een kunsthistorisch-ethische plaatsbepaling van tuin en woning in de Convivium religiosum van Erasmus* (Amsterdam: Amsterdam University Press, 1995).
[4] *The Oxford Companion to Gardens* (Oxford: Oxford University Press, 1986), pp. 390-391.
[5] Erik de Jong, 'Nature and Art, the Leiden Hortus as "musaeum"', in: *The Authentic Garden. A Symposium on Gardens* (Leiden: Clusius Foundation, 1991).
[6] Alexandre Vanautgaerden, *Hortus Erasmi*, Brussels 2001; this is an example of how Erasmian thought has found its way into contemporary garden design.
[7] Adriaan van der Staay, 'De tuin tussen oost en west', *Groen: vakblad voor groen in stad en landschap*, 56 (2000) no. 10 (October).

[fig. 6]
Courtyard of Vrouwe Groenevelt's Liefdesgesticht, Rotterdam 1816

The garden as counterpoint

[fig. 7]
Garden in the Generalife, Spain

Stillness, water and exuberant plant growth

[fig. 8]
The Persian Chahar-bagh

Quadripartite water garden

plementary source of inspiration in the modern world. It is regrettable that revolution, war and ideological struggle inflicted considerable damage on this tradition in China itself, where it is insufficiently recognized or honoured.

Although the Chinese hortus conclusus displays the general characteristics of seclusion, peace and quiet, harmony with the cosmos and concentration on the essential characteristics of nature, conceptually it is less dependent on walled-in exclusion [fig. 9]. The chief form is indeed the private urban garden, surrounded by a high, often undulating wall, which excludes the public, commerce-driven and tumultuous world of humankind and the city. But the effect of the enclosed garden is also achieved by seeking out places in the landscape where retreat and introspection are possible without enclosure: on remote hillsides, on islets in lakes, or on peninsulas along the banks of rivers. Moreover, the Chinese garden tradition developed innumerable devices to escape from an undesirable isolation and look outwards towards the landscape, the surrounding nature and the cosmos, for example with platforms to behold the moon or elevated viewing-points looking towards mountain landscapes in the distance. Lastly, there are the miniaturized table landscapes that offer the illusion of breaking out of any enclosure, even that of the vessel that contains them. The European hortus conclusus is relatively simple and straightforward compared with the complex and meandering enclosed garden of the Mother of Gardens, China.[7]

So there are traditions of enclosed gardens as cultural heritage from all round the world.

The obfuscation of the hortus conclusus from the consciousness of many of today's world citizens has many historical reasons. The rise of a market that sets more store by mass production and distribution of goods and services, an expansive consumerism that hardly encourages introspection or taking things easy, a modern conception of architecture and urbanism that has little interest in cosmic or natural aspects of life, and lastly, the tendency to see all the essential, metaphysical or religious urges and experiences as something that belongs to the private, non-public domain. If the amusement park were to be regarded as a symbol for contemporary culture in our globalizing civilization, then the hortus conclusus almost seems an anachronism, out of step with the spirit of our times.

However, there is one fact that contradicts this ideology: where a hortus conclusus has survived, it attracts a great deal of interest. This is not simply the case with monastery gardens in Japan, but is evident when private gardens are opened for public viewing here in the West [fig. 10]. Something that has satisfied needs for thousands of years is by definition resilient. Where new enclosed gardens are established, they can be seen as the maverick creation of individuals who have the wherewithal, the talent and the energy to realize them. The results remain, by definition, known only to restricted circles. The private dominates; the public is barely represented. In the Europe of the twentieth century, these enclosed gardens were designed by figures such as Russell Page, the Vicomte de Noailles, Major Laurence Johnston, Vita Sackville-West [fig. 11] and, more recently, the poet Ian Hamilton Finlay.

It cannot be denied that there is a real problem here. In a society where one's private life is becoming increasingly isolated and public life is becoming more and more mass-oriented, neither the market nor the government can be expected to be deeply concerned about the *giardino segreto,* the secret garden, even if the public has a demonstrable need for it. Public discussions quickly reach the populist conclusion that it is elitist. At this stage in the formation of public opinion one cannot expect much more than that the government conserve existing enclosed gardens for cultural and political reasons and open them to the public, and that it create opportunities

[fig. 9]
Private urban garden, Suzhou, China

The town is excluded

[fig. 10]
Monastery garden at Ryoan-Ji, Kyoto, Japan

Now open to the public

[fig. 11]
Vita Sackville-West, Sissinghurst, the white garden

Now open to the public

for experiments with alternative forms.

In addition, practically speaking, the hortus conclusus, as with every garden, demands more care than a strip of public green space. Not only because plants need attention and because a designed form must be protected against the brute forces of nature, but also because there must be supervision of the way it is used, as with a church or chapel. The enclosed garden is not a *terrain vague,* it is not a 'wasteland', nor is it an unmanaged green space where the homeless and drug addicts can hang out. This means that the hortus conclusus, just like everything that has anything to do with craftsmanship, continues to be a labour-intensive enclave in a society set on eliminating as much work as possible. In other words, the hortus conclusus is not only a physical entity but also a social and cultural one.

This brings up the question of whether the enclosed garden should only be dependent on the investments of well-heeled enthusiasts. Should not a wider public share this kind of experience? What is more, the enclosed garden in its most perfect form is not a standardized product, but a creation, i.e. a realization of profound personal desires. It can only succeed if it is a creative collaboration between the client and the garden designer. Creating an enclosed garden usually requires more money than is usually supposed.

This does not make designing this counterpoint easy in today's society. It is in fact throwing down the gauntlet, challenging the public domain, private initiative ('civil society') and institutions and artists to find a form that is suitable for our times. On the one hand, this can take the form of cultural conservation, i.e. safeguarding enclosed gardens that have survived from ages past, restoring them to their original purpose and making them accessible for the public in an appropriate manner. This is how the Hortus Clusianus mentioned above functions in the context of the botanical garden of the University of Leiden here in the Netherlands, where one can also find another, semi-enclosed hortus conclusus: the Von Siebold Memorial Garden, inspired by Asian tradition. The Begijnhof in Amsterdam has been mentioned above; once housing a religious sisterhood, it still has a sacred aspect and is managed by a foundation. This gives a pointer for the future: there must always be an agency or a group of volunteers willing to take on overall management and responsibility. These days, such organizations might well be universities, libraries, hospitals, museums, homes for the elderly, or municipal departments responsible for parks.

There is also the possibility of devising new forms: creating an enclosed garden at the top of a skyscraper or in the middle of a public square is by no means far-fetched [figs 12,13].[8] The experiences mentioned above can be evoked in new forms too. In the Netherlands there is a long tradition of inner courtyards, and nowadays buildings are often so big that it is worth considering including a hortus conclusus within a building. Besides, in a cultural climate where the invention of new forms is a global learning process, one can be certain that ideas can be drawn from a whole assortment of traditions and experiments. This makes the enclosed garden into a vital design task, not only for the West, but also for China, Korea and Japan, South-east Asia and India, Persia and the Arab world and beyond to Africa and Central and South America.

An experimental programme should develop a typology of new places as well as include cultural traditions from around the world. This programme could form a counterbalance to a one-dimensional and superficial understanding of globalization.

The garden as a mirror of culture

Even on cursory inspection, it is evident that the garden mirrors the insights and values of a culture, epoch or place. A weighty dissertation could be written on this sub-

[8.] Francesco Nuvolari, *Hortus Conclusus* (Milan: Mazotta, 1986).

[fig. 12]
**Burle Marx,
roof garden, Ministry of Education,
Rio de Janeiro**

[fig. 13]
**Burle Marx,
roof garden, Ministry of Education,
Rio de Janeiro**

ject, if one were to take the time to do more than scratch the surface. Here I must make do with presenting just a few examples.

I have already mentioned the first example: the old Dutch garden, which took its intimacy from the tradition of Thomas à Kempis and Erasmus. The Netherlands of the fifteenth and sixteenth centuries was, of course, part of a more broadly influential cultural structure: the Italian Renaissance. But the direction taken by the garden in the Netherlands imbued the Renaissance garden with a small-scale, civic, private, restrained aspect. I already mentioned the semi-public courtyards and the typical walled garden of urban properties. In the seventeenth century, the republican, decentralized and, in the circumstances of the era, free and egalitarian Netherlands had a garden design that held privacy in unusually high esteem.

These values did not constitute a general basis for the eighteenth-century European garden, because Europe as a whole was evolving in the direction of monarchal absolutism, rather than towards republican, democratic ideals. The trend-setting garden of the eighteenth century was no longer the garden of the aristocratic Renaissance, but that of Louis XIV. This French king broke away from the Italian influence, which still seems so strong at Vaux le Vicomte, and made the architect of that garden, Le Nôtre, into the new genius of a centralist monarchy with a desire to impress, a monarchy that had, or had taken, control of all around it [fig. 14]. Despite all the cosy Dutchness of Het Loo Palace, it has still become an example of a change of course in the culture of the Netherlands, when this shifted towards monarchy and accompanying pomp in the eighteenth century [fig. 15]. So the Netherlands had two garden traditions with highly different values as their backdrop: a civilian and a monarchal, at that time denoted as Dutch gardens versus French.

At risk of using examples that are perhaps unfamiliar to the reader, I want to mention another striking example, namely the development of the Mogul gardens in India. In the sixteenth century, Babur (1483-1530), the Turk who conquered North India, started to establish gardens there, bringing a heartfelt passion from Kabul. Later emperors of the Mogul dynasty shared this passion. These gardens are first and foremost an expression of the Persian traditions imported by the Turkish conquerors. They emphasize orderliness, using water as the structurally binding element and surrounding walls as a necessary defence against the hostile nature beyond. The early emperors, such as Babur and Akbar, were still fairly open to their Indian surroundings in terms of flora and fauna and culture. But as their successors alienated themselves from the conquered land, the language of the garden idiom became ever more distanced from the Indian vernacular and increasingly Persian. And this distant Persia, esoteric and pure, became the model. The conquerors did little in the way of assimilating, as had been the case in China. On the contrary: these idealized gardens record the growing distance between the invaders and the indigenous population. The gardens became increasingly Islamic amidst the surrounding Hindu culture. An important point in this process was the mausoleum garden of the Taj Mahal, which floats above the Indian landscape like a dream and refers exclusively back to Persia and the Islamic paradise [fig. 16].

It is remarkable how the British architect Edwin Lutyens (1869-1944), who designed a new colonial capital, New Delhi, including what is now the presidential palace, principally looked back to the tradition of the earlier Mogul emperors. He made just as little effort to fit in with an Indian 'vernacular', let alone Indian values. There are barely any Hindu elements to speak of. The gardens of the conquerors reflect each other more than they do the land where they are situated.

An example that does not stem from Western tradition, which in cultural-histori-

[fig. 14]
**André Le Nôtre,
Vaux-le-Vicomte**

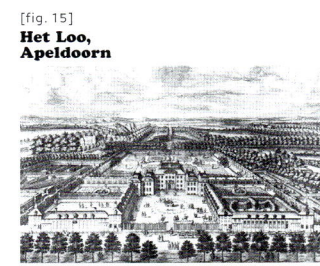

[fig. 15]
**Het Loo,
Apeldoorn**

[fig. 16]
**Taj Mahal,
Agra 1632-1643**

cal terms also includes the Mogul gardens, is that of the Chinese garden. The Chinese garden is based on completely different values and insights, on a conception utterly foreign to the Western garden. We have already noted this. On the surface it is immediately evident in the emphasis on symmetry within the Western tradition, an aspect that is completely absent in the Chinese tradition. An aversion to symmetry is one of the distinctive characteristics of the Chinese garden. More fundamentally, however, the Chinese garden seems to be rooted in a different relationship with the landscape. In Chinese culture, the landscape contains the garden, and human beings are also part of this landscape. People partake in a flow of energy that courses through the landscape, like the flow of blood in the human body. This is where harmony is found. And humankind can do no better than to seek to be in harmony with this force-field of nature, in concrete terms through geomancy, Feng Shui. The Chinese garden thus reflects a Taoist inspiration, in the same way as the house of the Mandarin does not repudiate its Confucian structure. The Chinese garden reflects values and insights that are not easily reconciled with Western ones.[9]

These four examples - the Dutch proto-democratic garden, the French absolutist garden, the colonial garden traditions of India and the Taoist garden concept of the Chinese upper classes - indicate that the garden is not an arbitrary aesthetic object, but that it mirrors a whole range of values and developments.

These different values can result from the need to display power or for diversion, but also from philosophies of life, and can embrace the public as well as the private domain. Though they determine the design of the garden, these principles remain, up to a degree, external to the garden. People can express their might in ways other than through garden culture; they can also seek diversion or pleasure elsewhere. One can even uphold a philosophy of life that shuns the garden, in the same way that there are ideologies that reject images.

However, one inalienable characteristic of the garden is its relation to nature. A garden without nature is unthinkable, and one's concept of nature will continue to define the characteristics of the garden.

If we accept that the development of the garden runs parallel with the development of agriculture, then one can talk about the garden being another form of dialogue with nature. While in agriculture the utilitarian function is uppermost, with the garden it is pleasure, power or contemplation that prevails. The design of the garden is freer than in the case of agriculture, and offers more expressive possibilities. At the same time, it is bound up with natural laws.

The inextricability of nature is demonstrated, for instance, by the importance of elements such as sun and water, plants and animals, as well as the requirements of the site in relation to the landscape or the specific characteristics of the ecosystem.[10] In relation to such natural elements, the garden can become a mirror of beliefs and ideals relating to nature. To me it does not seem too far-fetched to state that it is primarily this relationship with nature that determines the greatness or diminutiveness of an art of garden making. After all, man defines himself and his essence in a material sense if he gives shape and form to his relationship with nature. This means that the making of gardens reflects fundamental choices. Are these fundamental choices also made explicit in fundamental reflections? We have already referred to a Western tradition that separates the garden from raw nature in order to transform a section of it into a paradise. On the other hand, we have the Asian landscape garden, which has mankind blend with nature and landscape and regards the garden to be part of a cosmic whole. Because these choices are so fundamental, it does not seem unreasonable to enquire into the metaphysical foundations of garden making. This would not be the case were garden design merely decorative. It gives the art of garden making the potential of being culturally great or profound.

Here too, just a few examples must suffice to illustrate the garden's metaphysical significance. Lipsius (1547-1606), an ideologist from the south of the Netherlands employed by the Netherlandish State, found garden culture sufficiently interesting to devote extensive and detailed passages to it in his *De Constantia*, which he wrote in Leiden.[11] For this sixteenth-century figure, the garden was a great deal more than simply a collection of plants and animals that gave people pleasure, though that is a facet he does not deny. The garden provides space for the soul. The soul can regenerate there and transcend to a contemplation of creation. He even places gardens above churches, those gaols of the spirit. For him, the garden has a philosophical dimension.

There are indeed other examples of opinions about garden design that add a philo-

[9.] See note 5.
[10.] Adriaan van der Staay, 'Zon, water, landschap, garden', in: *Waterlandgoed Enschede essays*, Bureau B+B stedebouw en landschapsarchitectuur (Amsterdam: B+B, September 2001).
[11.] Justus Lipsius, *Over standvastigheid bij algemene rampspoed*, trans. P.H. Schrijvers (Baarn: Uitgeverij Ambo, 1983).
[12.] Charles Correa, 'In Search of the Hindu Garden', *Text of the Clusius Lectures 2001*, ed. Gerda van Uffelen (Leiden: Clusius Foundation, 2001).

sophical or metaphysical slant to the garden's relationship with nature. A single example from Asia will suffice here. In a recent study, the Indian architect Charles Correa offers an interpretation of nature.[12] In this essay – the Clusius Lecture given within the framework of Breeze of AIR – he fundamentally defined the Indian approach to nature as a relationship with something sacred. In the garden, in the landscape, in nature as a whole, the sacred element has precedence above everything else, even to the detriment of aesthetic aspects. The garden is first and foremost an opportunity to come into contact with what is sacred in it: tree, mountain, guru [fig. 17]. An aesthetic does not belong here, whether it be Renaissance or modern. For Correa too, the garden speaks a philosophical language.

I hope that these few examples have shown that the garden does not merely mirror the ideologies of a culture, but that it also adds its own dimension in which essential beliefs about nature can be read.

The contemporary enclosed garden: ten questions

I will restate my standpoint in order to underpin an assessment of the garden in contemporary culture. The garden seems to be a good indicator for cultural developments. One can see the contemporary garden as a metaphor for the state of today's culture, especially in its relationship with nature. This relationship is complex. The garden can mirror both the dominant culture and opposing movements against that culture. Cultural situations are seldom unambiguous.

Another example will serve to illustrate this. After World War I, when European culture entered a period of crisis and sought a way out in utopian dictatorships, the park became more collectivist. The enclosed garden was less useful for a dominant culture that rejected privacy. But contrary to this *Zeitgeist*, an underground garden culture continued to exist, rejecting collectivism and preferring the private garden (or the *dacha*) as an alternative for collectivist green space.

An example like the above shows how people must remain on their guard for at least two possibilities when considering garden design in the twenty-first century: that of a direct reflection of contemporary ideas, and that of a counterculture which will perhaps fall back on other, traditional values.

I now want to pose ten questions in an attempt to place the contemporary garden in the broader cultural context. These questions are not the result of a systematic judgement of contemporary culture, but arise from the inspection of the garden designs presented during the Breeze of AIR event.

1. Can the enclosed garden be regarded as a universal phenomenon that will appear time and again as a fixed component of the cultural needs in different times and places? This phenomenon will inevitably be influenced by the dominant culture, as I have argued. But isn't it an answer to a universal need in every civilized society? Even in a collectivist culture like that of the Muslims we see a withdrawal to the inner courtyard (and garden) of the family home. In the no less collectivist Confucian society of traditional China we see the possibility of withdrawal to the Taoist garden of the family complex. If this need for retreat to a private garden is abiding, where then is this manifest today? This need for seclusion is clearly illustrated in a number of designs, but is not caged in any one particular form.

2. Is the enclosed garden a place where the individual retreats in solitude, or is the hortus conclusus of today a place for intimate meetings of special groups? The concept of the Erasmian Garden was not meant for the solitary life of the hermit, but for encounter with people of similar mind. The Erasmian Garden is a reincarnation of a

[fig. 17]
The stupa at Barabadur

Coming into contact with what is sacred (tree, mountain, guru)

[fig. 18]
West 8, Erasmian garden

The garden for encountering others of similar mind

[fig. 19]
Elmgreen & Dragset, I never promised you a rose garden

Institutionalizing the 'cruising area' for homosexuals

Hellenistic concept, and more particularly an Epicurean idea, that saw the garden as the stage set for a community of friends [fig. 18].

Two of the designs for horti conclusi presented in Breeze of AIR, are a form of sexual retreat: the one for heterosexual prostitution, the other as an institutionalization of the homosexual 'cruising area' [fig. 19]. Is the garden, in its private or semi-public character, in fact meant as a facility for small or select groups? If enclosed gardens are specialized natural decors for club activities, how then do gardens fit in with the concept of emphatically public parks, accessible to everyone? The designs repeatedly demonstrate the tension between open and closed.

3. Is the enclosed garden intended to encourage stasis? A famous Dutch architect finds a perverse pleasure in drawing the most extreme conclusions about the dominant culture and giving these a three-dimensional form. This is expressed, for example, in his celebration of consumerism, glamorizing of mobility, endorsement of breaking with traditions, and even in an ode to an architecture of delirium. For me, much of the current interest in the enclosed garden derives from the idea of being a counterpoint to this dominant culture. So the hortus conclusus does represent a stasis in a rapidly turning world, expressed in a locus of obvious immobility. The enclosed garden thus embodies a critical message, becomes a countermovement, a reaction comparable with the 'slow-food' movement set up to counteract fast food.

4. Or is the enclosed garden merely a new space for consumerism, in this case the consumption of little chunks of nature? With the design for a zoological garden in the heart of a metropolitan railway station, the symbolic junction of traffic and mobility, the garden design by Atelier Quadrat seems to answer this question in the affirmative [fig. 20]. Nature is there to be consumed by the traveller. In his garden design for the Boijmans Van Beuningen Museum, a fountainhead among trees, Charles Correa seems to answer the same question in the negative [fig. 21]: nature cannot be consumed, because nature belongs to the sphere of the sacred.

5. Is the enclosed garden a form of 'intensive care' in a world that strives to be as carefree as possible? Undoubtedly every garden or park that bears the name with pride must be designed and maintained. But to what extent? How much care? Georges Descombes' answer is shatteringly clear. Rotterdam has a Museum Park with a number of attractively designed parts. But the City Council risks allowing the park to go to the dogs through its negligence and lack of concern. Rotterdam does not deserve new garden designs, as it is not able to care adequately for the existing ones. If an enclosed garden is to be established anywhere, then the appropriate care must be ready at hand, which means that the garden is understood, rather than lost from view, and is tended with a devoted hand and a professional eye.

6. Is enclosed garden another name for exoticism and nostalgia? In a world where more than half the population lives in cities, and where the aim is to increase production, distribution and consumption, traditional agriculture and eco-systems no longer seem terribly relevant and are primarily something to be nostalgic about. Traditional agriculture and garden design are a nostalgic way to spend time, comparable with sailing, horse riding or hunting, or going on photo safari in search of the last tigers or Tibetans. Is the hortus conclusus the museum of old agrarian and garden culture? In the way we tend to view community gardens and garden allotments? Or is a vital regeneration of the genre possible in new forms?

13. Nancy Gerlach-Spriggs et al., *Restorative Gardens: The Healing Landscape* (New Haven/London: Yale University Press, 1989).

[fig. 20]
Atelier Quadrat, a zoo in the heart of Central Station

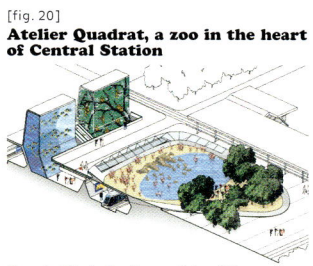

Symbolic interface of traffic and mobility

[fig. 21]
Charles Correa, the inner garden of Boijmans Van Beuningen

A spiral fountain amidst the trees

7. Could the enclosed garden be regarded as therapeutic? The contact with nature, the sound of water, the singing of birds, the perfume of flowers and the caring for unthreatened plants or animals all seem to be beneficial to physical and mental health, if experienced in gardens and parks designed for this purpose. At least this is the belief of a movement that we know from the name 'restorative gardens'.[13] Good for physical and mental recovery. Is hortus conclusus another name for some kind of psychiatric institution in a culture that has lost its way?

8. Who will assume responsibility for enclosed gardens, for their development and upkeep? Will the enclosed garden be the responsibility of the state, national and local, of project developers, of private investors, or of some other new form of semi-private or semi-public ownership? The public sector normally takes responsibility for cultural heritage, which includes old enclosed gardens but could also extend to new garden forms. Likewise, among private owners of enclosed gardens we can detect a growing willingness to temporarily open their gardens, or even make them public. On the other hand, a new hortus conclusus movement might perhaps develop, basing itself on the pronounced desire of neighbourhoods to have better parks and gardens in their surroundings. The reaction of neighbourhood representatives and residents to the designs by Hargreaves and Louafi was unexpectedly positive.

9. Does the enclosed garden have to remain connected to living nature? This is not a superfluous question, because the majority of the ideas for gardens by the artists who exhibited at Witte the With had only tenuous links to living nature. These interesting contemporary artists seemed more absorbed by the inner workings of the human mind, the technical solution to questions of privacy or peace, than by a dialogue with a living, growing or dying nature. One could not say this about the work of Cildo Meireles, a tree with one end sticking out of the window like a flag, but split into a forest of little matchsticks at its sawn-off base [fig. 22]. Here the artist is being more of a cultural critic, rather than someone concerned with garden design. Another artist in the exhibition, Zeger Reyers, used the growth of mushrooms, but primarily to make the decay of cultural products visible [fig. 23]. Even among the landscape architects there was one design, by the Japanese group SANAA, that did have some kind of relationship with nature, light and water but scarcely with living nature.

This widespread disinterest in living nature could indeed mark our culture's future focus on technology and artificiality as a means of creating individual space. There was one reviewer who protested about the cerebral character of the artists' reactions to the theme of hortus conclusus. The masses of garden-lovers stayed away.

10. Is the enclosed garden elitist by definition? If one regards the future of the dominant democratic culture in which we live as one of increasing uniformity and ever more large-scale experiences, a culture ruled by the masses, then the answer is yes. The enclosed garden seeks diversity and separation, also within a democratic culture. One might call this a noble endeavour, which is not necessarily inconsistent with a democratic political culture. The enclosed garden also seeks out intense moments of losing oneself in nature and culture, in one's own existence and that of others. If that proves impossible in a democratic society and is labelled elitist, then the outlook is bleak. Personally, as someone who has never ceased to believe in a democratic culture that includes that quality, I find that unacceptable.

To conclude

Revival of interest in the enclosed garden, for the philosophy of the hortus conclusus,

[fig. 22]
Cildo Meireles, Two trees III

A cultural-critical statement

[fig. 23]
Zeger Reyers, Onder-tussen II

Making visible the decay of cultural products

has evidently unleashed a Pandora's box, plucked a sensitive string that has not been played for a long time. In the expanding ambitions of landscape architects and urbanists to design ever-greater tracts of landscape, the small scale has been neglected. A no man's land has appeared between the rapidly developing market for the private garden and the large-scale commissions of project developers and governments. Modernism's disregard for the small-scale detail, the character of ornament, for the entire tradition of the ornamental garden did no good either. In the 1995-97 edition of the Dutch-language landscape architecture and town planning yearbook,[14] I complained about the dearth of designs for gardens and parks submitted to the editors. When I seized on a review about a study of the enclosed garden to illustrate the topicality of the problem,[15] I had no idea of the reaction that would follow.

The issue of the small-scale concentrated garden that is still public turns out to have many facets. Perhaps the time is now ripe to pay this some attention. During the Breeze of AIR event at least, it proved easy to prompt discussions about the typology of the modern public urban garden, about its sociology, about its history, about its patrons and its managers, and about the role of designers and artists. There was considerable interest from the general public. The whole subject enjoyed a brief but expert crystallization thanks to the AIR Foundation, and the event was held amidst the flurry of activities unleashed by *Rotterdam 2001*. I hope that the spark will not merely be a flash in the pan, but a burning torch.

[14] Adriaan van der Staay, 'Vignetten voor een landschap', in: *Landschapsarchitectuur en stedebouw in Nederland 95/97*, (Bussum: Uitgeverij Thoth, 1998).

[15] Rob Aben and Saskia de Wit, *De omsloten tuin. Geschiedenis en ontwikkeling van de hortus conclusus en de herintroductie in het hedendaagse stadslandschap* (Rotterdam: 010 Publishers, 1998). Translated as *The Enclosed Garden. History and development of the hortus conclusus and its reintroduction into the present-day urban landscape* (Rotterdam: 010 Publishers, 1999).

ERIK DE JONG

Hortus Conclusus: the law of the garden

One of the best-read books in the children's section of the Haarlem public library is the Dutch translation of Frances Hodgson Burnett's *The Secret Garden*. Since its original publication in England in 1911, the book has been through many editions, translations and retellings in the Netherlands and elsewhere. It is still a best-seller in England and America. What accounts for the enduring appeal of this book, which makes no claims to special literary merit?

The main role in the story is shared by a deserted, walled rose garden and three children. The door to the garden is locked and even were it not, the garden is so overgrown as to seem impenetrable: indeed, on the country estate where it stands, the garden appears to have been forgotten, its existence and potency denied. When the book opens, nature is wrapped in a death-like winter cloak and this contributes to the negligible, sombre character of the garden. That situation finds its parallel in the initially sullen character of the heroine, Mary Lennox, who comes to the estate as an orphan. Wandering around the huge house on her own she discovers the sickly, bedridden Colin, whose dead mother, it later transpires, created the walled garden. Then in early spring, guided by a robin, Mary discovers the mysterious wall and cannot rest until she knows what lies beyond. When she eventually finds the key and enters the deserted 'wasteland', a metamorphosis begins. Helped by Dickon, a humble country boy who understands the language of nature, she explores the silent garden, discovering all the surprises it holds in the way of plants, trees and animals: the *hortus conclusus* turns out to be full of enchantment. Its neglected state invites spontaneous gardening and during the spring the children nurture the garden back into a walled paradise. They are all affected by the walled garden's magic which cures Colin of his illness, harmonizes Mary's character and unites the three socially and temperamentally very different children in friendship with one another and the garden.

Hodgson Burnett's garden represents the essence of the *hortus conclusus*: there is the wall (separation and boundary, but also the link with a wider environment) and the door (entry and revelation). Closed becomes open and inside turns out to be outside – that is to say, nature. These elements contribute to the experience of discovery and rediscovery [fig. 1]. Inside the wall, beneath its patch of sky, the garden is a world of its own: a concentration of good and beauty and the magic of nature, uncovered and tended by human hands. The restoration of the garden is the restoration of harmonious order, free from sickness, ruin, neglect: the garden represents the world not as it is, but as it should be. Whereas the garden initially stood aloof from its surroundings, an invisible presence on the periphery of the estate, as it reveals its secret from within it establishes a new relation to life and the landscape beyond its walls. Even when it is restored and visible once more, the magic of the secret remains and the experience of its discovery and active restoration become part of memory, of spiritual awareness: 'being alive is the Magic – being spring is the Magic, the Magic is in me, in every one of us,' Hodgson Burnett has Colin say and the implication is, not just in the closed garden, but outside it, too. The springtime of the garden is childhood, a motif that other writers have also used in order, through the metaphor of the closed garden, to say something about life itself. In his autobiographical novel *Feast in the Garden* (tr. 1992), György Konrád writes: 'Again and again the garden is the original stage, the place where the delight of the vision becomes complete. The house

[fig. 1]
Rie Cramer, *Juli. Hooimaand. Tekeningen en versjes,* The Hague/Batavia, G.B. van Goor Zonen's Uitgeversmaatschappij, 2nd impression

[fig. 2]
Villa Lante, Bagnaia (near Rome), late 16th century

[fig. 3]
Simon Benin or his atelier, Book of Hours with miniature of an enclosed garden, ca. 1525

[fig. 4]
Enclosed garden in a manuscript of *Le Roman de la Rose,* late 15th century

[fig. 5]
Willem Buytewech, *De Tuin van Holland,* etching 1615

is built on a hillside: to the right is the cemetery, to the left the mental asylum. Garden, childhood, paradise, they vanish and reappear' – thereby neatly encapsulating the meaning and appeal of the closed garden.

Topographía and topothesía

The motif of the enclosed garden has a long literary and visual history in Western culture. Since antiquity, the enclosed garden has been seen both as topographía, a particular, real place, and as *topothesía,* an imaginary place [fig. 2]. The strength of the hortus conclusus is its ability to alternate, mix and metamorphose the real and the imaginary.

Much of the meaning of the closed garden is contained in the etymology of the word. Hortus is related to the Indo-Germanic 'ghort' or enclosure, 'conclusus' reinforces that closed and secluded character. 'Tuin', the Dutch word for garden, is related to the Old High German 'tun' and modern German 'Zaun', both meaning fence. This is still reflected in the Dutch verb 'omtuinen', meaning to demarcate a piece of ground with a fence, wall or hedge. From this we may infer that 'tuin' refers both to the fence itself and to the area within the enclosure: the territory that we still call garden. Both are essential for the creation of the hortus conclusus [fig. 3]. This dual meaning of the word for garden is universal. The French 'jardin' and the English 'garden' (together with the related Dutch word 'gaard' that appears in the word for orchard, 'boomgaard') mean 'fence' or 'enclosed space', just as the words 'court', 'park' and 'paradise' originally referred to spaces shut off from the outside world by some form of partitioning. The garden is thus in essence a smaller or larger open space screened from the outside world by fence, hedge or wall so that it suggests safety and seclusion within and at the same time defines itself vis à vis its surroundings. It can be realized in many places. Because of its closed nature, the garden also stands for security, safety, wholeness and individuality.

In medieval literature these meanings turn the hortus conclusus into a *locus amoenus,* a pleasant place, a microcosm of nature with water, trees, grass and flowers, separated from the wilderness [fig. 4]. It is a place of enjoyment, of the senses, of love, a dream as in Guillaume de Lorris's *Roman de la Rose* (mid-thirteenth century) or the *Hyperotomachia Poliphili* of Francesco Colonna (late fifteenth century). But seclusion can, via the imagery of allegory and symbol, convey other meanings, such as the immaculateness of the Virgin Mary or the impregnability of the Dutch Republic (represented by the Dutch Maid) to Spanish intruders [fig. 5]. The garden may also be interpreted in spiritual terms, as a place of retreat, as is so beautifully described in Erasmus's *Convivium Religiosum* of 1522, where a herb garden, surrounded on three sides by arcades painted with allegories, provides the setting for a learned discussion on Christian ethics. The Flemish humanist Justus Lipsius set part of the discussion about fate and constancy in his *De Constantia* of 1584 in a garden. For him the garden was a wholesome refuge, the place where the soul is nourished by repose and gains inspiration for new life [fig. 6]. To the garden, he wrote, we owe the works about nature and human morality by the ancient philosophers; as a green academy the garden inspires natural philosophy and insight into life and death. For this neo-Stoic humanist, the true purpose of the garden was to provide a quiet and secluded setting for thinking, reading and writing. Much of that contemplative ideal lives on in many a modern garden, although few would go so far as the late-eighteenth-century English artist and poet William Blake and his wife, who were wont to sit naked in their little walled London garden, reading aloud verses from Milton's *Paradise Lost.* Still, the act itself is very telling.

For actual garden design (*topographía*), the closed garden proved to be an influ-

[fig. 6]
An enclosed garden in Crispijn van de Passe, Hortus Floridus, 1615

[fig. 7]
Hans Vredeman de Vries, Corinthia, etching in Hortorvm Viridariorvmque elegantes & multiplicis formae 1583

[fig. 8]
D. Stoopendaal after I. de Moucheron, Bird's-eye view of the gardens of Heemstede (Houten, Utrecht), after 1700, etching

[fig. 9]
Martha Schwartz, Splice Garden, 1986, Whitehead Institute for Biomedical Research, Cambridge (Mass.)

[fig. 10]
Modern Japanese roof garden

ential spatial motif. In the Dutch tradition, the closed medieval cloister was transformed at the end of the sixteenth century into a mathematically constructed space, as can be seen in the first, Northern Flemish/Dutch, garden treatise by Hans Vredeman de Vries (the *Hortorvm Viridariorvmque elegantes & multiplicis formae*, 1583) and its imitators [fig. 7]. Here the garden became an architectural design of a dignity, purity and harmony comparable to that of the three classical orders. The architecture of the closed garden was an expressive system whose simple or complex power was based on a design grammar of walls, entrances, axes, parterres containing topiary and plants, fencing, berceaux and fountains laid out in relation to the surrounding buildings. This formal language was to be further developed in the seventeenth and eighteenth centuries, fuelled by the imaginative power of the *topothesía*. As an expressive system, the closed garden could stand on its own (initiating a tradition that extends to the modern town garden), but it could also link up to form a larger whole, so that garden designs from the late seventeenth century, with their arrangements of protective windbreaks, can be seen as an enlarged hortus conclusus made up of a succession of introverted but interconnected, rooms or boskets, to be discovered by the wanderer. When attitudes to nature underwent a change at the end of the eighteenth century and geometry vanished, the landscape style continued to cater to the need for intimacy and seclusion, even if that was achieved more by atmospheric scenography than by physical separation. Although... in the Dutch landscape the strict geometry of parcellation is never far away, so that the composition of the landscape, constrained to take place within taut outlines, soon reverts to a hortus conclusus.

Experience and discovery

Those who interpret and view the garden in purely stylistic design terms – a stance encouraged by many bird's eye views and plans – will fail to discover the strength and significance of the closed garden as a cultural phenomenon of the first order. The garden was a staged, eye-level experience intent on subjecting the public to its own world, seducing them into a novel experience, a unique adventure that colours memory, provides insight and gives direction. In the garden of Heemstede te Houten laid out around 1680-1700, the design grammar of axes, rooms and plantings was deployed in such a way that the visitor was coaxed into discovering and exploring the various gradations between nature and culture: from wilderness to cultural landscape to art [fig. 8]. Via various closed spaces with a 'star' wood (the architectural treatment of the theme 'wood') and ponds (the 'water' theme), the visitor passed a game preserve and menagerie (the tamed world of the wild animal) finally ending up, by way of a walled fruit and vegetable garden (the horticultural adaptation of nature) and a grotto (representing the sea), in what was the apogee of nature transformed by art: a large outdoor architectural space with a parterre and open-air orangery, filled with countless exotics. The staged experience focused on the varying gradations in the creations of nature and human art, work and technology and it functioned, as some put it, as God's second book, a text about divine creation to be read for edification and enjoyment. The visitor, coming from the flat, geometrically laid out agricultural landscape, encountered the architectural presentation of the first, 'ur' nature of wood and water and wild animals, passed then through a second nature of fruit and vegetable cultivation that was strongly reminiscent of farming, finally arriving at the ideal third nature, the edifying arrangement of both first and second nature. Thus was the visitor made aware of all the gradations in the relationship between nature and human beings.

In such an approach, the hortus conclusus represents to this day the symbiotic rela-

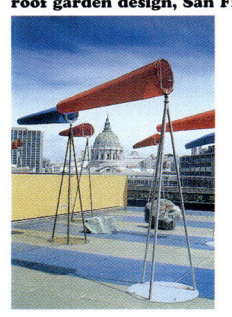

[fig. 11]
Delaney, Cochran & Castillo, roof garden design, San Francisco

[fig. 12]
Garden of Villa Noailles, 1991, Hyères. Reconstruction of the design by Gabriel Guevrekian, 1928

[fig. 13]
C.T. Sørensen, design for a garden, 1954

[fig. 14]
Philip Johnson, garden of the Museum of Modern Art, New York

tion between *topographía* and *topothesía*, between nature and art, between place and imagination. Both share in one another's essential features so that when nature allies itself with art, it becomes a creative force and is raised to the same level as art. Depending on time, place and task, the two may give rise to something new, something that in the Italian garden treatises of the sixteenth century was referred to as a 'third nature', the product of an almost alchemical process in which nature and art play an equal role and in which wilderness, natural artificiality and artificial nature alternate and intermingle. And where the outcome is not art, but intensified nature. As such, the hortus conclusus may be a small, even empty, oasis, but equally a large urban park, a scene of concentrated nature, or a space where inside and outside, seeing, experiencing, nature, wilderness, town and culture are placed in dialogue with one another or commented on in a different way [figs 2, 9-14].

Town and garden

The meaning of the hortus conclusus applies also, and to a great degree, to the Dutch 'stad' or town, in which context it should be noted that the English word 'town' and the Dutch word for garden – 'tuin' – have a common etymological source in the Old High German word 'tun'. They are not opposites, in other words, but cognates. Both garden and town provided protection and seclusion. In the Netherlands one may discern a similarity in the streets, squares and courtyards of the town, the intimacy of corridors and rooms inside the home and the avenues and closed 'rooms' of the garden – a characteristic of Dutch towns that has persisted into the present age with its predilection for perimeter blocks enclosing inner courtyards [figs 15, 16]. In the seventeenth and eighteenth centuries, many foreign visitors saw Dutch towns in terms of 'urban landscape', although that phrase conjured up a rather different picture than it does today. The unity of canal, street, stoop and house was extended mentally to include the yards behind the house. As early as the sixteenth century these rear areas often included a garden, or elements thereof such as an orchard, bleaching field or parterre. In the seventeenth-century extension of Amsterdam, the garden became a standard element of the 'keur' blocks laid down in the new town planning regulations. The various regulation blocks and their gardens, invisible and thus unknown to most visitors to Amsterdam, still bear witness to the close connection that existed between town and garden at the start of the Dutch town planning tradition. Unsurprisingly, seventeenth- and eighteenth-century travellers compared the city of Amsterdam, built on a forest of piles, with its gardens, semi-public courtyards and almshouse courts (the Begijnhof is prototypical of this kind of green urban space), its tree-lined streets, squares and bastions and its harbour bristling with ships' masts, to a wood or garden. The same comparison was also drawn in other Dutch towns like The Hague and Leiden. For some visitors the Dutch canals resembled the pleasances along the rivers Vecht, Amstel and Vliet (and not the other way around), others compared the tree-lined streets of Leiden to 'so many avenues of a finely laid out garden'. Gardens, like Leiden's Hortus, lay concealed behind facades like a peep-show [fig. 17]. With its collections of medicinal and rare botanical plants and ethnographic artefacts, brought together here from around the world and later supplemented by classic sculptures, the Hortus presented itself in garden and gallery as a public museum, a place of study, knowledge and wonder, an object of civic pride and *salus publica*, civic welfare. If we add to this the many painted landscapes and plaster allegories of nature in the seventeenth- and eighteenth-century parlours of the Dutch town house, which often looked out onto a garden, it becomes clear how closely connected the intimacy of garden, nature and landscape is with the history of the Dutch town. It is equally clear that the history of the town has rarely been written from this perspective.

[fig. 15]
Rotterdam courtyards, Agniesebuurt

[fig. 16]
Rotterdam courtyards, Vreewijk

[fig. 17]
The Hortus in Leiden, W. Swanenburgh after J.C. Woudanus, engraving 1610

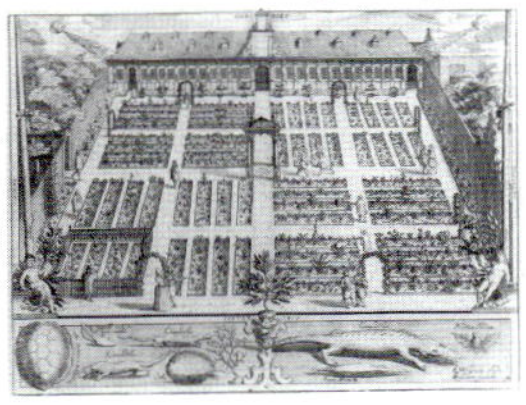

[fig. 18]
Fast-food box with instant park, 1999, 'The Park of the Future', Rietveld Academie, Amsterdam

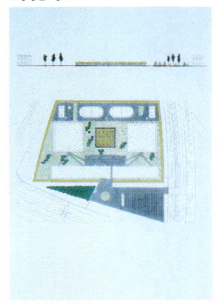

[fig. 19]
Bureau B & B, design for penitentiary in Lelystad, 1993-96

Revitalization

This brings us to the question of the viability of the hortus conclusus today. Do ideas about it still live on, consciously or unconsciously, and if so where – and can they be utilized for new solutions?

When the Gerrit Rietveld Academy organized an International Student Seminar to mark its 75th anniversary in 1999, it chose as its theme 'the Park of the Future'. Some of the entries showed not only that the idea and the world of the hortus conclusus was still a valid model for young artists, but also how complex it had become. For example, there was the fast food box containing various garden elements that could be assembled according to personal preference to create a park or garden [fig. 18]. This contrivance reflected the current demand for 'instant' experiences but it could also be read as a longing for an urban pocket park that provides for an unspecified green space with flora and fauna. Both possibilities mirror the fragmented nature of the modern city with its new networks where both globalization and the search for a new definition of locale and place are at work. Another design showed a caged garden, as if to say that the viability of the hortus conclusus is imprisoned in an excess of urban violence and must be confined and protected as a rare museological artefact. It also suggested that the tradition of the hortus conclusus has connotations other than the familiar humanistic and romantic ideals, that 'conclusus' may also invoke the tragic and the subversive. An early example of this is the medieval picture of Christ's agony in the Garden of Olives which also calls to mind the way urban gardens and parks have become a place of refuge and shelter for the homeless [fig. 18]. For them, too, garden and park are a hortus conclusus – often involuntarily, but a refuge nonetheless. A refuge, however, of a kind that, like nocturnal practices in public parks, falls outside the category of socially acceptable behaviour and is consequently accorded no place in the historiography of the hortus conclusus and in the regeneration of parks and gardens.

In several major works of Dutch twentieth-century literature, the enclosed garden is revealed not only as a place of self-realization and of the good and beautiful, but also as a place of such oppressive bourgeois morality and uniformity that the immediate impulse is to escape. For that matter, legal wrangling over property boundaries goes back to Roman times. A similarly contradictory picture of the hortus conclusus emerges from a recent competition for prison gardens (1993-1996). No other living space is so hermetic as these repositories of order and discipline, so that the closed garden – sometimes conceived as a representation of free nature outside, with fields of sunflowers, a rockery and stands of trees – becomes a symbol of freedom, hope and regeneration, even though in this situation 'outside' is always 'inside' [fig. 19]. A comparable yet different role is that of the hortus conclusus as therapeutic ideal as reflected in the modern tendency to surround hospitals and mental institutions with gardens.

The hortus as a performing art

However complex and contradictory, these examples also indicate that there are possibilities for a modern revitalization of the hortus conclusus on the threshold between private and public. If we interpret the hortus conclusus as a metaphor for the regeneration of the garden and for designed nature in the city in general, something may yet come of Professor Dirk Frieling's proposal to use the design and typology of the garden as basic elements for the composition and proportioning of the spatial order of town and landscape. The word 'compose' was also used by Clemens Steenbergen who, in his 1994 inaugural lecture as professor of landscape architecture at Delft University of Technology, compared the design of nature and landscape with

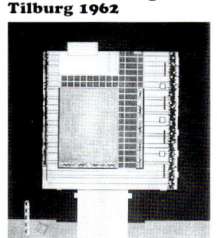

[fig. 20]
**P.A.M. Buys,
design for a courtyard, R.K.
Economische Hogeschool,
Tilburg 1962**

[fig. 21]
**Mien Ruys,
urban garden, design 1960,
Tuinen Mien Ruys,
Dedemsvaart**

[fig. 22]
**Allotment garden in Haarlem,
Schalkwijk 2000**

[fig. 23]
**Allotment garden in Rotterdam,
Heyplaat 2001**

a symphony. As performing arts, garden and landscape architecture are constantly reinterpreting old and new nature, taking the original material as their starting point, with a view to maintaining relevance and vitality. Such an orchestra also has its gradations, from solos to basso continuos, which together produce a single timbre.

This is somewhat different from the way the urbanist John Habraken compared his profession in 1961 to 'the gardener who steers and stimulates the growth of the organism by means of numerous measures. He prunes and guides future development, he must be able to oversee the whole. The organism of the city would grow and live even without the interventions of the town planner, but the result would be chaotic and the plant would quickly suffocate.' He was unable to give any indication of the position of gardens and parks during post-war reconstruction, for in his view the supervision of 'future development' was reserved only for architects and urbanists of a modernist bent. Nonetheless, in the hands of garden and landscape designers of the likes of P.A.M. Buys, Mien Ruys, Hans Warnau, Wim Boer and others – all contemporaries of Habraken – the garden has remained a source of experiment that has enabled it to survive, be it often invisibly rather than as a conspicuous element of public space [figs 20, 21]. The position of the garden in urban management often still depends on a modernist-inspired architecture and urbanism that manages to ignore the distinctive character and tradition of garden and landscape design. This is abundantly clear in the lack of ideas among local authorities concerning the management, conservation and development of existing parks and gardens. People still seem to have difficulty acknowledging that garden and landscape designers had a strong tradition of clean and uncluttered simplicity long before modernism appeared on the scene: a discipline that, instead of divorcing tradition and modernity, nature and culture, combines, merges and transforms them into oases of high quality. One proof of this proposition is the fact that when the postmodernist critique attacked modernism's technocratic-scientific world view (as Stephen Toulmin so nicely demonstrated in his *Cosmopolis. The Hidden Agenda of Modernity* of 1990), landscape, ecology and landscape architecture could count on renewed interest among the public, government and the design community. But despite the steady renaissance of garden and landscape architecture over the past ten years and recent discussions about the management, conservation and development of existing parks and gardens, the correction of the modernist vision has not yet penetrated everywhere. The lack of an integrated policy is especially evident in the absence of a modern public patronage and the failure of urban and other authorities to assume responsibility for making the garden as designed creation part of cultural policy.

The garden as a cultural phenomenon

But other conditions also need to be satisfied: given that the garden is a constant in human culture there should be more opportunities for an integrated and interdisciplinary study of its history and current condition, of management, conservation and evolution in the context of future developments in town and landscape. At present this is not possible in Dutch academia. Even environmental and nature studies undervalue the cultural significance of the garden. The profession of garden and landscape architecture would benefit from further independent development in education and design practice. Paradoxically, it sometimes seems that the garden is not even a matter for concern within the discipline of landscape architecture itself and that it is fated to lose out to the larger, and more urbanist, designs – at least if *De Blauwe Kamer* the leading magazine for landscape architects and planners, and the *Yearbook of Landscape Architecture and Urbanism in the Netherlands* are anything to go by. As if the garden cannot be a vehicle of modern imagination and con-

LITERATURE

Rob Aben and Saskia de Wit, *De omsloten tuin. Geschiedenis en ontwikkeling van de hortus conclusus en de herintroductie in het hedendaagse stadslandschap*, 010 Publishers, Rotterdam 1998.

Peter Ackroyd, *Blake*, Random House, London 1997.

Diane Balmori and Margaret Morton, *Transitory Gardens, Uprooted Lives*, Yale University Press, New Haven/London 1993.

Catherine Benoît, *Corps, Jardins, Mémoires. Anthropologie du corps et de l'espace à la Guadeloupe*, CNRS Editions/Editions de la Maison des Sciences de l'Homme, Paris 2000.

Augustin Berque, *Être humains sur la terre. Principes d'éthique de l'écoumène*, Editions Gallimard, Paris 1996.

Hervé Brunon (ed.), *Le jardin, notre double. Sagesse et déraison*, Editions Autrement, Paris 1999.

Humphrey Carpenter, *Secret Gardens. The Golden Age of Children's Literature*, Boston 1985.

Gilles Clément, *Le Jardin en Mouvement de la Vallée au Parc André-Citroën*, Le Govic SA, Saint-Herblain 1994.

Gilles Clément, *Le jardin planétaire. Réconcilier l'homme et la nature*, Albin Michel, Paris 1999.

Lorette Coen (ed.), *Lausanne jardins. Une envie de ville heureuse*, Editions du Péribole et Ecole Nationale Superieure du Paysage de Versailles, Lausanne 1998.

Michel Conan (ed.), *Perspectives on Garden Histories*, Washington DC, Dumbarton Oaks Research Library and Collection, 1999.

Terence Conran and Dan Pearson, *The Essential Garden Book. Getting back to basics*, Three Rivers Press, New York 1998.

Anne van Erp-Houtepen, 'The etymological origin of the garden', *Journal of Garden History* 6 (1986) no. 3, pp. 227-232.

L.A.Tjon Sie Fat and Erik de Jong (eds), *The Authentic Garden. A Symposium on Gardens*, Clusius Foundation, Leiden 1991.

Dirk Frieling, 'Vooruit, naar een hoger besef van tuinkunst', *Forum. Het Hollands landschap als Kunstwerk* 37 (1993), pp. 16-18.

Stanislaus Fung and John Makeham (eds), *Chinese Gardens I, Studies in the History of Gardens and Designed Landscapes*, 18 (1998) no. 3.

Stanislaus Fung (ed.), *Chinese Gardens II, Studies in the History of Gardens and Designed Landscapes*, 19 (1999) no. 3/4.

Pierre Gangnet (ed.), *Paris côté cours. La ville derrière la ville*, Editions du Pavillion de l'Arsenal, Paris, 1998.

Gert Gröning and Joachim Wolschke-Bühlmahn, *Von Ackermann bis Ziegelhütte. Ein Jahrhundert Kleingartenkultur in Frankfurt am Main*, Verlag Waldemar Kramer, Frankfurt 1995.

Grey Gundaker (ed.), *Keep Your Head to the Sky. Interpreting African American Home Ground*, University Press of Virginia, Charlottesville/London 1998.

Allison Hardie (translator), *The Craft of Gardens. Ji Cheng*, Yale University Press, New Haven/London 1988.

Frances Hodgson Burnett, *De geheime tuin*, retold by Els Pelgrom, with drawings by Mance Post, Wolters-Noordhoff, Groningen 1984.

H. Patricia Hynes, *A Patch of Eden. America's Inner-City Gardeners*, Chelsea Green Publishing Company, White River Junction, Vermont 1996.

Erik de Jong, *Natuur en kunst. Nederlandse tuin- en landschapsarchitectuur 1650-1740*, Thoth, Bussum 1995 (second edition).

[fig. 24]
Allotment garden in Rotterdam, Eigen Hof 2001

[fig. 25]
Urban Gardening in New York, 'Nueva Esperanza', Upper East Side, 111th Street/Madison Ave, 1993

[fig. 26]
Piet Oudolf, 'Evolution', prizewinning entry design for Chelsea Flower Show 2000

temporary ideals, has no place for the individual or the masses and belongs in the garden supplement of a women's magazine. If the hortus conclusus has any future, it is in the hands of amateur and professional gardeners in countless allotments and front and back gardens scattered throughout the Netherlands: it is there that the garden has survived the urbanist rationalism of the twentieth century [figs 22-24]. Such gardens contain a wealth of knowledge about the function of the garden and gardening in our society that has scarcely been tapped, doubtless because they do not belong to the official design circuit or are not seen as a vital element of urban space. 'Wild gardening', in the sense of designing one's own surroundings, long predates Carel Weeber's discovery of 'wild housing'.

Like modern park and garden design, all these closed gardens belong to our garden culture, at least if we define this as a much broader phenomenon than design culture alone. In that broad culture, the garden is part of the process of making rather than of any eventual result. The quality of the garden lies in the experience of the seasons and of slow time; it tells of everyday life and of the continuous involvement with and design of one's own place as an extension of oneself, is connected with the fulfilment of personal ideals and desires; the boundedness of the garden spurs the gardener to a boundless creative process of give and take. There, in dialogue with nature, tribute is paid to the small scale which, in the words of Rob Leopold 'is in fact greater than any measurable size'. In that culture, aesthetics is *aisthèsis*, in the original Greek meaning of the word, namely sensory experience that leads to personal expertise, taste, understanding and spiritual insight. The enclosed garden stands for our place in the world and constitutes a special locus of myth, fiction and illusion; it is a melting pot of the tangible (*phenomena*) and the intangible (*noumena*). The garden – and landscape architecture in the broader sense – is a key concept in what the French geographer Augustin Berque has called 'ecumene', that is to say places where human habitation marks and shapes the landscape and which the earth allows us to inhabit as human beings. Nowhere else is the 'imperative to garden', as Gerrit Komrij so eloquently described it in his 1990 Huizinga Lecture, more evident than in the American 'urban gardening' movement, where enclosed gardens – with names like 'nueva esperanza' – are wrung from real estate developers on behalf of the often impoverished Latin-American and Afro-American population. Their gardening, as part of a social-cultural emancipation, engenders a new relationship with the city [fig. 25].

Despite the lingering effects of modernist traditions, change is afoot in the Netherlands, as evidenced by various initiatives during the past decade. For example, 1998 saw the publication of Aben and de Wit's *De Omsloten Tuin* (The Enclosed Garden), a study of the history and evolution of the hortus conclusus and its reintroduction into the contemporary landscape. The book is part of an ongoing research project being conducted at Delft University of Technology into the principles of garden and landscape architecture. Change is also evident in the NVTL's Year of the Garden in 2000 – the year in which Piet Oudolf won a Gold Medal for his garden design at the Chelsea Flower Show [fig. 26] – which was so successful that it was extended into 2001. The Breeze of AIR event was the first interdisciplinary investigation of the meaning of the enclosed garden for the modern city and for the first time invested the garden with a truly cultural significance.

As a result of such initiatives, the garden is once again a laboratory and a site of experiments that may enrich not just the garden but also the city and the landscape with new ideas. There is a great design task here, and not only in the Netherlands. In France, England, Sweden, Germany, Switzerland, Finland and Spain, traditional

[fig. 27]
Bureau B & B,
Kromhoutpark, Tilburg,
design of 1991

[fig. 28]
Gilles Clément,
Jardin en mouvement,
Parc André-Citroën, Paris,
design/execution from 1990-91

[fig. 29]
Gilles Clément,
Jardin Orange,
Parc André-Citroën, Paris

[fig. 30]
Patio in the Alhambra,
Granada,
reign of Charles V

[fig. 31]
Old woman and two wise men in a garden, Iranian miniature,
1520-40

open and communal urban spaces – especially that 'other side of the city' (private gardens, courts, yards, pocket parks, roof terraces) – are being reexamined and redefined with a view to constructing a new grammar of enclosed urban space [fig. 27]. This has all sorts of consequences for the 'stone' and 'hard' design of architecture and urban fabric. It is gradually becoming clear that instead of viewing the enclosed garden as the antithesis of the city – as an escape from reality – we should see it as a particularization and intensification of urban life and as a carrier of authentic values of human existence that do not get an airing elsewhere.

A non-Western focus
In a cultural situation in which the discovery of new functions and meanings is also a global process, non-Western approaches to the garden may prove a source of great inspiration and correction and for this reason more attention should be paid to them in history and theory as well as in design. This implies less attention to style and more interest in the relation between design and experience and a more comprehensive study of other ways of seeing and interpreting the garden.

The drawn Western design has long championed point, line, plane and volume as the essentials of garden design, thereby keeping the enclosed garden within a specific dimension of time and space. It is a practice that places more emphasis on general outlines (direction, distance, volume) than on the experience of details; that is more often static than active, defining, quite literally, the boundaries. Such an approach can prove rather one-sided, reducing design grammar to an international vocabulary of forms that ignores a time- and place-bound experience and a dialogue between nature and culture. In France, Gilles Clément has tried, with his 'jardin en mouvement', to break through this practice by abandoning the architectural design and permitting plantings to change over the course of months and years. In Parc André Citroën, in the centre of Paris, one can also see how, through a variety of gradations in design and planting, Clément gives the enclosed garden a new, magical meaning and so inspires people to see, experience and understand wilderness and culture from a different perspective [figs 28, 29]. His ideas about the 'jardin planétaire' are the consequence of a global orientation and arise from his desire to understand the meaning of garden, landscape, nature and ecology in a globalizing society via an inter-cultural approach.

Is the twentieth-century interest in the closed Japanese Zen garden the product of a genuine desire to understand the essence of this creation, or was and is Western interest purely a matter of seeking affirmation for its own striving after modern emptiness and abstraction; in other words is the Western gaze colonizing the Japanese garden out of an unconscious exoticism? Those who feel attracted by the simplicity of the architectural garden in the Islamic tradition, should realize that their gaze, too, is selective and probably denies them a true understanding of this complex culture which also boasts, alongside the architectural courtyard, a rich veneration of nature [figs 30, 31]. Form is not the same as experience which is rooted in life itself.

Within the framework of different cultural traditions the garden appears to be an easily understood reality. But to the extent that the garden is an instrumentalization of the world around us it must of necessity entail different worlds of experience, with other rites and other social identifications.

In the Creole tradition, nature is the domain of spirits and ancestors. Gardens in the Caribbean region consequently contain strategic plantings of medicinal herbs designed to guard and protect the house and its inhabitants against evil influences from outside. Such gardens, which strike Western eyes as disordered, act as a magic

[fig. 32]
Garden in Pointe-à-Pitre, Basse-Terre, Guadeloupe

[fig. 33]
Mandia Smith's yard, Georgia (US)

[fig. 34]
Edith Windom in her garden, South Carolina

Erik de Jong and Marleen Dominicus van Soest, *Aardse Paradijzen I. De tuin in de Nederlandse kunst 15de tot 18de eeuw*, Snoeck Ducaju, Haarlem/Ghent 1996.

Erik de Jong and Wouter Reh, 'De tuin en de Stad. De Amsterdamse grachtentuin in vogelvlucht' in: *Amsterdamse Grachtentuinen. Keizersgracht*, Waanders, Zwolle 1997, pp. 15-49.

Erik de Jong, 'De tuin als derde natuur. Een beschouwing over natuur en kunst', *Theoretische Geschiedenis* 25 (1998) 2/3, pp. 97-112.

Erik de Jong and Marleen Dominicus-van Soest, *Aardse Paradijzen II. De tuin in de Nederlandse kunst 1770-2000*, Snoeck Ducaju, Haarlem/Ghent 1999.

Erik de Jong, 'Gärten auf Papier. Hans Vredeman de Vries und sein Hortorvm Viridariorvmque elegantes & multiplicis formae von 1583', in: U. Härting (ed.), *Gärten und Höfe der Rubenszeit im Spiegel der Malerfamilie Brueghel un der Künstler um Peter Paul Rubens*, Hirmer Verlag, Munich 2000, pp. 37-49.

Maggie Keswick, *The Chinese Garden. History, Art & Architecture*, Academy Editions, London 1980.

Richard Koek (ed.), *Tuinen in detentie 1993-96* [garden and landscape designs in penitentiaries], Ministry of Housing, Spatial Planning and Environmental Management, Central Directorate for Information and External Relations, The Hague 1994.

Gerrit Komrij, *Over de noodzaak van tuinieren*, Bert Bakker, Amsterdam 1991 (Huizinga lecture 1990).

György Konrád, *Tuinfeest*. A novel. Van Gennep, Amsterdam 1992.

Margriet Kruyver (ed.), *The Park of the Future. 75 Years Gerrit Rietveld Academie – International AIAS Student Seminar*, Gerrit Rietveld Academy, Amsterdam 1999.

Rob Leopold, 'Een plek van afzondering en overgave' in: Erik de Jong and Marleen Dominicus van Soest, *Aardse Paradijzen II. De tuin in de Nederlandse kunst 1770-2000*, Snoeck Ducaju, Haarlem/Ghent 1999, pp. 211-253.

Amina-Aïcha Malek, *Le sentiment de la nature dans les domus de l'Afrique romaine -IIème-Vème siècles* [unpublished thesis], Ecole des Hautes Etudes en Sciences Sociales, Paris 1999.

Toby Musgrave, *Courtyard Gardens. Imaginative ideas for outdoor living*, Jacqui Small, London 2000.

The assignments. Innovative concepts for City Gardens in Rotterdam, Architecture International Rotterdam/Breeze of AIR, Rotterdam 2000.

Attilio Petruccioli, *Il giardino islamico. Architettura, natura, paessagio*, Electa, Milan 1994.

Adriaan van der Staay, 'Vignetten voor een landschap', in: *Landschapsarchitectuur en Stedebouw in Nederland 1995-1997*, Bussum 1998, pp. 12-26.

Clemens Steenbergen, *Symfonie van water, land en lucht* [inaugural lecture, Delft, 12 January 1994], Thoth, Bussum 1994.

Willem van Toorn, *Dooltuin*, Amsterdam, Em. Querido, 1995.

Jean-Louis Vincendeau, *Petit traité du jardin en ville*, Desclée de Brouwer, Paris 1993.

Richard Westmacott, *African-American Gardens and Yards in the Rural South*, The University of Tennessee Press, Knoxville 1998.

Ad Zuiderent, 'Een zwerftocht door een wilde tuin. Tuinen in de twintigste-eeuwse Nederlandse literatuur', in: Erik de Jong and Marleen Dominicus van Soest, *Aardse Paradijzen II. De tuin in de Nederlandse kunst 1770-2000*, Haarlem/Ghent, Snoeck Ducaju, 1999, pp. 175-211.

This essay was largely written during my Harvard Fellowship as Fellow in the History of Landscape Architecture, Dumbarton Oaks, Landscape Studies, Washington D.C., USA, in the spring semester (January to May) 2001. I would like to thank the Trustees of Harvard University, the Director and Senior Fellows in Landscape Architecture of Dumbarton Oaks for this appointment. My research was inspired by many professional and friendly discussions with Catherine Benoît, Michel Conan, Philip Hu, Amina-Aïcha Malek and Kenjii Wako. A Dutch version was previously published as the Clusius Lecture, Clusius Foundation, Leiden 2001.

shell or shield, as an invisible hortus conclusus [fig. 32]. Just as a medicine man or woman may use these plants to heal and protect the human body, so the garden as a whole serves as an amulet against cosmological influences. In the Afro-American tradition, this magical function is fulfilled by bottles and other 'worthless' objects. In the 'yard' or garden they are part of ritual, physical acts that contribute to the notion of 'self' vis à vis nature, ancestors and society [figs 33, 34]. It is not the resulting form or visual ordering and demarcation that is important here, but where objects are located, the power they possess and the way the whole can be experienced as a magical order. That order, which defines and protects, is invisible to the uninitiated, however.

The classic Chinese garden – to the extent that it can be categorized as such – belongs to an extensive and rich culture [figs 35-37]. The enclosed court and garden occupies an important place in this, although as a design principle it is rapidly declining in cities like Beijing under the influence of international architectural styles. Yet it would be a misunderstanding to interpret the classic Chinese enclosure as a need to establish boundaries, to impose form, to define. The Chinese manner of enclosing is more a means of emphasizing the centre whereby the wall is experienced as permeable and elastic. Rather than defining and confining, the fence around the Chinese garden organizes space and time in a continuous flow. The landscape inside the enclosure is in fact unbounded and incomplete. Moreover, Chinese cosmology does not distinguish between nature and human culture which are seen as belonging to the same order; nor does Chinese culture make the kind of distinction between nature and artificiality, between natural and cultivated, as is made in the Western world with its contrast between *physis* and *nomos*. This means that the Chinese garden is a landscape with the same ontological status as its 'natural' surroundings. The Chinese enclosed garden is not an imitation of nature, nor is it a transformation of nature: the construction of the garden as a work of art involves the cultivation of nature and as such maintains the continuity between nature and artificiality. The Chinese enclosed garden is not 'organic' either, but organized and coordinated: objects are placed in relation to one another with respect and esteem for their own particularity and quintessence. Multiplicity, diversity and individuality can exist side by side. Western tradition separates the dimensions of time and space: time moves forwards in one dimension, space stands still in three dimensions. In the Chinese garden, time and space are inseparable, part of the ceaseless transformation in which phenomena are events rather than fixed, formal and bounded objects. Time and space are as concrete and particular as the other elements that make up the inventory of the garden. They are not absolute or abstract but are on the same ontological level as the plants, rocks, pavilions or pools, and like these they too can be selected, constructed and arranged.

To conclude

Such examples can be an important corrective to our Western notions about the enclosed garden. The area of tension between closed and open may well be the secret of the hortus conclusus. An open garden can be experienced as closed, a hortus conclusus as open. In a multicultural society, non-Western examples can enrich and revalidate the enclosed garden as an integrated phenomenon of the first order. For this it is necessary that we rewrite our own history from a comparative perspective. Which leads to the conclusion that the art of making a new hortus conclusus resides first and foremost in the chambers of our mind, for there, as Willem van Toorn wrote in his poem 'Hortus conclusus' of 1995, 'The first thought is rounded off.'

[fig. 35]
Passage in the garden of Shih Tzu Lin, begun 14th century and later drastically altered, Suzhou, China

[fig. 36]
Tuin He Yuan, Yangzhou, Jiangsu, China, late 19th, early 20th century

[fig. 37]
A Chinese courtyard, woodcut from Hung Hsueh Yin Yuan T'u Chi by Lin Ch'ing

IVAN NIO

Weak Boundaries

It goes without saying that an event around the theme 'hortus conclusus' is concerned with the meaning of boundaries. Boundaries are emphasized much more by an enclosed garden than by an open garden. Demarcation of the enclosed garden with hedges, walls or water defines spaces between interior and exterior, between private and public, between proximity and distance. A boundary also indicates the arena for social and mental activities. The enclosed garden marks a private space, within which certain rules apply. This localized boundary is an essential precondition for both the contemplative mood of the Erasmian garden and the playfulness in the *hortus ludi*. According to the historian Johan Huizinga, the tracing of a boundary expresses something whimsical. 'There is a natural tendency,' he wrote in *Homo Ludens*, 'to see the potential for a space for play in every enclosed garden.'[1] Just like the enclosed spaces themselves, the boundaries can be interpreted in myriad different ways. The garden designs created within the context of Breeze of AIR examine and variously highlight the question of the garden boundary.

For Breeze of AIR, the garden was no counterbalance to the city but an unmissable component of urban culture. The spatial form and modern-day meaning of boundaries were investigated at nine different sites. Old dividing lines, say the result of functional zoning and infrastructural networks, have often lost their meaning. At other places – especially in undifferentiated green space – new borders need to be drawn. The hortus conclusus can offer a solution in the quest for new demarcations of green public space. However, the distinction made by the cultural sociologist Richard Sennett between strong and weak borders is another important consideration in the reintroduction of the enclosed urban garden.[2] In Sennett's opinion, the strong boundaries of functional zoning in public space should be replaced by weak boundaries, transitions between the different spheres in the city. These weak boundaries control the confrontation between and intermingling of diverse activities and cultures in the city. Rather than fostering segregation or retreat into the private domain, weak boundaries in fact stimulate interchange in the city as a patchwork of public domains with different levels of activity and ambiences.

Enclosures

Due to its clear-cut boundaries, the urban garden is more in the transitional zone between private and public domains than is the city park. Access to the garden is restricted by an enclosure or the imposition of rules. The design and meaning of the boundaries mirrors this fraught grey area between private and public. The designers participating in Breeze of AIR have interpreted the enclosure in a variety of ways. The design of the perimeters ranges from transparent fences (Museum Park, the new square in the Agniese neighbourhood), water (Valkeniersweide), existing walls (Boijmans Van Beuningen Museum) and glazed partitions (Central Station, Hofplein viaduct, Arboretum Trompenburg and Las Palmas). In the Spinoza park, a coulisse hedge with openings frames an enclosed garden. The use of transparent boundaries is a surprising choice. Openings in the walls and glazed partitions emphasize that the interior of the garden is relative to an exterior state.[3] It marks a revival of the spatial paradox of the enclosed garden as infinity within enclosure.[4] It also points to the ambivalent meaning of the enclosed garden, a meaning primarily to be found in the adverse effects of privatization. Fencing always shuts out something or someone.

[1] Johan Huizinga, *Homo Ludens* (Haarlem: Tjeenk Willink, 1938).
[2] Richard Sennett, *The Conscience of the Eye. The Design and Social Life of Cities* (New York: Alfred A. Knopf, 1990). For an analysis of Sennett's term 'weak boundary' see: René Boomkens, *Een drempelwereld. Moderne ervaring en stedelijke openbaarheid* (Rotterdam: NAi Publishers, 1998).
[3] The use of glass does not necessarily mean a weak boundary. According to Richard Sennett it can in fact signify the very opposite.
[4] This spatial paradox is a central theme in Rob Aben and Saskia de Wit, *De omsloten tuin* (Rotterdam: 010 Publishers, 1998), translated as *The Enclosed Garden* (Rotterdam: 010 Publishers, 1999).
[5] The authors arrive at a similar conclusion in Maarten Hajer and Arnold Reijndorp, *In search of new public domain*, trans. Andrew May (Rotterdam: NAi Publishers, 2001).

Valkeniersweide, summer 2001
Relaxing by the water

Valkeniersweide, summer 2001
Football

Valkeniersweide, summer 2001
A chat after shopping

That is why the concept of the hortus conclusus has not been embraced by all the designers. In the Lijnbaanhoven, Hargreaves has opted to use the concept of the park rather than that of the garden, because of the public significance of these spaces. By increasing the clarity of organization and avoiding the placement of fencing, Hargreaves increases the openness of both these courtyard gardens and retains their role as a component of public space. The plan for the Lijnbaan gardens puts the debate about the privatization of public space using fences, walls and closed-circuit cameras into finer focus.

While enclosed public space in the USA – where life increasingly turns inward in the guise of guarded shopping malls and gated communities – is tainted with strongly negative overtones in discussions about the contemporary city, the fenced-in garden in Europe seems, for the time being, to have a less charged connotation. Public spaces such as Amsterdam's Vondelpark and the Parque del Buen Retiro in Madrid are physically fenced in, yet they are still perceived and used as freely accessible urban gardens. A fence can indicate that the park is a special space, where clear-cut rules apply compared with other public spaces. Fences can establish symbolic boundaries without necessarily leading to barriers or exclusion, providing they are designed as weak boundaries.[5] The demarcation of the hortus conclusus can define the public space in a spatial as well as a social sense. In a heterogeneous society some spaces must be clearly marked in order to allow different cultures and a variety of uses to coexist. Possible strategies include enclosure with a fence, establishing rules, putting up signs and the appointment of wardens, so that visitors know what is, and is not, permitted. However, formalization of the space using a fence is only appropriate if the spaces lose as little of their openness as possible.

By focusing on the boundaries of the horti conclusi, the designers put the design of the enclosure on the agenda. Currently, formalizing collective public space in the post-war neighbourhoods by means of fences, planted borders and water, so that the distinction between public and private becomes more explicit, is an important task in urban restructuring. The dilemma here, however, is that fences and walls do not sit well with the openness and fluid space of post-war urban planning. The fences employed are often too high and too massive, and they are usually the lowest priority in the budget. Like garden making, giving shape to the boundary needs injecting with new vitality. It does bring up the question of which particular places are appropriate for siting boundaries. In spatial terms, weak boundaries can be defined in various ways. In a multiform society they are perceived differently by different groups, depending on lifestyle and culture or subculture. The garden border does not have the same meaning for all residents. Here we are faced with the impossibility of unambiguously defining the border of the hortus conclusus. There is no blueprint for the enclosure of a garden.

Enchanted spaces

The boundaries of the horti conclusi can transform poorly defined spaces into meaningful ones. The concept of the enclosed garden introduces a hiatus in the omnipresent transport and communication networks. Yet the contemporary Erasmian garden proves to be more than just a place of repose. Above all, the plans constitute poetic intensifications of the fluid public space of the modern city. In the same way that modern urban planning strips the public space of its mystery, so the concept of the hortus conclusus proves to be a means of restoring the sensual or even sacred character of sites. The water-filled spiral by Charles Correa for the inner garden of the Boijmans Van Beuningen Museum is a literal reference to the metaphysical dimension beyond the surface of visible space. Other gardens have been designed as

Valkeniersweide, summer 2001

Tennis

Valkeniersweide, summer 2001

Play area

Valkeniersweide, summer 2001

The annual neighbourhood festival

enchanted places for memories or dreams. In the orchid-filled greenhouse of Gross.Max. and the garden with ornamental grasses and shrubs of Piet Oudolf, visitors are intoxicated by the shapes, colours and perfumes of the exotic plants and perennials. The enchantment in SANAA's design derives from the distorted panorama it gives of the city and the overwhelming impact of the enclosed space. On the station square designed by Quadrat the flamingo pool and the 20-metre-tall glasshouses briefly wrest the onlooker away from daily life, and in West 8's design the boat trip through the wisteria is meant to evoke a sense of rebirth. The designs call on sensuous experience and the imagination. By re-instilling public spaces with meaning and atmosphere – even by way of an illusion – they facilitate a need for escape as well as an intensification of the quotidian.

As a prosaic locus of repose, the Erasmian garden is likewise variously interpreted. Its use is intensified into a spectacle for the benefit of collective or urban life. The distinction between the meaning of the garden as a meditative space and as a space for such display is often vague. Valkeniersweide and the Spinoza park are set up for sport activities yet still reserve space for meditation by means of zoning. The hortus conclusus of the Arboretum is intended for the staging of presentations. In the dome atop Las Palmas and along the route of the former Hofplein line, the spectacular panorama of the city arouses a sense of awe of the infinite. The game of seeing and being seen happens around the pool fronting Central Station, on the green stairway at Valkeniersweide and in the Lijnbaan gardens. And Hargreaves has stated that additional programmatic elements can be added to these courtyard gardens, such as a café and a public toilet. The enclosed, private space of the hortus conclusus lends itself to various programmes on the continuum from sacred to profane *in extremis*. Gross.Max.'s glasshouse has specifically been designed as a hedonistic pleasure zone for marginal users driven from other public spaces, from drug users to prostitutes.

Gardens divide and unite simultaneously. Because of their boundaries, the horti conclusi always stand in a different relation to the outside world. Given their programmes they also remain part of the public space of the metropolis. Sometimes the hortus's boundaries are even more important than the space within, as at Museum Park, where the curved fence of the Erasmus University garden clarifies the pedestrian route through the park and over the Westzeedijk. The garden designed by Piet Oudolf is a place for lingering as well as a place for passing, set as it is at the intersection of four routes. At Central Station, Quadrat has shifted the station underground in order to underscore the structure of the city. In the Lijnbaan gardens, too – albeit on a smaller scale – the focus is connection rather than enclosure or privacy. Here the designs not only condition a retardation of the circulation flows in the city, but also affect spatial and cultural mobility. The weak boundaries of the hortus conclusus can engender interfaces between busy and peaceful areas. Moreover, the garden as public domain can result in surprising or meditative spots where the diversity of the urban fabric surfaces without being threatening.

Crossing borders

The theme of the hortus conclusus not only pertains to defining boundaries for specific groups or activities, but also to breaking them down. It entails the examination and overstepping of the bounds between nature and culture (as can be seen in the designs by Gross.Max., Teresita Fernández and Zeger Reyers), as well as the exploration of the borderline between the visible and the invisible, the profane and the sacred. It was primarily the artists who adopted the breaking down of boundaries as a tactic. In their proposals they seek out conditions for transforming the material as well as cultures/subcultures and accepted values. In the *hortus ludi* of Dennis

Spinoza park, summer 2001

Spinoza park, summer 2001

Sitting and admiring the flower garden

Spinoza park, summer 2001

To the shopping centre

Spinoza park, summer 2001

Youth hang-out

Spinoza park, summer 2001

Skating

Adams, children play in an imitation *afwerkplaats* or drive-in 'sex service station', this time for pedal cars, and the pavilion of Elmgreen & Dragset serves as a meeting place for homosexual men as well as for more public activities. During the symposium, Fiona Raby reproached the garden designers for avoiding these controversial dimensions of urban life. However, in the case of Valkeniersweide and the Lijnbaan gardens there was indeed an attempt to position dissimilar groups of visitors alongside each other, so that encounters might occur there. Hargreaves' response to Raby's criticism was that in the final analysis the use of the Lijnbaan gardens embodied more culture than her own work. One can see in both gardens a confrontation between diverse users on a daily basis, from the shopping public, schoolchildren, the homeless and drug users to tourists. And while Elmgreen & Dragset's white pavilion is fairly unambiguously designed with a view to sexual encounters, Correa's 'Kund' – the walled pond for ritual cleansing – in the public park of the Boijmans Van Beuningen Museum treads a contrary and more subversive path. As a sacred structure it can also signify a place for play, even sexual interplay. The kund is an ambivalent place where the religious and the profane commingle. The hortus conclusus does not exclude the crossing of borders in a cultural sense. The gardens respond not simply to the need for escape from reality, but also to the need to step up their public character.

Aghain, the horti conclusi blur the distinction between 'high' and 'low' culture. No longer elitist, the hortus conclusus can host reciprocal exchanges between high and low, between avant-gardism and popular culture. In SANAA's Las Palmas garden visual culture is transformed into a sublime hortus conclusus. The use of the hortus conclusus is also democratized. Oudolf's sumptuous garden is open to all and sundry. His gardens in Enköping, Sweden, have become an attraction daily visited by hordes of tourists. The station area designed by Quadrat is even explicitly designed as an attraction. It is as though the garden is being integrated in the 'experience economy', where the experience of a panorama, a journey through the wisteria of the Arboretum, or even the celebration of peace and quiet, are increasingly becoming public attractions. However, it may be better to experience some quiet gardens on one's own. In this age, even the meditative dimension of the hortus conclusus rubs up against its own weak boundaries.

Engagement and appropriation

The role that public space plays in the life of society is dependent on the extent to which users and wardens engage with it. Implementing the urban garden can reinforce that engagement and identification with the public realm. This engagement relates to the design and programming, as well as to upkeep and management. The plans facilitate the identities and lifestyles of users in a variety of ways.

The ways in which the programming of the designs reacts to the heterogeneity of Rotterdam's population can be subdivided into various methodologies. The designs for the Lijnbaan gardens and the Hofplein line viaduct with the new square are neutral, so that a diversity of groups can attach themselves to the spaces. Hargreaves anticipates potential use forms. In Gross.Max.'s design more has been left unprogrammed. Here the aesthetics of the design overshadows the social dimension. Will people really go cycling on the Hofplein viaduct? How can the glasshouse be kept intact? In Valkeniersweide, Louafi has opted for another approach. Here the demarcation of spheres gives specific areas a meaning for particular activities and groups, from separate paths for cyclists and pedestrians to zones where families can hold barbecues. The hortus conclusus, surrounded by water, is conceived of as a multicultural meeting place. The plan is marked by an element of spatial determinism. Its

Spinoza park, summer 2001
Walking

Spinoza park, summer 2001
Fishing

Spinoza park, summer 2001
Cycling

garden boundaries must result in the overlapping of and exchange between different social worlds. The approaches adopted by Gross.Max. and Louafi illustrate the dilemma of public space in the multicultural city. Alongside a partial theming and programming of the public space, designers have also to determine the conditions for flexible or simultaneous use by different groups. The task is to strike a balance between programming and non-specificity, making use of weak boundaries. On the one hand, the hortus conclusus provides a model to clearly programme certain places; on the other, it is still important to create multi-purpose or ambiguous places, so that each visitor can attach his/her own meaning to public space.

Engagement and appropriation require intensive maintenance and management. Someone or some organization must feel responsible. In the horti conclusi to be managed by private organizations, this seems to have been taken care of. In the public realm, however, the government falls short. At the symposium there was consensus about the need for more money to be made available for the upkeep of gardens and parks. Effective maintenance requires rules of play. Rules regarding upkeep occupy a prominent place in the plan for Valkeniersweide. The establishing of rules extends as far as self-management by residents, which seems to be the best way to stimulate engagement. The hortus conclusus in Valkeniersweide puts this point at the top of the agenda: what are the potentialities and limitations for that self-management in a heterogeneous city district? The other designs refrain from broaching this issue, yet it is possible that the self-managed hortus conclusus could define a new intermediate space elsewhere in the city where private and public spheres touch and overlap.[6]

The city as garden

The hortus conclusus has proved to be a fertile spatial and cultural construct. Also very much alive is the garden as metaphor. This concerns, among other things, the city as a human biotope. Back in the 1920s, the sociologists of the Chicago School viewed the city as an ecological system. The whole city is a garden, a living organism with different communities that adapt themselves to an environment, grow in number, disappear as a result of competition, and are supplanted by new groups. The metaphor of the city as garden also holds for the design and management. In 1961, the urbanist John Habraken compared his profession with that of the gardener who trains and stimulates the growth of the organism using a whole armoury of techniques.[7] Compared with the attempts of recent urban planning to control the chaos and the diversity of the city and prune back the vegetation with all speed, today's designers and planners must espouse a more multiform concept of the garden, with places that give room to the city organism. In addition, it is no longer a question of a lone gardener, but many: governments, organizations, institutions, business concerns and residents. In this respect, the geographer Marwyn Samuels once compared the city with a garden: 'Whether benign or evil, the city is also a "garden", which differs from other gardens primarily in that its authors are plural and involve all those who live in and contribute to the design of the landscape.'[8] What does this mean for our handling of the public realm and the role of the garden within it?

In his last essay, written a few months before his death at the age of 86, the landscape historian John Brinckerhoff Jackson qualifies Huizinga's 'play-space' concept.[9] Jackson concluded that play is not always tied to boundaries. Lone skiers, snowboarders, sailors and surfers move over and through matter with relative freedom. They are always searching for new surroundings where no binding rules yet apply. The discovery of virgin territory is coupled with a taste for excitement and uncertainty. Perhaps this attitude can also be applied in the quest for places where the concept of the hortus conclusus is relevant, and in the search for commissioning bodies that

[6.] Margaret Crawford, 'Blurring the boundaries: public space and private life', in: J. Chase, M. Crawford and J. Kaliski (eds), *Everyday Urbanism* (New York: The Monacelli Press, 1999).
[7.] The reference to Habraken is derived from Erik de Jong, 'Hortus Conclusus': open of gesloten, zichtbaar of onzichtbaar?' *Text of the Clusius Lectures 2001*, ed. Gerda van Uffelen (Leiden: Clusius Foundation, 2001).
[8.] Marwyn S. Samuels, 'The Biography of Landscape', in: Donald W. Meinig (ed.), *The Interpretation of Ordinary Landscapes* (Oxford: Oxford University Press, 1979).
[9.] John Brinckerhoff Jackson, 'Places for Fun and Games', in: *Landscape in Sight. Looking at America* (New Haven: Yale University Press, 1997).

Lijnbaanhoven summer 2001

Walking the dog

Lijnbaanhoven summer 2001

A breather after shopping

Lijnbaanhoven summer 2001

Rotterdam tourists

might best serve garden design. These are places similar to those focused upon during the Breeze of AIR event, but also places elsewhere, for example on the enclosed inner spaces between blocks of buildings, along motorways, in shopping centres, theme parks, business parks, suburbia, allotments and recreation areas. The urban landscape provides a fertile layer of humus for revivifying the art of garden making. If the garden is indicative of the state of culture then we should not resist the everyday urban landscape. Instead of rejecting that culture, we should embrace it and make it special.

**Lijnbaanhoven
summer 2001**

Sleeping-place for a vagrant

**Lijnbaanhoven
summer 2001**

Walking and talking

**Lijnbaanhoven
summer 2001**

Youth hang-out

ERIC LUITEN & FRANK DE JOSSELIN DE JONG

Four Shades of Green

The number of town dwellers who depend on public parks for their open-air recreation has declined strongly since the post-war reconstruction period, when large new residential suburbs were tacked onto the densely occupied pre-war cities. Since then there has a huge rise in indoor recreation. Car ownership has made it easy for people to explore the countryside, and present-day incomes make the option of exotic holidays available. On top of that, the average house occupancy has fallen from a one-bedroom house for five people to a four-bedroom house for two. The large city parks, which were originally designed for intensive year-round enjoyment, are now used for much shorter periods but all the more intensively for both individual and mass recreation: walking, skating, jogging and pop concerts. The large areas of green in the post-war suburbs generally lie empty and abandoned for much of the year.

An altogether different situation prevails in the inner cities and adjacent late nineteenth-century districts. Planners exert themselves to find ways to make these busy areas attractive for modern living. With much difficulty, they find some space for the construction of public squares and small city parks. Park designers follow the examples of foreign cities in producing high-grade layouts which contribute a touch of elegance to the urban surroundings. The intensive use of outdoor space associated with these densely built-up urban areas calls for robust and (owing to the application of architectural facilities) expensive layouts. Rigorous maintenance is required to counteract wear-and-tear and to prevent deterioration. The budgets applicable for park creation and maintenance in the outlying expansion districts would be insufficient here. At the same time, in these districts there is relatively little prospect of supplementing the budgets for high-quality green-space management with the proceeds from land sale.

These two opposing characteristics of urban green space make it essential to reassess its value to the city and its significance in the future. The aspiration to sustainable, high-quality and above all compact cities that dominates government policy will have an impact on the development of parks and public gardens, and in this respect it is a good thing that the unquestioning attitude towards green urban space is now a matter of debate. Parks have lost much of the quality they used to have. We examine three aspects of this deterioration in a little more detail below. These aspects are over-programming, negatively argued zoning decisions and growing technical uniformity of management.

First, the programmatic overkill. This is not something that has always been there. The parks created in the nineteenth and early twentieth centuries were deliberate investments in land in or near the city by the well-to-do. Building plots adjacent to such green space could be sold for high prices. The Vondelpark in Amsterdam, with its generous ratio of border length to surface area and its quasi-endless ground plan, is the shrewdest and most famous example of this approach in the Netherlands. There was hardly any functional programme to speak of. The main design motif was the evocation of an idyll, which manifested itself as an informal composition of lawns and open water, grouped trees, shrubbery and winding paths. Here and there room could be found for a poetic feature or a subtle amenity. The first city parks of this period were created on plots that became available more or less incidentally, with a preference for sites already planted with greenery such as private estates and cemeteries. After 1920, the city park became 'democratized' under the influence of

Deterioration of the urban park

ideas about public health and recreation. The enjoyment of public gardens now fell within the reach of all walks of society. The design and furnishing of the larger Dutch public parks was increasingly determined by social/physical planning policy, future need estimates and standardization. Their construction was feasible due to the work-creation programmes designed to attack the rampant Dutch unemployment between the wars. City parks of this period were multi-functional leisure amenities whose surface area and layout was dictated not by the idyll but by the position in the city and visitor capacities. The site was first indicated on a planned basis; the surface area was based on practical experience.

The tendency towards the programming and theming of green areas has been pursued further and refined in recent decades. The design and management of city parks have become increasingly subject to trends in leisure activity, to very strictly defined sports and games criteria, to pressure from the urban ecological movement and to a multitude of commercial activities of a thematic nature. On the margins of the metropolitan areas in the western part of the Netherlands, higher government authorities have taken it upon themselves to establish 'green star' sites. In the city, an expanding range of user categories has been defined, with a distinct green land-use optimized for each. In rural areas, sophisticated amusement parks and theme parks have risen up with immense visitor capacities as well as inward-looking and lavishly equipped buildings for visitor use, based on the completely closed consumer expenditure model of the family at leisure.

In his dissertation *Der kommende Stadtpark* (1995), Norfried Pohl describes how the city park phenomenon has undergone huge differentiation in the course of the twentieth century. Starting from a simple green civic amenity which bore roughly the same connotations for everyone, the park has been adopted by city planners and spatial designers as a compliant laboratory for experiments in shape, materials and atmosphere. We could compile a veritable alphabet of park types, indicating that the intended topographical and functional differentiation has also produced a postmodern parks vocabulary. Here is a selection from that alphabet:

Amusement park, Archaeology park, Botany park, Brain park, Centre Parc, Countryside park, Ecopark, Energy park, Equestrian park, Fairytale park, Farm park, Health park, History park, Homo park, Indoor park, Industry park, Jurassic Park, Lunapark, Media park, Museum Park, Picnic park, Pony park, Residential park, Safari park, Science park, Sculpture park, Senior citizens' park, Sports park, Technology park, Transmitter park, Waterway park, Windmill park, Zoo park.

A list of park 'types' like this is a useful means of eliciting new ideas about the contemporary meanings of the park. But the main thing about the list is that it demonstrates how the park concept has been eagerly embraced by functional categories and groups that traditionally have nothing to do with parks but are conscious of the mollifying effect that the attribute 'park' has on the image of their activities. This tends to undermine the associations residents and users form with the traditional city park. In this connection, the German art historian Osterwold (1977) slates the endless proliferation of green space types as a perverse development.

The second obfuscating aspect is spatial sameness. The history of urban green space may be summed up as a process in which rational planning methods have gradually gained the upper hand over a more intuitive approach. The first parks were invariably products of a positive and often artistic land-use decision, and in many cases were the result of individual initiatives. Site qualities such as a panorama, the urban backdrop or existing vegetation were usually crucial to the siting of a green place of repose. The establishment of these urban oases was the outcome of a private creative impulse rather than a civic policy. The city has, as it were, adopted

[fig. 2]

Appropriated green space: the leisure garden as indigenous domain

[fig. 3]

New green space at low-grade sites: woods along the A15

[fig. 4]

New green space at low-grade sites: park on filled waste dump

them as its own in the course of time. Around the beginning of the twentieth century – partly due to the Dutch Housing Act which was passed at that time – the creation of parks came under the sway of urban economic and physical planning criteria, a development which manifested itself in guidelines for area and facilities. The gradual transition of the city park from being a form of public art ownership to being a green area marked on the city planners' maps has furthered the standardization of public green space. After the war, during the reconstruction of the Netherlands, the planning and laying out of park space was subject to a hierarchical system of dividing up surface area and tasks. Functionalist standards for allowable distance from dwellings and the green surface area per resident led to a distinction between city, district and neighbourhood green space. Greenery provision has since been a routine component of urban planning, with a strongly uniformizing effect on urban expansion and urban renewal practice.

This rigid approach has been turning against park planning itself in recent years. In order to meet quantitative standards and at the same time prevent salable plots, designatable as building land, from being sacrificed, the designation of 'public green space' is in most cases given to sites that cannot be assigned a more positive use on account of soil contamination, noise, instability or other unpleasant deficiencies. Park-making therefore increasingly serves as a camouflage and expedient treatment for urban anomalies. In some cases – the Griftpark in Utrecht, the park on the site of the former gas works (Westergasfabriek) in Amsterdam, and the park to be laid out in the heavily polluted Oost-Abstpolder – green space was the only conceivable option left.

Finally, a third alarm bell is ringing: compartmentalized planning processes and low-grade maintenance impede the pursuit of quality. The distinction between living, working, recreation and traffic, based on the ideas of the modern city, impacted on the organization of practically every municipal department and corporation in the Netherlands. A division of responsibilities developed among the various bodies, as well as between government and market actors. The increasing self-sufficiency of various municipal departments manifested itself not only in territorial respects but also in the division of responsibilities within the single task of physical planning.

The main features of the plan were determined by the Urban Planning Department, the design and planting of public green space was managed by the Open Space Planning Department and the paving was provided by Public Works. Lighting systems were installed by the Illumination Department, waste-bins by the Sanitation Department, and benches and other park furniture by Parks and Public Gardens. The countenance of open space could thus never be more than a sum of well-meant but poorly matched parts.

The political reorganization of the main cities has also left its imprint on the quality of public space. The establishment of sub-municipalities and their associated administrative corporations has involved residents more closely with decision-taking about the development and maintenance of their surroundings. The other side of the coin has been a loss of differentiation at city level. Each sub-municipality wants to have the complete palette of green categories in its own area, and this has increased the fragmentation and lack of variety at the scale of the city as a whole. There is now a numbingly correct distribution of open-air recreational amenities around the urban parks of Rotterdam. There is virtually no difference between one park and another as to programme or topography; at first sight they are practically interchangeable. There are sportsfields and allotments everywhere. Everywhere too, grass fields, lakes and woodlands occur in the same proportions. You can walk on the footpaths, cycle on the cycle paths or ride your horse on the bridle paths wherever you go; and of

[fig. 5]

Green theming: a children's wood, Clara-Kinderbos

course, you must always park your car in the area provided.

A second effect of the new situation in urban politics is a widespread reticence about taking action on urban green space, even when it is essential from a purely technical and maintenance point of view. Collective sentiments about urban green space have achieved bizarre proportions. The administrators in the urban districts, for understandable if opportunistic reasons, have grown cautious about suggesting the transformation, ownership change or piecemeal selling of green space. Only very rarely are areas of public green space disposed of or privatized. Such cases apply only to small, labour-consuming areas of planting adjoining private gardens. The remainder of public green space is evidently considered so inviolable that the authorities have little stomach for redesignating poorly sited or little used areas of parkland or neglected coppices for building purposes.

The difficulty of making unequivocal choices in this situation is also apparent from the apportionment of funds for creating and maintaining green areas. The cost of making parks and public gardens in the Netherlands is low compared to urban parks in other countries like France or Spain. Layout budgets generally range from 7 to 25 Euros per square metre, while a budget of 135 Euros per square metre is regarded as low in, say, Barcelona. The new parks in Paris, such as La Villette, Bercy and André Citroën, have been accorded a layout budget of some 450 Euros per square metre. In the case of La Villette, this funding rate was applicable to no less than 55 hectares. Comparable budges are unknown in Rotterdam except for a central-city public square like Schouwburgplein, a wholly paved area for which the city reserved 385 Euros per square metre.

The maintenance budgets for Dutch parks and public gardens are correspondingly modest. Many cities in the Netherlands moreover economized on maintenance costs in the 1980s. Two rounds of cutbacks resulted in a budget reduced by no less than thirty per cent. This led not to a reduction in area but a decline in maintenance level. Expensive, rare or exotic plants were removed and replaced with simpler, generally native varieties. The pursuit of a 'more natural' look served as an excuse for more extensive mechanical mowing of meadows, while traditional garden tasks such as hoeing and weeding were discontinued.

Although a general diagnosis on parks and public gardens in Dutch cities suggests a chronic lack of meaning, quality and differentiation, there has been an undeniable revival in the paved public realm. Interest in the quality of open spaces, especially in inner cities, has grown furiously in the last fifteen years. Prompted by inspiring examples from abroad and in search of new vehicles for the urban image, administrators and civil servants became fascinated by the prospect of a thorough, high-quality renovation of streets and public squares. Cities such as Groningen, Breda, The Hague, 's-Hertogenbosch and more recently Amsterdam are good examples of this trend. A combination of official determination, unequivocal project management, decisive planning, controlled differentiation and the consistent application of materials has given the street remodelling projects of these cities the success they enjoy. We consider the same approach should work for green public spaces too.

In 1997, in his contribution to the Rotterdam 2010 Spatial Plan, Luiten proposed adopting new key categories for public green-space policy, based on an old, familiar typology. The desire existing in Rotterdam to develop a clear differentiation within such policy was answered by a recommendation to use no more than four categories of green space in subsequent discussions and decisions on its siting, design and upkeep at city level. The legend that was adopted for the urban plan comprises city gardens, city parks, city woodlands and city landscapes. This almost archetypical legend has a number of concrete advantages. The four categories are non-hierarchi-

[fig. 6]

The Zen garden; the original theme garden

[fig. 7]

Differentiation in upkeep: weeding and trimming

cal with respect to one another. Moreover, they are topographical – in other words, physical, concrete, simple to interpret and communicable. They provide adequate coverage with regard to the desired diversity, and have an organizing and disciplining effect on the municipal departments involved. They moreover support differentiation in both sociological and environmental-psychological attitudes towards public green space in and around the city, and introduce gradations in legal, ecological and spatial respects. The input for the typology is linked to physical properties and to ownership, management and maintenance regimes, and to a lesser extent to functional, programmatic or evaluative allocations, or the nature of the amenities. The survival of the typology is thus encouraged beyond trends in urban society, ad-hoc insights of individual aldermen, the will-to-form of incidentally involved designers and passing fashions in general.

The *city garden* is a very clearly bounded, wholly or partially closable green space in an arbitrary location. The garden is a floating category and thus lacks emphatic anchoring in urban design respects. It is monofunctionally or monothematically conceived, and changeable in time, with a cultivated, well-tended, intensively managed character and weekly maintenance cycles ('trimming and sweeping'). The experience of symbolically manipulated nature or groupwise utilization of instrumental nature is primary. Openness to the public is generally conditional, on the basis of contracted-out responsibility. Use varies with the seasons, and the users are members, interested persons who are willing to be actively involved, or walkers aware of being only visitors.

The *city park* is a clearly bounded green space of some size, with a multifunctional, more or less programmed atmosphere and a cultivated character. There exists an emphatic orientation towards the surrounding urban structure. The layout is gauged to peak visiting volumes and is scarcely susceptible to change with time. Here the experience of staged or catalogued nature is primary. City parks are unconditionally open to the public and as far as possible accessible from all sides and all year round. The upkeep is carried out in monthly cycles ('mowing and pruning') by the municipality itself or is contracted out on the basis of municipal guidelines and control. Usage is regular, and is variously individual or collective and aimed at interpersonal contact.

The *city woodland* is a more or less bounded green space of substantial size, in which ecological quality and usage intensity are mutually attuned. It occupies a peripheral position at the transition of urban and rural structures. Openness to the public is conditional on a natural 'carrying capacity'. The woodland has a very limited level of programming, a modest degree of layout design and an uncultivated character. Urban woodlands are accessible all year round. Maintenance is carried out by the municipality or is contracted out on the basis of guidelines with an annual maintenance cycle ('lopping and dredging'). The users and visitors walk the pathways with a weekly frequency and a duration of several hours. Their behaviour is gauged to the perception of tranquillity and a neutral environment.

The *city landscape*, finally, is an unbounded green space with an urban boundary effect. Non-urban land use and ownership are dominant there. It is multifunctional and has a rural topography. It is publicly open conditional to the interests of 'others' (e.g. farmers, woodland owners and naturalists). The management is delegated and wholly contracted out. Maintenance takes place in a multi-year cycle ('grazing and cleaning'). The users are either owners, i.e. persons with a permanent, existential involvement, or visiting cyclists or motorists who are prepared to travel some distance and spend at least half the day for a visit, generally in the company of others.

The new green-space legend at city level implies a drastic reconsideration of the

[fig. 8]

City garden type

[fig. 9]

City park type

LITERATURE
Municipality of Rotterdam, *Ruimtelijk Plan 2010 – Samenvatting/Verkenningen*, Rotterdam 1998.
Municipality of Rotterdam, *Ruimtelijk Plan 2010. Meer stad, meer toekomst*, Rotterdam 2000.
J. Goosens et al. (ed.), *Buitenruimte. Ontwerp, aanleg en beheer van de openbare ruimte in Rotterdam*, Rotterdam 1995.
Louwerse, D. et al. (ed.), *Groen in Rotterdam. Heden, verleden en toekomst van het landschap in de stad*, Rotterdam 1985.
D. Louwerse, 'De wederopbouw en de vormgeving van het stedelijk groen', in *Nederlandse Landschapsarchitectuur. Tussen traditie en experiment*, Amsterdam 1993.
E. Luiten, *Tuin Park Bos Landschap. Differentiatie van Rotterdamse stadsparken*, Barcelona/Rotterdam 1998.
N. Pohl, *Der kommende Stadtpark. Über urbane Grundbefindlichkeiten und die Einmischung der Natur*, Delft/Wageningen 1995.

ever-expanding list of policy categories for green space. It offers a relatively appealing alternative to the bureaucratic division into city, district, neighbourhood and urban block greenery, and for such metaphors as green corners, wedges, linkages or streamers. Above all, however, it fosters a shifting of budgets for layout and maintenance. With this typology, it becomes possible to adjust the more or less uniform and locally imbalanced expenditures, and to defend financial restraint on the one hand (for the city landscapes) and revitalization and intensification on the other (the city gardens). The four categories moreover make it possible to determine the appropriate direction of transformation of individual objects, which objects should be scratched from the municipal agenda, and which 'shade of green' should be assigned to planned new outdoor areas.

With the reintroduction of this somewhat traditionally coloured-in typology, two important questions were adopted by the AIR Foundation immediately after publication of the Structure Plan. The first of these related to the distribution and appearance of the existing city gardens in Rotterdam; the question was whether an open city like Rotterdam is well served by the introduction of the city garden phenomenon. The second question was a wish to test the green-space typology, and in particular the 'city garden' type, for its capacity to represent and elicit contemporary landscape-architectural forms, materials, styles and insights. These questions formed the basis for the Breeze of AIR event.

[fig. 10]

City woodland type

[fig. 11]

City landscape type

The Public Garden

The Public Garden

Designers' Proposals

THE SITE

Situated between the Lijnbaan shopping promenade and Schouwburgplein (Theatre Square) are the Lijnbaanhoven – the gardens of Jan Evertsenplaats and Joost Banckertsplaats – surprising green oases in Rotterdam's concrete-dominated city centre. In fact they constitute the only garden-like spaces in the centre and present a tranquil green contrast with bustling new Schouwburgplein. The gardens nestle somewhat hidden between the blocks of flats on the Lijnbaan. Residents look out from their apartments on these little parks, which were intended as communal inner courts. Although the southern sides of both gardens border directly on fairly busy shopping streets, Van Oldenbarneveltplaats and Aert van Nesstraat respectively, these spaces are rarely visited. In the course of time, they have degenerated primarily into a hang-out for urban nomads, and a place to walk dogs.

THE BRIEF

How can the original meaning of the Lijnbaanhoven as public city gardens be reinforced in a city centre that is becoming increasingly compact and vital? The brief seeks a new form and content for the contrast between the sensual experience of peace and quiet in the gardens and the dynamics of commerce, going out and recreation in their immediate vicinity. The character, use and ambience of the gardens in the design should appeal enough to make them widely loved, used and cared for as public urban gardens. The desired result is a type of urban garden that elaborates on the romantic layout of Jan Evertsenplaats and the orthogonal design of Joost Banckertsplaats, using a richer variety of plants and flowers that change colour with the seasons. Benches, rubbish bins, lighting and a dog toilet must be included in the design. The brief also calls for a management and maintenance plan that involves local residents and shopkeepers.

Schouwburgplein and Lijnbaanhoven, 2001

photo: Pandion

THE DESIGNER ON THE DESIGN

'The currently deteriorated condition of both gardens discourages most visitors and residents from lingering or using the gardens in any other way. The gardens have devolved into a type of no man's land: neither public nor private. They give the impression that only a few people make use of these spaces, with the exception of those engaged in illicit drug transactions. The Lijnbaan gardens are in fact part of the public space of the city, and everyone should be able to enjoy them.

'The approach is simple: reduce the negative and reinforce the positive. Residents of the enveloping apartment towers are uniquely positioned to exert their influence over the space, helping to determine the management and operational issues that can help drive out the negative uses of the spaces by vagrants and drug users, dog waste, general littering and the increasing sense of a lack of safety. Many of these issues are related to poor operational management and a declining respect for and appreciation of these gardens.

'The redesign embraces editing the existing garden components and continuing the ongoing evolution of the gardens. The single biggest improvement to be made to the Lijnbaanhoven is to increase visibility and security. When the gardens were initially planted, the young trees undoubtedly looked small and weak in relation to the soaring residential towers. The low-growing ground-covering plants and shrubs that were planted originally have now grown into thickets more than a metre high. Cutting back some of the shrubs will eliminate undesirable activities that this cover currently harbours. This will help to increase the sense of safety and will foster the return of positive use of the gardens. Certain garden walls need to be renewed, and worn or deteriorated surfaces need replacing with new materials.

'The "moderne" design of Joost Banckertsplaats is used as a starting-point for adding additional layers of detail. Small, rectangular bands of water, ornamental grasses and flower beds are inserted into the existing grass panels, bringing a finer scale and "hyper-modern" quality to the space. New stone paving is installed around the lime tree.

'The new Joost Banckertsplaats contains four rectangular pools with aerating jets that gently agitate the water; the pools form a background and counterbalance to the noise of the adjacent street. The design of Jan Evertsenplaats is in fact a palimpsest upon which aspects of previous designs are selectively retained while others eliminated. Certain paths and walls are retained, while shrub beds are reconfigured or eliminated. A new path cuts across the square diagonally, paved in new stone and set on concrete spread footings to combat future subsidence. This path is set 15 cm above the level of the lawn, reinforcing the idea that this diagonal cuts through the garden as a shopper's shortcut to Schouwburgplein, and to ensure that pools of rainwater do not impede pedestrian flow across the garden. In essence, the path becomes an overlay to the palimpsest. The pond will be renovated.

'In both gardens, the majority of the 17 species of tree will be retained. These mature trees lend a vertical presence to the gardens, and the current park-like character is due to these full-grown trees. There are a few that could be replaced by more attractive species that would provide more seasonal interest. Removal of the shrub undergrowth allows each tree to be viewed individually. Upon removal of the shrubs the garden space will extend as one continuous space from building to building. The "behind the shrubs" zone will be eliminated. New varieties of low-growing shrubs with a variety of foliage colour and berries will enliven the colour palette.

'As a counterpoint to the openness and activity of Schouwburgplein, the "silent gardens" on the Lijnbaan offer a respite amidst the bustling urbanity of Rotterdam. Additional benches are added to encourage residents and visitors to stop and linger in the gardens. The benches are positioned with either low shrubs or trees to the back, providing an increased sense of security and affording a better vantage point to look out over the garden.

'The dated lighting standards and fixtures will be replaced with contemporary fixtures with metal halide lamps, casting a white light that emphasizes the plants and trees. This reinforces the perception that the Lijnbaan gardens are a valuable pedestrian space at night, too. Photovoltaic panels can supply the lighting and filtration and circulation systems for the pools with a minimum of generated energy.

'The city council, building owners and residents need to develop a common strategy for security, routine maintenance, timely garbage collection, and revenue-generating activities. The proposal is to paint portions of the lower facades, which will be exposed after the removal of the high shrubs, in the colour that corresponds to the colour of the awnings. The use of these two bright, modernist orange and yellow colours achieves a number of objectives: the domestic sphere will extend into the garden, the blank walls will be livelier, and it deters graffiti. In the event that tagging and graffiti does persist, the blocks of colour can be repainted easily.

'The portico under the residential block to the east of Jan Evertsenplaats is the proposed site for a food or teahouse concession. Beyond the revenue-generating aspect of providing food and drink to garden visitors, the concession would also increase the sense of safety. In order to encourage more intensive use of the gardens, the proposal includes the programming of performances and organizing temporary art installations or exhibitions in the gardens. A more fundamental change is the proposal to make selected cafés or restaurants, which currently only overlook Schouwburgplein, double-sided. Similarly, the ground level facades of the residential towers could be reconstructed to afford a more direct visual link between the living rooms and the garden. The installation of a self-cleaning, unisex toilet would provide a much-needed amenity.

'The redesign of both gardens seeks an intensity of modernity, an intensity of pedestrian usage, and an intensity of greenness to enliven the gardens. The long-term objective is to attract pedestrians to both gardens with the goal of animating the spaces. Visitors and residents who enjoy the reconfigured gardens will become the gardens' wardens. Restoring both gardens as an attractive, "hyper-green" zone will ultimately enrich the experience of Rotterdam city centre.'

The Lijnbaan gardens
Hargreaves Associates

GEORGE HARGREAVES
in association with
KIRT RIEDER
KATE ORFF
JOONYON KIM
ATTAPORN KOBKONGSANTI
ALISSA PUHM
MATHIEU CASAVANT

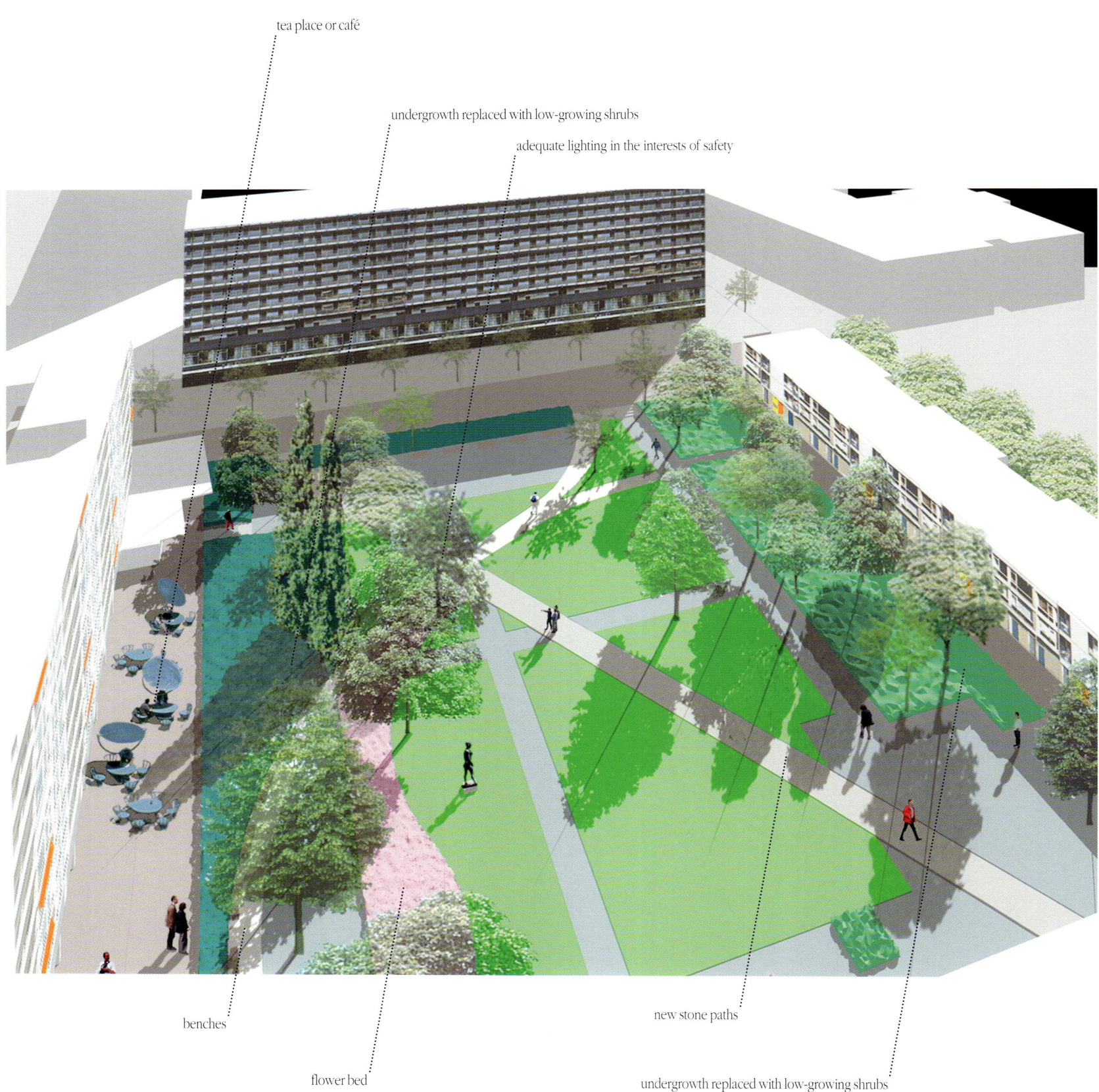

Jan Evertsenplaats: a palimpsest upon which aspects of previous designs are selectively retained and others eliminated

The Public Garden

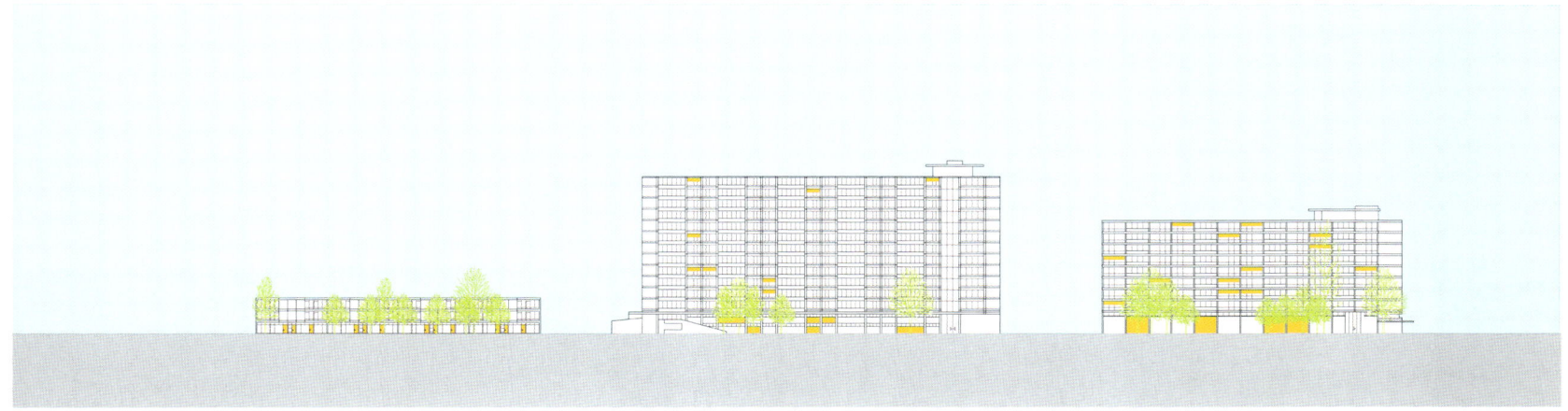

Blocks of colour to deter graffiti correspond with the colour of the awnings

present situation

proposal for new situation

situation in 2000

photo: Rob Ponsen

The new path cuts diagonally through the garden to Schouwburgplein

The 'moderne' design of Joost Banckertsplaats gets an additional layer of detail

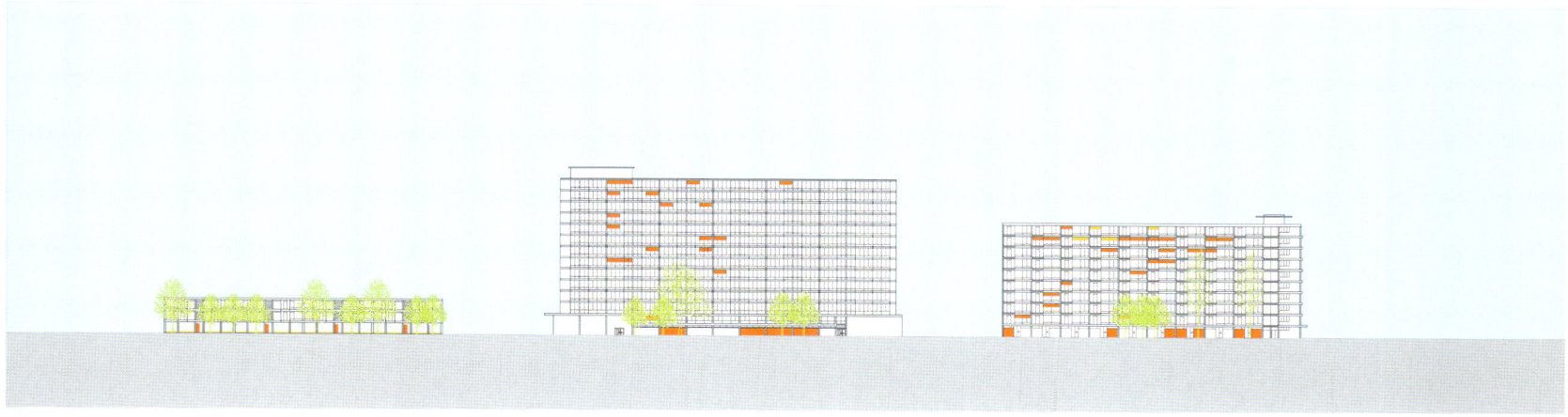

Blocks of colour to deter graffiti correspond with the colour of the awnings

current situation

proposal for new situation

situation in 2000

photo: Rob Ponsen

THE SITE

Rotterdam's Central Station is to be expanded into a terminal, a high-grade mobility hub that functions at a European, national, Randstad-regional and metropolitan level. This adaptation is necessary to accommodate the high-speed railway line or TGV, for which Rotterdam will be the first stop in the Netherlands on its completion in 2005, and also to realize the Randstad rail link. British urban designer William Alsop of Alsop & Störmer, presented the master plan for this massive project in mid-April 2001. The twenty-hectare site around the terminal must become a fully integrated component of the city. There will be housing, offices, shops, 'urban entertainment' facilities and parking areas between the north side of the existing station and Kruisplein and between Statenweg and Pompenburg. One of the priorities is urban quality and good pedestrian access to the public and semi-public space of the forthcoming zone from the immediate surroundings. Because it is not only infrastructure but also offices, housing and various urban amenities that are to be developed, Rotterdam Central Station will be much more than just a place for stopping. Every day large numbers of passers-by and visitors will spend brief or longer periods of time in the terminal area. The new Central Station will not only be a place of arrival and departure for the city, but a place for tarrying, meeting and waiting.

THE BRIEF

There were two parts to the brief. To start with, it called for an analysis of the pedestrian areas in the existing and forthcoming urban programme. It also specified a design study into the agenda of public and semi-public space for travellers, visitors and city residents, and into the role of gardens as places for informal activity.

Central Station and Weena, 1999
photo: Aerocamera

THE DESIGNERS ON THE DESIGN

'The city centre seems to be shrinking all the time. Before World War II, the city had a comprehensive system of boulevards, streets and alleys where the functions of shopping, work, dwelling and leisure fused into a metropolitan whole. Post-war reconstruction and the later urban renewal projects have resulted in a compartmentalization of these activities along with an urban concentration in what we now call the centre. This compartmentalization and concentration has left other, usually long-standing urban places 'divorced' from that centre. Rotterdam is therefore known as a city with a modern centre where you need to know how to find the nice places, but with connections between them that are often anything but attractive.

'To be able to accommodate the growth of urban amenities and mixing of functions, we can distinguish between two tendencies, two angles of approach to the urban planning. One is further concentration and clustering of urbanity within the existing structure; the other is the introduction of new, urban morphological structures to decentralize and expand that urbanity.

'The recent transplantation of the market, the museums around Museum Park and the Beurstraverse sunken shopping mall are examples of concentration and clustering. This is usually accompanied in the end by a weakening of the areas beyond the concentration. The Kop van Zuid project is the supreme example of decentralization and expansion. It not only constitutes an expansion of the centre, but forges new links with other existing and interesting loci of urban life.

'The Central Station building and former Hofplein station will cease to be the focus of activities in the station area. The station concourse and its refreshment kiosks will then no longer serve as the pre-eminent gathering spot. Improvement of the transport hub roughly at the site of today's station forecourt (Stationsplein), will provide a diffuse network of routes to the nodes of the various transport modes on several levels. It will be a world of transport and movement, of coming and going. In order to make the area urban, the aspect of informal social space will need introducing in a new form.

'Weena and Pompenburg currently define the outer limit of the urban area. Anywhere north of here only holds an interest for commuters and office workers. The reason that few others cross these busy boulevards is not so much the volume of traffic, but more the area's current position in the urban morphology: it is the edge of the centre. As a peripheral zone, the station area must emanate a strong force of attraction in order to seduce residents and visitors into crossing the busy traffic artery.

'If the current position of the station area in the city's morphology is not to be altered, then it will have to become an attraction in its own right, something really worth visiting. This will require a large-scale urban programme with sufficient critical mass, as a complement to the existing. Should the decision be to replace existing attractions, it will result in a more extreme concentration of urbanity, weakening areas elsewhere. If the choice is to add new urban programmes, then these will have to be permanent. The history of urban design shows this to be a sensitive point.

'In contrast to this scenario of concentration within a restricted area, we propose a scenario of decentralization and expansion. Giving the station area a different status in the morphology of the city, so that it is no longer the edge of the centre, would make it possible to establish links with existing urban areas further away.

The agenda of public space

'While the garden and the urban place disappeared with the assimilation of the house into the modernist urban landscape of the twentieth century, we are currently seeing the garden undergoing a revival. The city garden is now regarded and designed as a place with its own programme, a theme of its own; a finite space that creates the illusion of being a different world to the one around it. To each his own, a place for every target group. But each individual belongs to many different categories of target group, resulting in considerable exchange and interaction. That is why it is probably a more important task (the well-designed urban garden aside) to understand how we can facilitate the interaction and exchange between those activities, themes and places.

'The urban garden is specific, and the position it occupies in the urban morphological structure is important for the exchange process. The more opportunity for exchange, the more vital and enduring an urban garden will be. If there is little exchange or interaction between groups, then a garden will only be vibrant if fostered and tended by a caring private owner.

'Apart from places with a fixed programme, in the European city it is the unexpected activities and the so-called 'unfamiliar' places that make a lasting impression. It is essential that the city allow that spontaneity and flexibility. That is why the city itself must not be approached as an urban garden: boundaries are restrictions, regulations are boundaries.

'It is impossible to plan change, growth and exchange or interaction in the long term, never mind design for it. However, it is possible to provide the conditions for it. Those conditions are anchored in a structure. A structure indicates how the parts relate to the whole. A structure is not always immediately intelligible or explicit. Sometimes the underlying structure is not even made visible, having only played a role in devising an eventual composition. Even then, the chosen structure is the key to the essence of how something will be perceived as a whole. A structure can exist on many different levels. For example, a garden can incorporate several gardens, in which the ensemble of gardens forms a whole. That compositional entity is defined by the chosen structure. One section of the garden will appeal to an individual more than another, and whether one eventually leaves the garden feeling good will depend on one's empathy with the underlying structure. Despite the fact that few people will consciously experience a structure, it is a deciding factor for the lasting impression. When there is structure, the whole and its parts can work in harmony; private, collective and public initiatives can flourish, serving their further development and leading to a dynamic transformation, growth and exchange.

'In the station area it is not just the substance but above all the structural significance that has to predominate. It has to be a project on the "in-between-scale". How can new connections be established, how can other areas be integrated in the urban development? After that structural place has been defined, the spaces for waiting, resting or simply spending time can be slotted into it.

'The station area should not be an urban garden. It is advisable to design it as a flexible, neutral public space with the potential for all kinds of public and private activities and for growth and development, especially beyond the planning area.

'Within Rotterdam's urban structure, the street level is pre-eminently the neutral, public structure, with the special functions set higher or lower to it. That is why it is desirable to have pedestrians, cyclists, cars, trams and buses at street level and trains below ground, and not the other way around.

A garden in the station area

'For many years, the development of the city took place mainly along an east-west axis because of the orientation of Rotterdam's port. Recently we have been seeing increasing development in the region along the north-south axis, directed more towards other national and international urban regions. The city is evolving from being a port city into a services city. This means that the centre's level of amenities will keep improving.

'This results in consolidation, which means that the city centre will be more focused on a

Central Station area
Quadrat, studio for urban planning, landscape and architecture

PAUL ACHTERBERG
ROY BIJHOUWER
STEFAN GALL
in association with
CONNY BOS
DANIÉLLE VAN DEN BERK
PAUL BROEKHUISEN
MAURICE DUMAS
ERIK VAN DER ELST
SABINE GEERLINGS
MAURICE HARTEVELD
ASTRID HÖLZER
ELLEN HOUTMAN
MATTHIAS HUIJGEN
ANNELIES KERKUM
JÖRGEN OLESEN
JOEKE STOECKART
JACQUI STRADLING
WARD VANSTEELANDT
JOYCE DE VCOGT
MATTHIJS WESTHOEVE

north-south axis, especially now that Kop van Zuid is starting to develop as an urban area. The old, long service streets running east-west, such as Middellandstraat, Binnenweg and Hoogstraat, are losing their significance. North-south connections by contrast will become increasingly important. The new metro, urban railway network and tram lines play a key role in this switch. A third and perhaps even a fourth city bridge would make a great difference for south-north road links. As road links from the north, the two main thoroughfares, the Maas Tunnel route and Schiekade, are becoming overtaxed and a new link from the northwest, parallel with the railway, would be a useful complement. However, the "railway triangle" at Blijdorp Zoo still stands in the way of this possibility.

'The station area is presently a fault-zone, a cut-off point in the urban structure. The area around Hofplein and Pompenburg, where the railway branches off towards the south until it has passed beneath Binnenrotte and where the Hofplein line is located, is a particularly tricky leftover space. Being a fault-zone, it will quickly become an autonomous area. This is reinforced by the level of the railway track, which is so problematic that accessing the area involves all kinds of changes in level.

'This broaches a number of issues. In the context of Rotterdam, even a small difference in level makes us feel that we are entering a new terrain. Does this mean that the whole fault-zone area might end up resembling "a finite space that creates the illusion of being a different world to the one around it"? Would the whole station area, up to and including Pompenburg, then become an urban garden? Would the two neighbourhoods of Provenierswijk and Agniesebuurt disappear from view behind it? Will trams, buses, cyclists and pedestrians have to pass through tunnels under the tracks, and will parking and road access have to be accommodated above the tracks on bridges and viaducts?

'As an alternative we propose the scenario of completing the railway-tunnel project so that the station will come to lie underground, a solution that is undoubtedly radical but not inconceivable. This will give rise to utterly new conditions. A new system of roads could be devised to draw other areas into the urban development. Complexes of buildings such as the penitentiary on the Noordsingel and the Van Nelle factory would then occupy a different position in the city structure. The corridor to the Hofplein line, which is to be taken out of service, can gain new structural relevance too.

'Shifting the station underground frees us from the present-day tangle, making it possible to think more creatively in terms of larger- and smaller-scale structures. The Central Station-Pompenburg area would then amount to an "in-between-scale" space. The urban garden can be devised on a smaller scale and in one of a variety of forms, from public area to private atrium.

'With the disappearance of the station concourse as the central space and the inevitable development of a diffuse network of connections, we propose creating a new, central public space, between the platforms of the train station, the metro station, car parks and cycle shelter underground and the tram and bus stops at street level. This is where commuters, tourists, city residents and travellers must be able to meet and interact. The central point is a pond filled with amorous and quarrelsome flamingos, with space for terraces, a point of repose in the world of travel. Behind the flamingos stand two 20-metre-high structures, one a terrarium inhabited by monkeys, the other an aquarium containing fish.

'These rise up from the subterranean world. It is an annex of Rotterdam's Blijdorp Zoo, where tourists can buy a ticket to travel to the zoo proper by shuttle. The shuttle will leave every quarter of an hour from the same platform as the high-speed international trains. Amidst the flamingos, the monkeys and the fish, it can also be the starting point for a long and adventurous journey by high-speed train. The ideal garden awakens yearnings for far-off places.'

situation before 1840

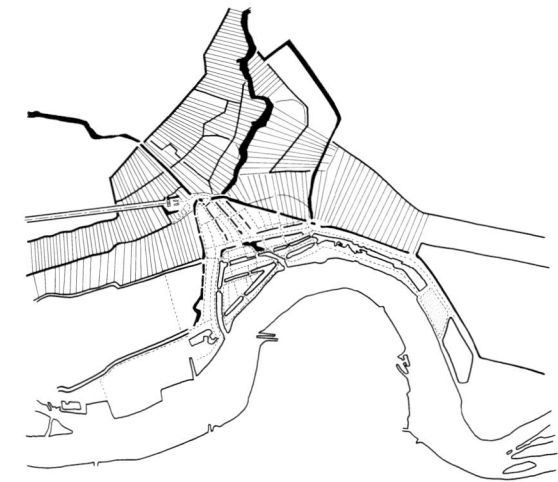
situation in 1850

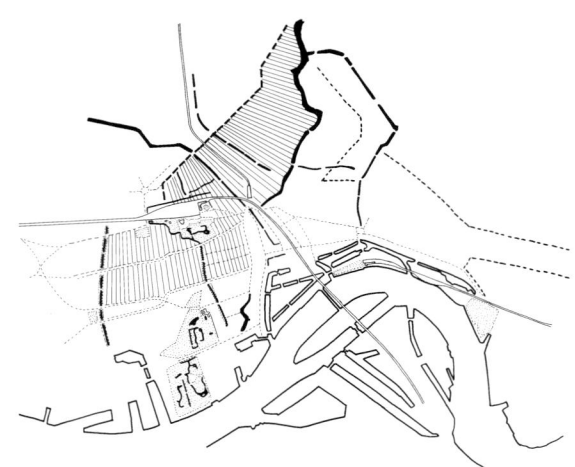
situation in 1930

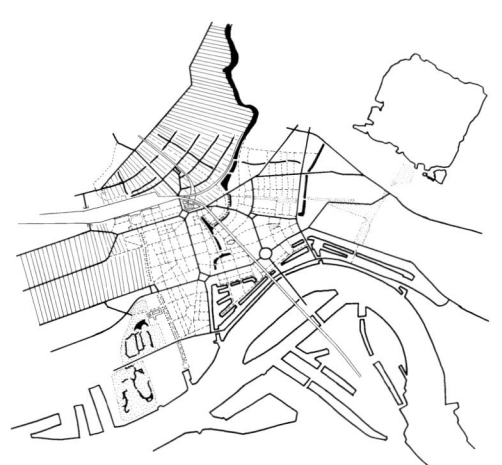
situation in 1946 (Basic Plan for the reconstruction of Rotterdam)

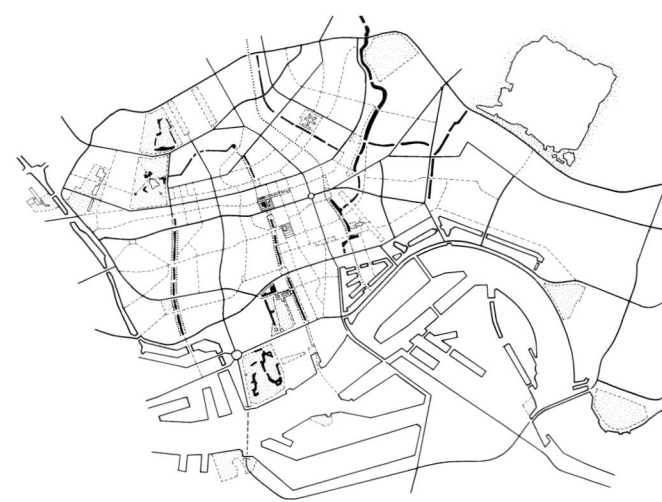
possible future situation

examples of appropriated spaces in Rotterdam

Het Oude Westen local park sculpture garden, Westersingel forecourt of Unilever building Schouwburgplein

future scenario: redevelopment of station area after extending railway tunnel as a linking structure

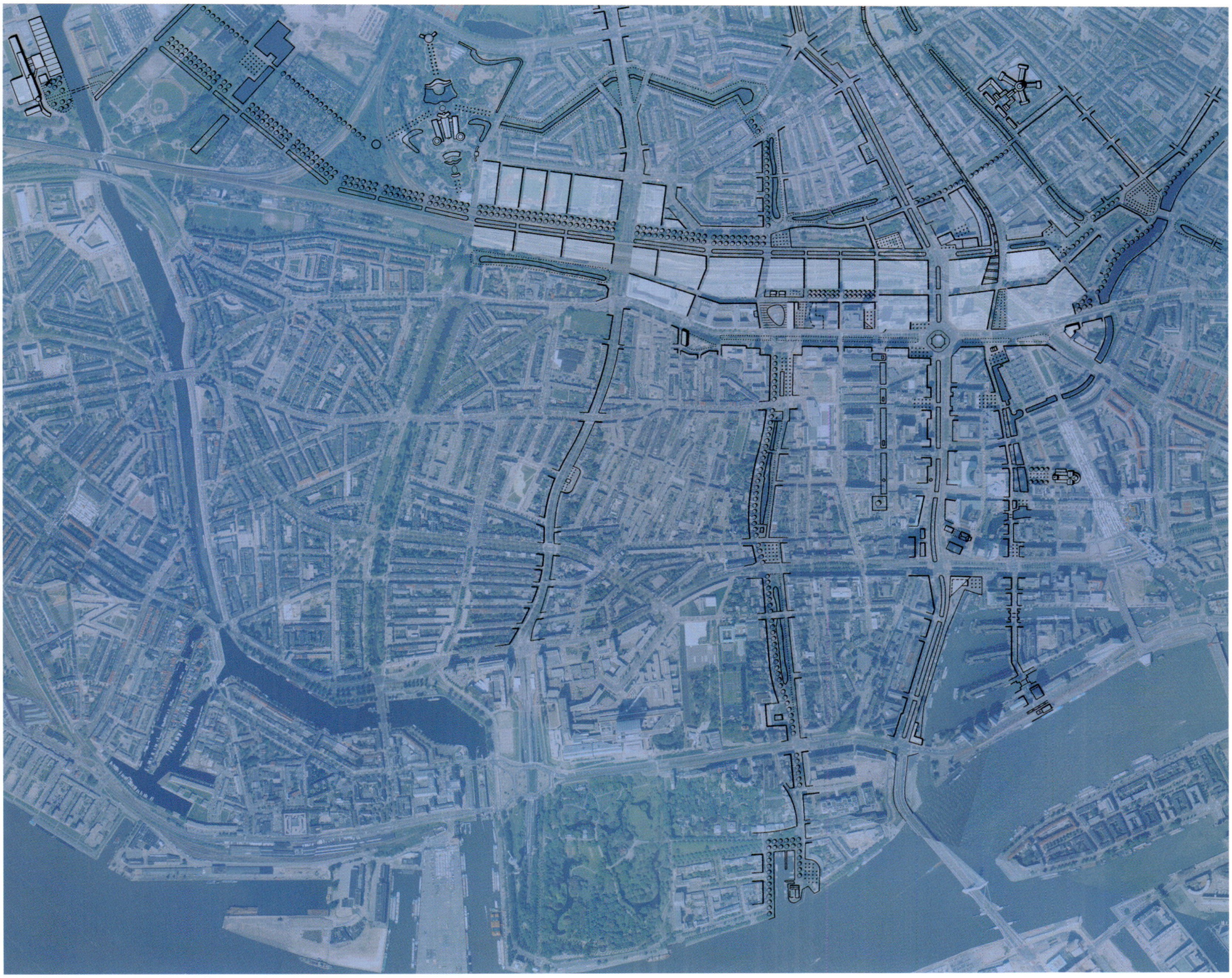

skate park on Westblaak Beurstraverse shopping mall Maritime Open-air Museum, Leuvehaven Boompjeskade

examples of appropriated spaces in Rotterdam

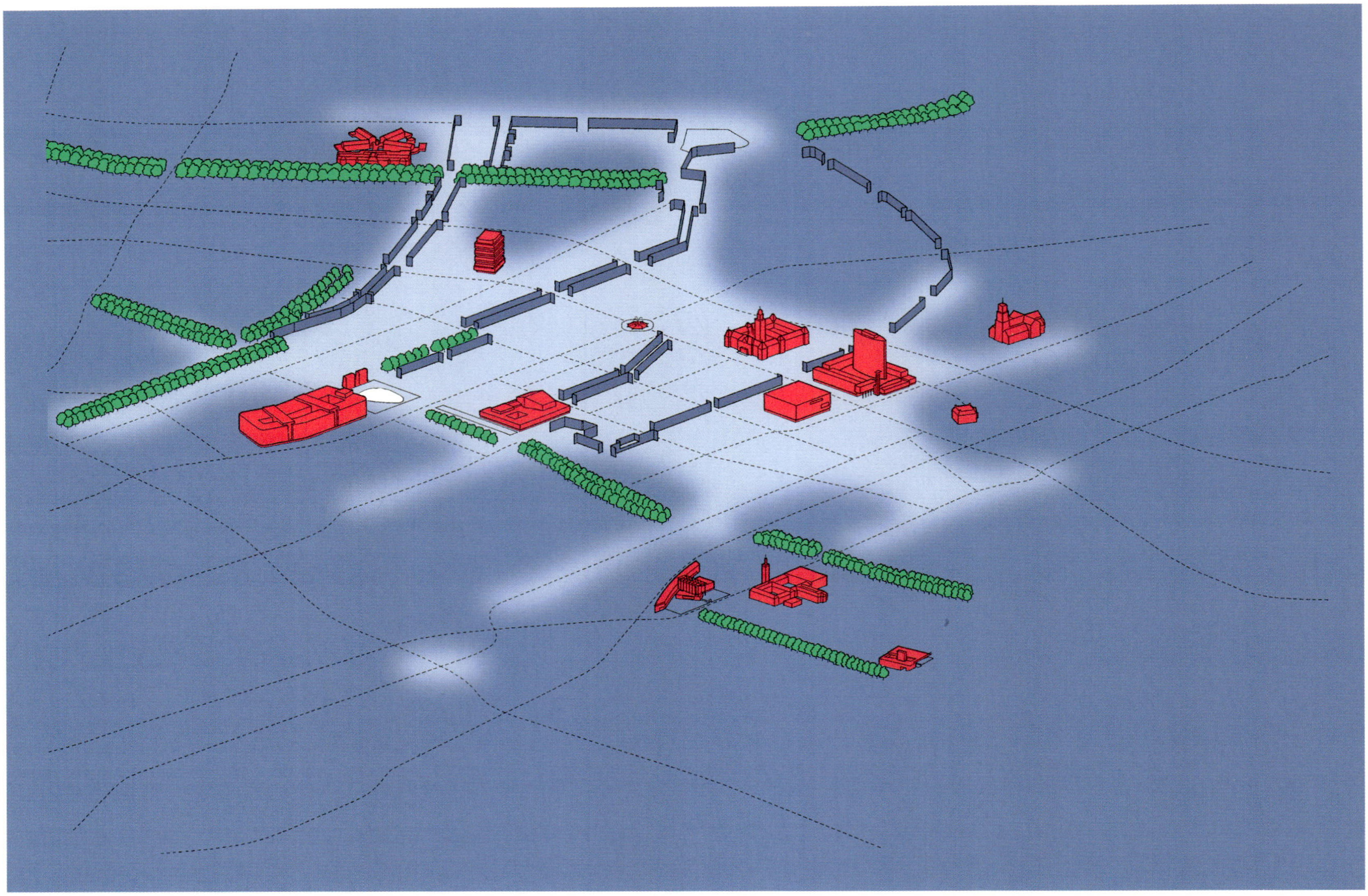

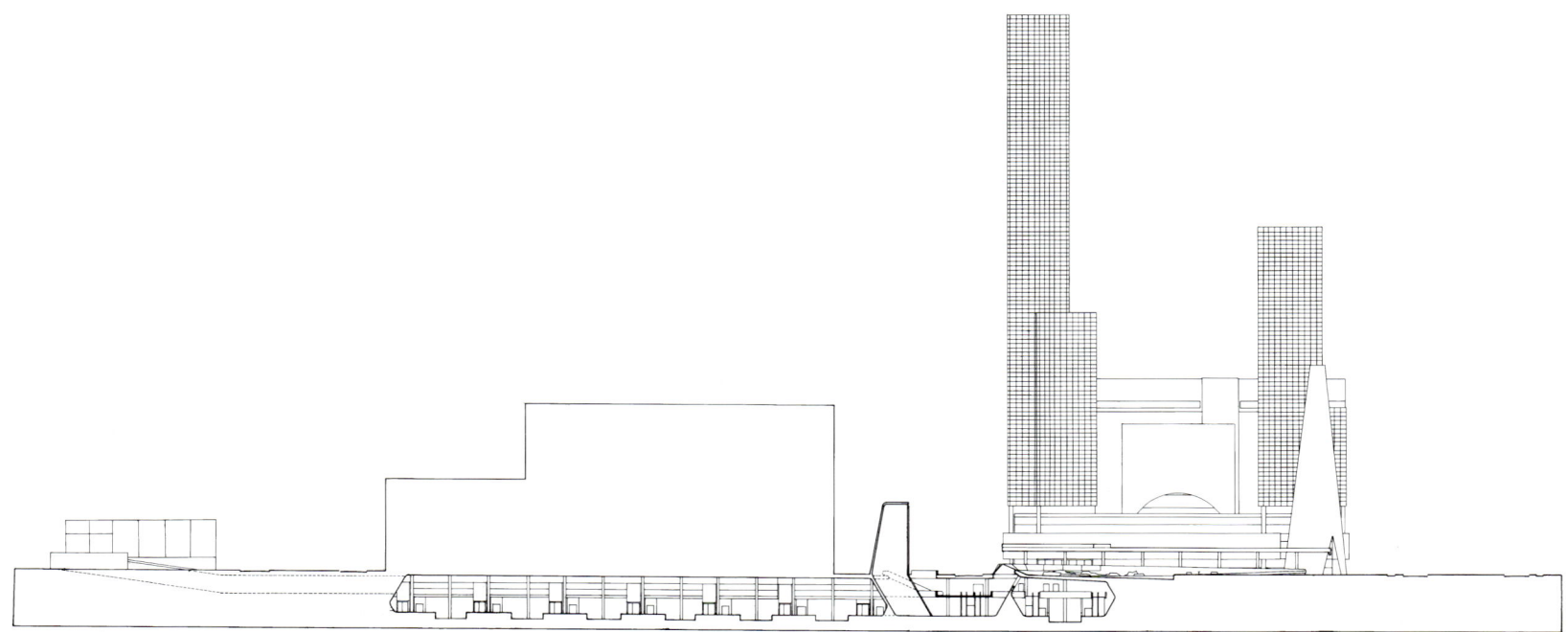

city centre expanded across the railway zone

north-south section through underground station with platforms

flamingo pool above the underground station with terrarium and aquarium

section including metro shuttle to Blijdorp

the ideal garden awakens yearnings for far-off places

terrarium, aquarium and underground station concourse

flamingo pool with terrarium and aquarium at rear

photo: Tom Kroes

THE SITE
The inner garden of the Boijmans Van Beuningen Museum is an open-air space laid out in the 1930s that has remained exceptionally intact. Museum Park, the area between Mathenesserlaan and the Westzeedijk, was part of a larger-scale design by architect A. van der Steur for the then undeveloped grounds of Land van Hoboken, once a family estate. Van der Steur created an experience of cultivated nature, proceeding gradually from the museum's contemplative court to a public park. The planting and architecture of the outdoor space around the museum building have been altered at various points, but the structure of the inner garden has remained untouched. Now that the reorganization and extension of the museum to a design by Paul Robbrecht and Hilde Daem is under way, the design of the inner garden must update its function as a hortus conclusus.

THE BRIEF
In tandem with the spatial reorganization and extension of the museum, the inner garden is due for a reinterpretation of its function as a hortus conclusus. Because all the inner garden's architectural elements as originally designed by van der Steur are still intact and because the building is now a municipal monument, the starting-point for the design naturally requires conservation of all the existing architectural elements (the layout of the paving and the central water feature with fountain). The garden could be a true work of art, a sublime space for garden making. The garden could also be largely composed of water and plants.

The goal of the rearrangement of the museum itself is to afford a more clearly defined experience of art inside the building and to emphasize the special architectural qualities of the museum. The inner garden must be experienced as a space that is equally special. A much more carefully planned planting and layout must reinstate the uniqueness of this place, on condition that 'fixed' elements of the inner garden are respected.

Boijmans Van Beuningen and museum garden, 2001

photo: Pandion

THE PROPOSAL
Correa studied the altered context of the inner garden due to the museum's new Henket Pavilion extension. For Correa the orientation of the garden is both inward and outward. The centre is also the source of energy. The centre of the enclosed garden, which is characterized by water, is an expression of this energy. A spiral of water positions visitors in relation to the centre as they descend the incline. While the water in the spiral remains at ground level, the visitor descends the spiral ramp. The design alludes to historic Indian objects in which the spiritual, metaphysical world encounters the palpable, physical world. Alongside the proposal for a sublime garden within the walls of the museum, Correa proposes a second garden that plays a role in everyday life. The design calls for the construction of a walled stone garden, for example in a public park. The form is based on the typology of traditional 'kunds'. These are small buildings around a rectangular pond where the faithful wash and purify themselves before they enter a mosque. This strictly geometrical garden is the place for meeting, debate and meditation.

THE DESIGNER ON THE DESIGN
'Of course the mindset we are discussing is just one of many that exist in India. For instance, at Sabali Kund, built in the tenth century by the first Muslim sultans of Gujarat, the steps on three sides of the kund are the same as those in front of a Hindu temple – but on the fourth side is built a pleasure palace. Being partly submerged underwater, it is a wonderfully cool place to stay during the hot summers, to while away your afternoons with friends, reading poetry, and so forth. Why did the sultans modify the kund in this matter? Because when Islam came to India, it brought with it the mythic Persian image of the Garden of Paradise – a garden of earthly pleasures. And so the architecture becomes sensuous, hedonistic, voluptuous.... as for instance, at the Taj Mahal in Agra, or at Humayun's magnificent Tomb in Delhi.

'And then again, starting in the sixteenth and seventeenth centuries, there comes another mindset. For the European colonialists bring with them a new system of mythic beliefs: Rationality, Science, Progress – which leads to quite a different understanding of the context of our lives. And so the architecture changes once again: for man believes he now has the freedom and power to invent his own future.

'Through all these various mindsets, we can see that Man does not change – but there are decisive shifts in his perception of the context in which he exists. Over the centuries, this has happened in almost every society – but the contexts usually follow one another in sequence, each obliterating the presence of what went before. In India, on the other hand, these diverse contexts all coexist – like the transparent layers of a palimpsest. (As Nehru used to say: "In India, the centuries live side by side.") Thus the shift from one context to another can become vivid to any one of us, at any given moment, as we go about our everyday lives.

'And the experience of such shifts might be extremely relevant to the programme of nine urban gardens that the city of Rotterdam is proposing. The very term "urban garden" implies that in the heart of the crowded city there is a small oasis which transports you into another state of mind. This could be achieved just by making each one of them a delightful place for rest and relaxation. But wouldn't it be extraordinary if these urban gardens could also make us understand another context, another truth, another reality – so as to help one see, if even for only a few moments, one's life in perspective?'

The inner garden of Boijmans Van Beuningen Museum
Charles Correa Architects & Planners

CHARLES CORREA
NONDITA CORREA-MEHROTRA

Concept

In the heart of the urban context - another presence, reminding us of Nature and of the invisibilia of the metaphysical world that underlies the physical one in which we exist.

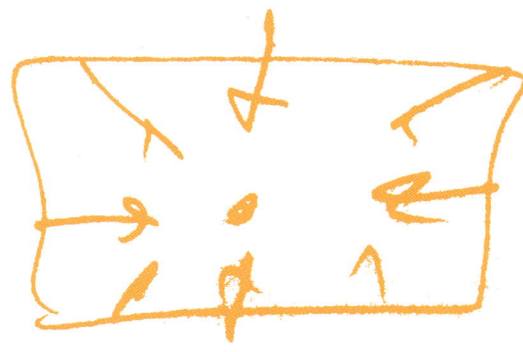
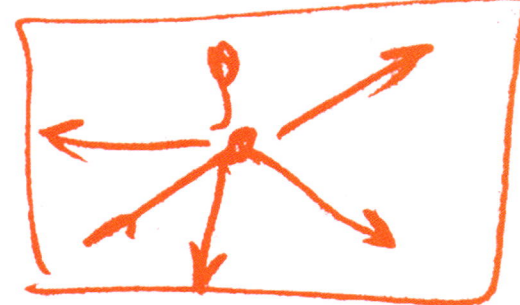

The paradigm of the walled garden has two crucial aspects: *centrality* and *energy*. The paradox is that the centrality of the Void becomes the source of all energy (i.e. Bindu)

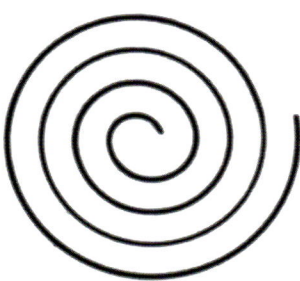
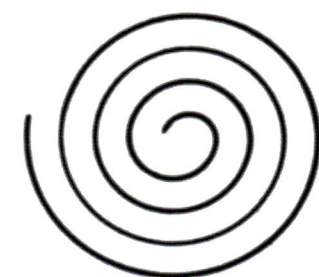

The energy of *Bindu*, representing Matter and Anti-matter, and the Evolution and Dissolution of the Cosmos

Mandu

Traditional Warli drawing

British Council, Delhi

At the Boijmans Van Beuningen Museum

In the centre of the courtyard is Bindu, expressing the opposing forces of Void and Energy. The spiral draws us within, ramping down, until we reach the centre. The water level of the spiral is a constant, but Man is now on Earth... which gradually descends lower than Water.
In the garden outside, we propose another variation of the *Kund*. The traditional kunds generally located next to temples, are rectangular water, ponds where the faithful come for ritual purification before entering the temple to worship. The form of these kunds is derived from *vastu-purusha-mandalas,* those ancient Vedic diagrams which conceived of Architecture as the Model of the Cosmos. Like many other aspects of India, these diagrams are both ancient and contemporary, both pragmatic and metaphysical.

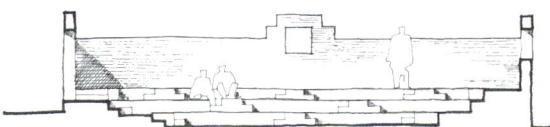
Town centre, New Bagalkot

The Kund, Modhera

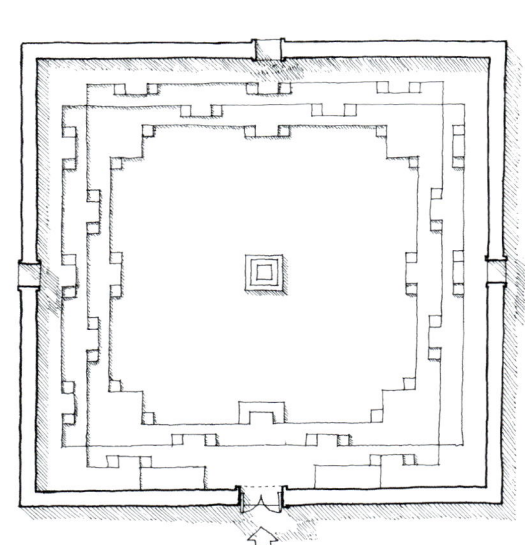

Kapur think tank, Delhi. A place for meditation and debate

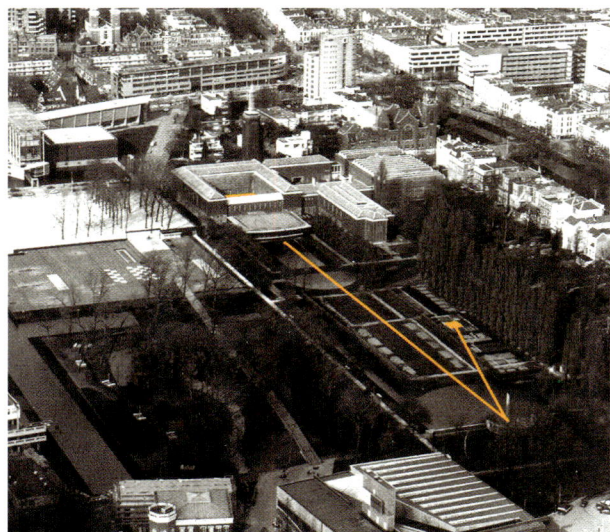

Invisibilia

Bindu and *Kund* complement each other and show both the fountainhead and the invisible lines of action that are of influence on our daily existence.

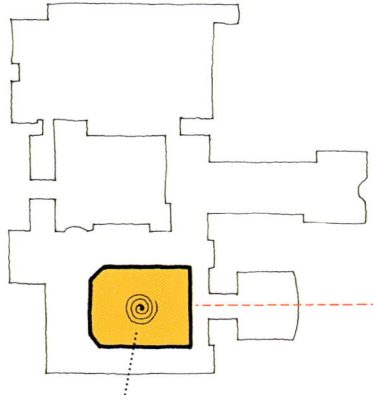

Bindu – the walled garden in the museum

Kund – the walled garden within the museum garden
The kund proposed for the museum garden is a reincarnation of the traditional kunds and like its prototypes, its orientation has been precisely determined by the cardinal directions of the compass.

fountain

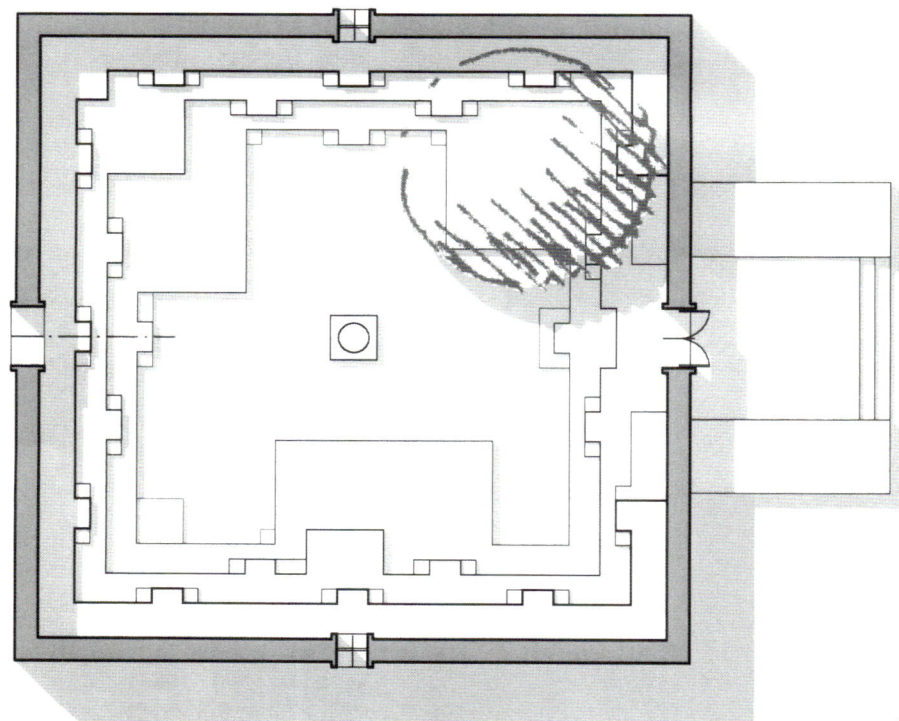

Kund

the walled garden for meditation and encounter in the museum garden

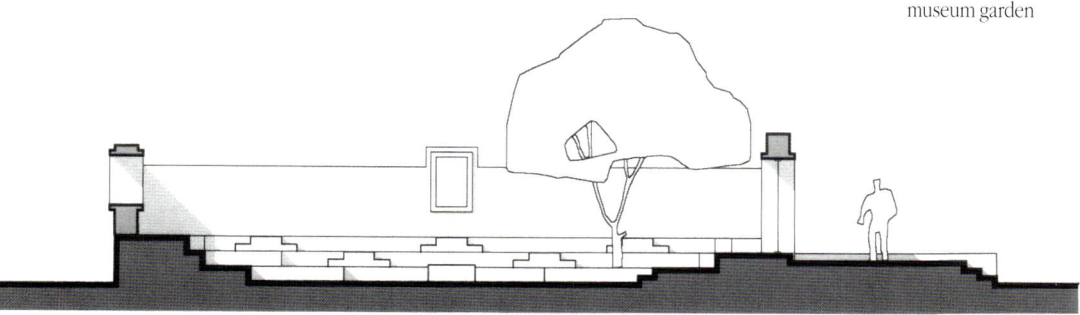

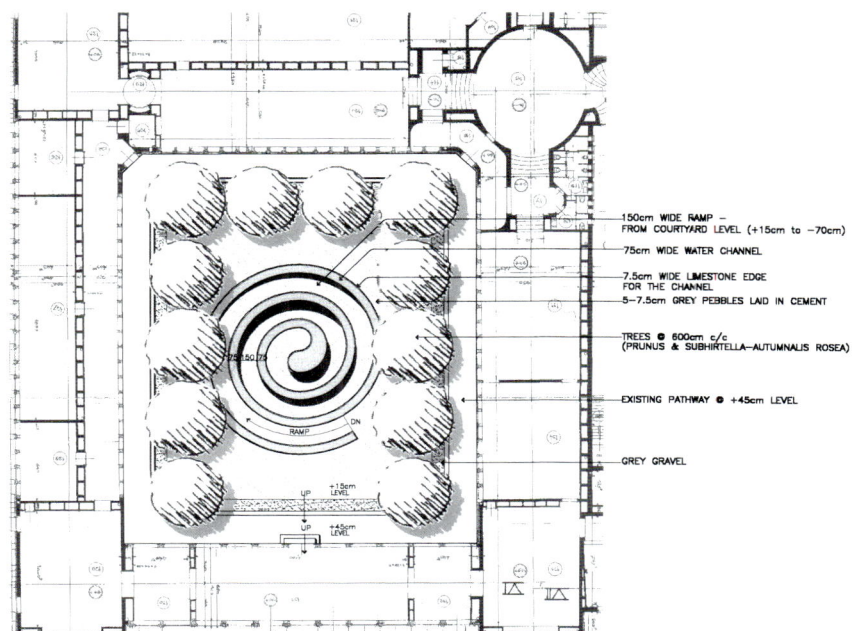

Bindu
the walled garden in the museum for reflection

THE SITE

Until recently, the former workshop building of Las Palmas was intended to house an International Centre for Photography, Film & Media Technology – to wit, the Institute for Visual Culture. The building stands on the Wilhelmina Pier (at Kop van Zuid, the development on the southern banks of the Maas river), where high-rise office and residential buildings will spring up over the coming years. There are plans for an open-air cinema on the roof of Las Palmas. With a sturdy foundation and the dimensions of a football pitch, the roof has small buildings on it and is accessed from both the main building and the street. This is an inspiring site with a stunning view of the skyline of Rotterdam's city centre.

THE BRIEF

The brief was to design a semi-public, enclosed roof garden: in the sun, out of the wind, a short escape from the pressure of work to recuperate and relax. A place for reflection, meditation and contemplation on the roof of a public building, with the elements of water, earth, air and fire and the principles of a Zen garden interpreted using contemporary means.

Wilhelmina Pier with Las Palmas at centre, 2001

THE DESIGNERS ON THE DESIGN

'A private garden is a rarity in the modern Japanese metropolis. Sky-high land prices mean that having a garden is a luxury reserved for the lucky few. Even in the suburbs the houses are packed so closely together that you could hardly describe the interstitial spaces as gardens. Nevertheless, in Tokyo you do see that people take care of the public space close to their homes. In a radius of five metres around their front doors you will find little plants in all kinds of pots, old tumble-driers and other improvised containers. The Zen garden is a historic type that is now no longer consciously employed. In a few gardens, however, you can detect a wistful reference to this once so supernatural archetype, in the use of gravel and water, for example. An interesting aspect of the Zen garden is the freedom for individual interpretation. The garden is not a rigid structure, but an enclosed space arranged with a feeling for harmony that can be interpreted in different ways.

'In our proposal for a garden on the roof of the future Institute for Visual Culture, which was to be housed in the Las Palmas warehouse on Kop van Zuid, we propose mirroring the volume of the existing building in transparent, solid acrylic on the roof. One continuous space will be hewn from this block of plastic. Inside, it is silence that reigns. Solid, concave walls deform the images from outside, transforming the surrounding buildings into abstract masterpieces, like a memory of the city. The garden carries you off from the superabundance of information, away from the visual stimuli and cacophony of the city. During the day, the garden is almost invisible against the Rotterdam skyline, because of its transparency and reflection. At night, the brightly lit volume shrouds the surroundings in a mysterious glow.

'Over a number of years, when Kop van Zuid has developed into the intended link between Rotterdam-Noord and Rotterdam-Zuid, north and south of the river respectively, and has crystallized into the desired mix of housing, businesses and shops, this transparent garden will be like an ice-cold breath of fresh air in that urban euphoria.'

Rooftop of Las Palmas
Kazuyo Sejima & Ryue Nishizawa, SANAA Architects & Planners

KAZUYO SEJIMA
RYUE NISHIZAWA
YOSHITAKA TANASE
TAKAYUKI HASEGAWA
JUNYA ISHIGAMI
JONAS ELDING
FLORIAN IDENBURG
YORITAKA HAYASHI
YUKO ONARI
KOJI YOSHIDA
KEY KAWAMURA

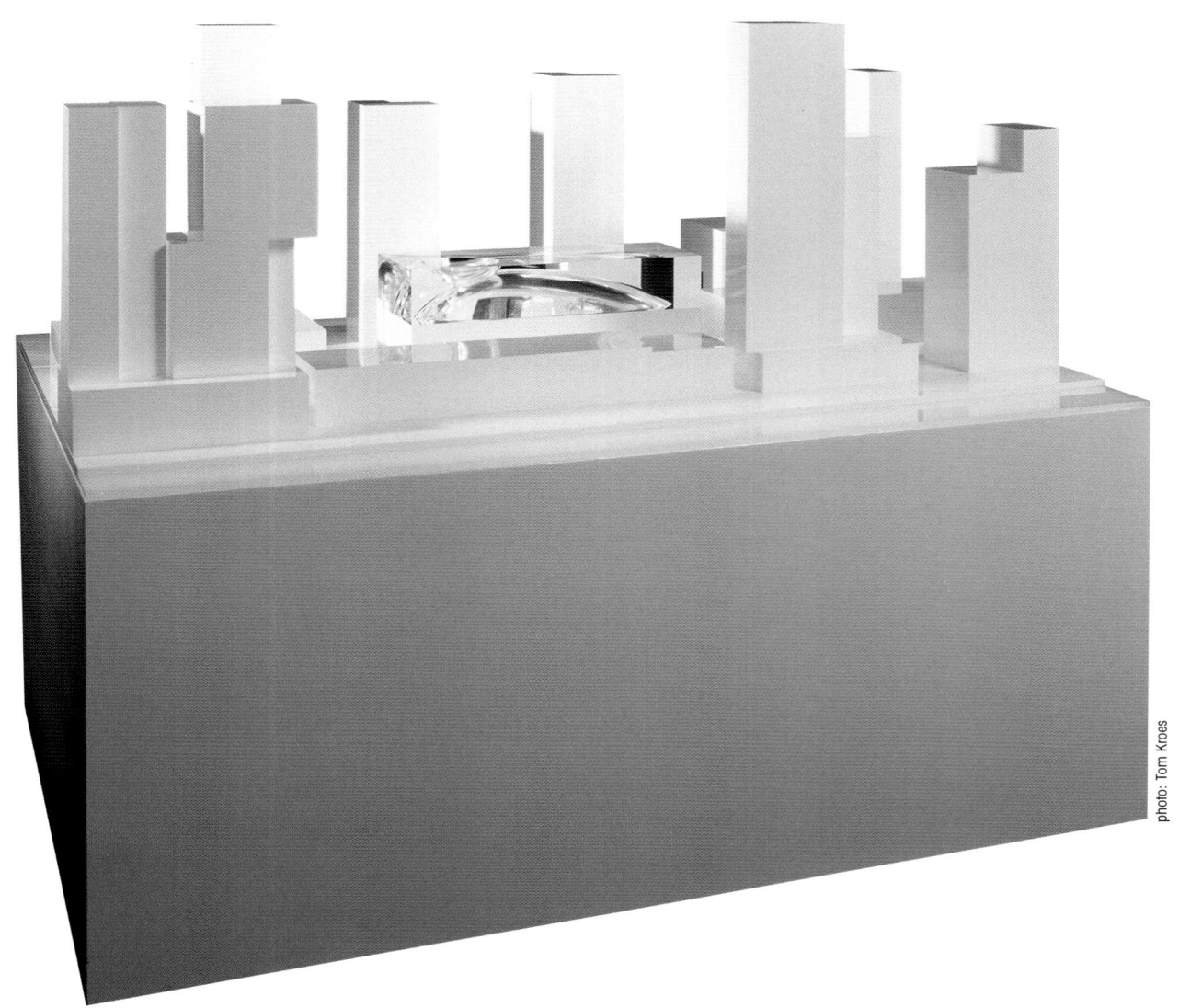

view of facade

section through botanical garden and sky café

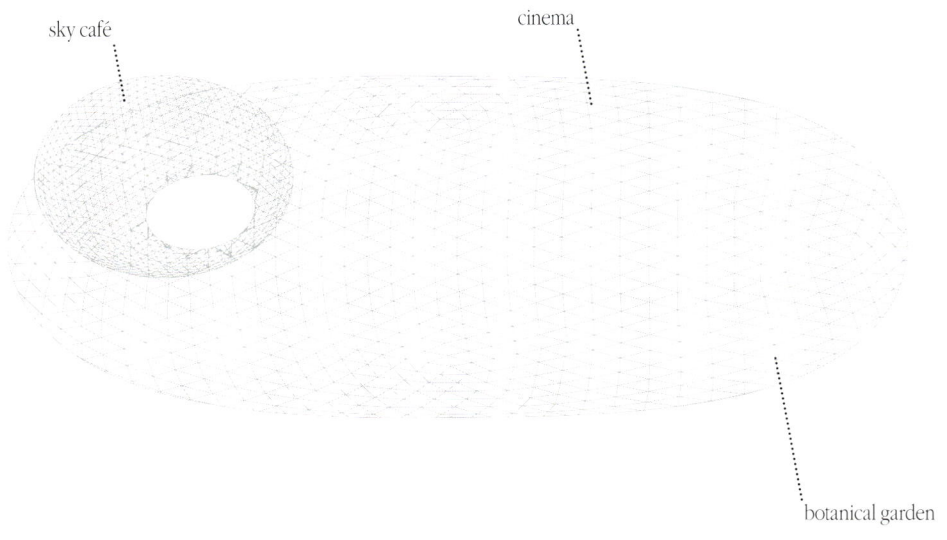

sky café   cinema

botanical garden

botanical garden

The garden transports you away from the superabundance of information, the visual stimuli, the noise of the city

77

view of the city through the wall of the botanical garden

Solid, concave outside, transforming the su abstract masterp

view from the botanical garden of the airhole and the sky

alls deform the images from
ounding buildings into
ces, like a memory of the city

THE SITE

Originally a historic country estate in Kralingen, Arboretum Trompenburg has grown into a group of gardens that includes nurseries for the propagation and maintenance of botanical collections. The park therefore is of great scientific value alongside its function as a high-quality recreational area. Though not that familiar to Rotterdam's residents, the internationally prized Arboretum is an unmissable section of Kralingen's green belt which stretches unbroken from the Esch polder as far as the woodlands of Kralingse Bos. The area is an urban nature reserve that could be termed 'the green lung of Rotterdam'. The Arboretum was recently enlarged with an additional seven hectares to the north of the adjacent football pitches.

THE BRIEF

The brief calls for a design for a garden of the twenty-first century in the tradition of the Erasmian Garden, a 'hortus conclusus', located in the most recent extension to the Arboretum. This Erasmian Garden is an enclosed garden where one can briefly withdraw in the company of others from a hostile world, from wars and the lack of inner harmony, there to focus on the better things in life. The essential elements of the Erasmian Garden are safety (the surrounding walls), shelter (a loggia) and intimacy (the restricted access). Other requisites are peace and quiet; there is also water in the form of a central fountain. Erasmus even thought to include an aviary, while inspiring expressions of culture are present as a library with a reading room and educational murals.

Arboretum Trompenburg with the design site (above right), 2001

THE DESIGNER ON THE DESIGN

The Erasmian Garden, a place where you read a book and celebrate silence, a garden within a garden, the university, wine.

'Whereas the landscape was once the natural counterpoint to the city, and a beautiful urban park was laid out in every city of standing, today this logical situation has disappeared. The modern-day urbanized landscape with its bundles of infrastructure, fragments of archaeological landscape, sprawling suburbs and business parks, does not invite anonymous parks. Parks, after all, need a vibrant urban culture. The planting of greenery and park design must be given another form. From the clichéd medium-scale concept that seems implanted in the genes of urban planners and landscape architects, the focus should shift towards the design and execution of large-scale new nature and garden design. This ambition should play an important part in creating the contemporary landscape.

'New nature of any calibre creates space and brings silence, ecological regeneration and the round of the seasons to the urbanized landscape. In the built-up Netherlands there are characterless areas that extend for 40,000 hectares. Campsites and military ranges, for example, could be transformed into Yellowstone-like parks, a national park stretching from the river Rijn to the lakes behind the sea defences; the delta could be transformed into a landscape of dunes, sea inlets and wetlands, and the Green Heart into one of marshy polders and imposing horizons. At the same time, there is a desperate need for new gardens in today's cities. Gardens that serve no other purpose than simply being gardens. Isolated, enclosed, concealed in the midst of the metropolis. Garden design is an important medium for self-reflection and for creating illusions. Small, well-maintained gardens will be cherished and thus reach full maturity.

'The design for the Erasmian Garden is proposed as the newest extension to Arboretum Trompenburg. Covering the botanical garden's system of waterways with pergolas creates an extended, continuous and navigable tunnel bedecked with wisteria, offering visitors the feeling of reincarnation as they travel through it aboard a flat-bottomed boat. The silent boat trip through the morning mist and the lilies, through the azure clusters of flowers in the shimmering dawn, is disarming. The hidden Erasmian Garden emerges from behind the verdant vegetation of the Arboretum, surrounded by sloping contours covered in ferns and red walls.

'The Erasmian Garden includes a pavilion and an enclosed garden, and examines the theme of evolution, life and mortality. It toys with the illusion of fossils and living nature. The garden is designed as a still life and textural composition: fossil trees, toppled and broken like Greek columns, alongside living mammoth trees with fibrous, hairy trunks; angular blocks of slate standing upright, soiled by the crows; fast-growing prehistoric horsetail in shallow water, its shadows etched onto the glazed enclosure. The glass wall that folds itself around the garden is connected to the pavilion. The glazed panels can close off the pavilion space, or they can be opened, offering a vista of the garden from the pavilion. Shafts of light passing through the perforated red walls of the pavilion intensify the mysteriousness of the garden. In the pavilion one can meditate and read. Representative meetings for the city and the university will take place there. A small kitchen will supply the garden with food and wine.

'The Erasmian Garden will make Trompenburg a fully-fledged green icon. More than is currently the case, the Kralingen district will gain a secret, inward-looking oasis.'

Arboretum Trompenburg
West 8 landscape architects

ADRIAAN GEUZE
in association with
THEO REESINK
NIGEL SAMPEY
RIËTTE BOSCH
JOYCE VAN DEN BERG
SABINE MÜLLER
JEROEN MUSCH

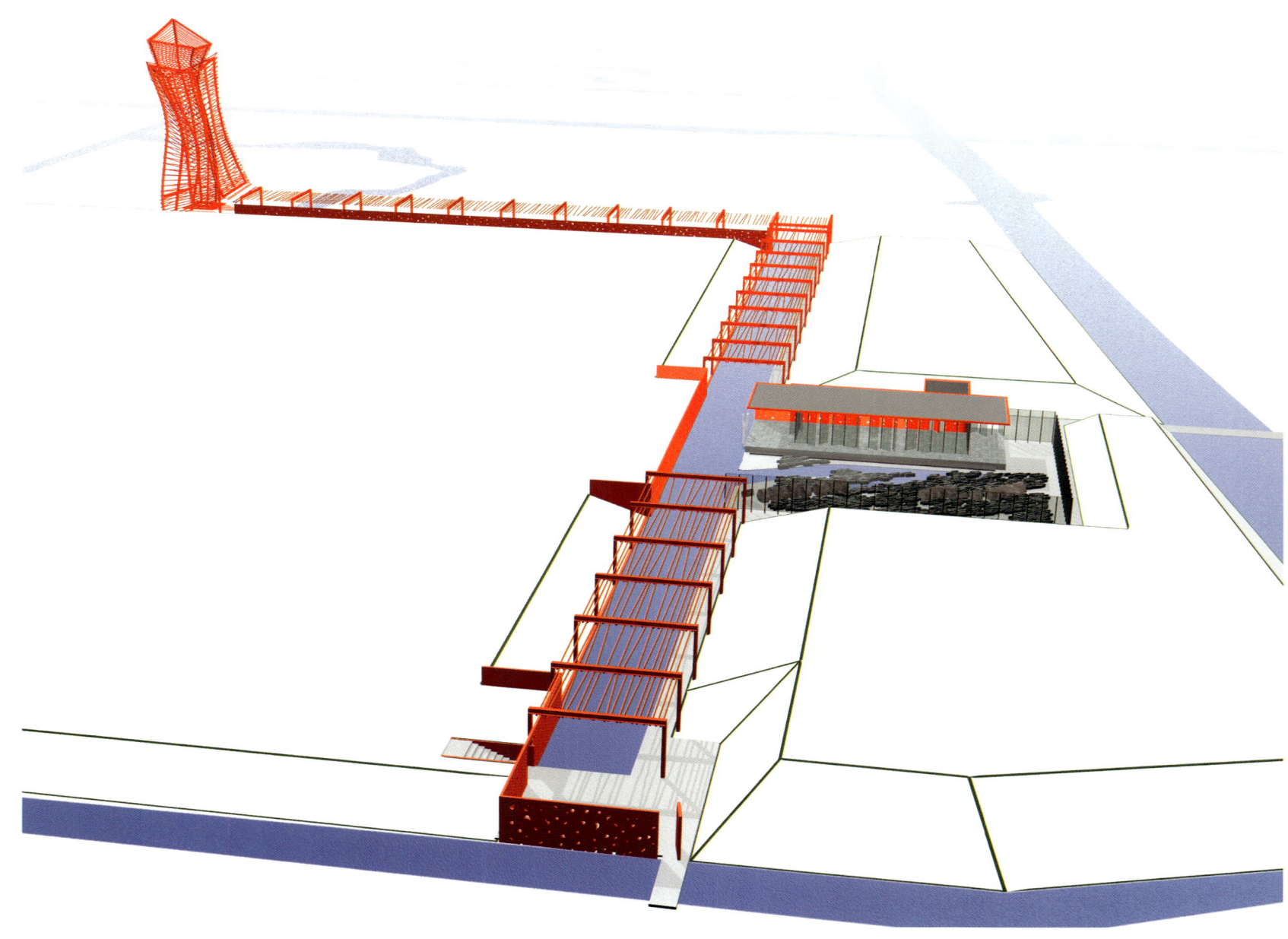

The second entrance to Arboretum Trompenburg on Laan van Woudestein via a path and a drainage ditch to the Erasmian garden and the gardens of the Arboretum.

The silent boat trip through the morning mist and the lilies, through the azure clusters of flowers in the shimmering dawn...

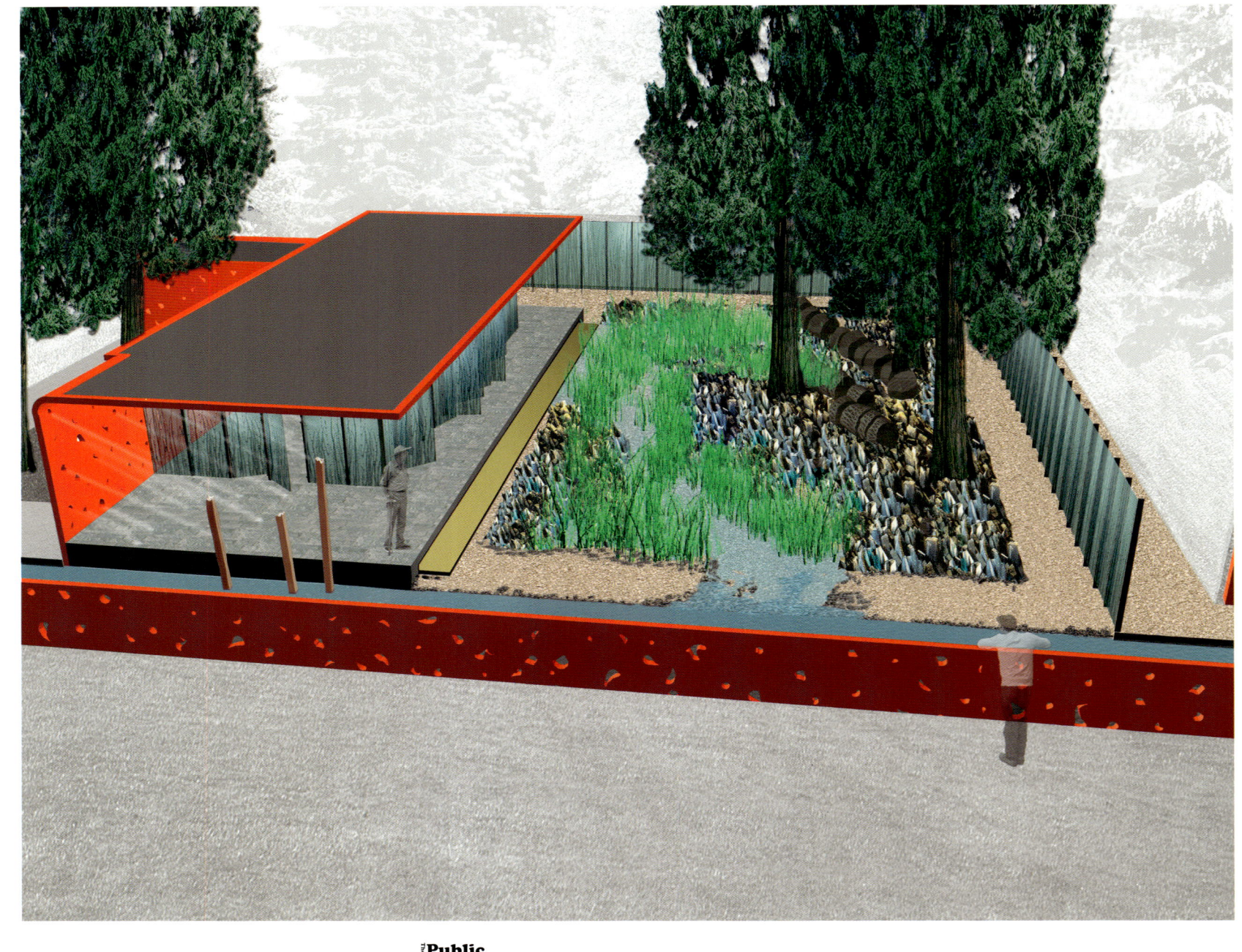

The illusion of fossils and living nature

The Erasmian Garden, a place and celebrate silen

where you read a book
, a garden within a garden...

THE SITE

Agniesebuurt lies to the north of Rotterdam's Central Station, between Schiekade and Noordsingel. This 'Agniese neighbourhood' was built more than a century ago, partially rebuilt after World War II, and has been renovated again since then. The Hofpleinlijn, an elevated track on a long concrete viaduct, has cut through the middle of the neighbourhood for almost a century, too. When the Randstadrail urban railway network, which will run from Central Station below Statenweg to Kleiweg station, is completed in 2005, this two-kilometre-long elevated track will be redundant. The space under the viaduct is currently occupied by start-ups and established companies. A monumental structure running crosswise through this northern city district, the local council believes it can become a high-quality, extended green walk. Because Agniesebuurt has far too little public green space according to planning norms, there are plans to demolish one block alongside the viaduct. What is the role, form and significance of new gardens in the public space of a densely built neighbourhood in a nineteenth-century district close to the centre of the city?

THE BRIEF

This entails a design proposal for the public space in Agniesebuurt related to potential future functions of the Hofplein viaduct for the neighbourhood and for the city. It additionally calls for a design for an enclosed garden as part of the neighbourhood's new, central open space.

The Hofplein line cutting through Agniesebuurt, 2001
photo: Pandion

THE PROPOSAL

The deck of the viaduct will become an extended walking and skating route, a monumental structure cutting through the northern city district, leading away from the city. Arches under the viaduct afford spaces for new workshops for the neighbourhood. The designers propose placing a hortus conclusus in the form of a big, transparent glasshouse at the end of the viaduct. The glasshouse will have exotic plants, vegetables and fruit that visitors can see, smell and feel - a nod to the horticulture of the Westland market gardening area. The minimalist architecture of the glazed box stands in stark contrast with the organic forms of the plants. This glass pavilion will be illuminated in the evening and at night. Alongside the viaduct, on the ground freed by the demolition of half of two of the built blocks, there will be a neighbourhood park with trees and play equipment. The medium-rise building on Ammersooiseplein will be matched by a similar building at the other end of the park.

THE DESIGNERS ON THE DESIGN

This recent interest in the garden seems a rather sentimental regression; gardens being something you do in private behind enclosing walls but of little or no import in the current debate on public space in a city like Rotterdam. 'For a long time we have been interested in the notion that experiments in garden design can be instrumental in the development of urban concepts. Laugier wrote in the seventeenth century that whoever knows how to design a park well will have no difficulty in making a plan for building a city.'

But surely something went wrong along the way? You yourselves once wrote: 'In the twentieth century a delicate green tissue turned into a monstrous green blanket….' 'If you study historic maps of Rotterdam you see the most amazing pleasure gardens. Really, the whole city was surrounded by weird pattern-book gardens; nature reshaped according to fashion and taste. This whole notion of Rotterdam as a hard-core no-nonsense work-city is obviously relatively recent…. As much as we admire the modern movement, with respect to garden design they were far too moralistic to produce work of interest. However, twentieth-century garden design is also a kind of **terra incognita**. It is amazing how little is known about some of the great garden experiments of the past century!'

Can you enlighten us? 'Take, for example, Ivan Leodinov's 1932 proposal for a small neighbourhood park in Moscow, which included an 11-metre-high canvas for a colourful neon painting of flowers and trees, and at night a neon-lit illumination would highlight the colours of the flowerbeds to an unnatural intensity; and the Italian Futurist, Felice Azari, who wrote a manifesto entitled **Futurist Flora and Plastic Equivalents of Artificial Scent,** which proclaimed the abandonment of all natural flowers; Le Corbusier's Beistegui rooftop apartment with its periscope and electrically operated sliding hedges; the Surrealist expeditions into Buttes-Chaumont so wonderfully described by Aragon in **Le Paysan de Paris** and the rediscovery by the Surrealists (soon followed by the Situationists); of gardens like the Palais Idéal created by the postman Ferdinand Cheval, the Désert de Retz created on the eve of the French Revolution, Bomarzo, and the rooftop Winter Garden at Neuschwanstein Castle by "mad" King Ludwig II of Bavaria, complete with alligator-infested pool, and his Blue Grotto in the grounds of Schloss Linderhof with a painted backdrop of the Venusberg. In Britain we had our own Archigram's proposals for Hedgerow City and visionary ideas for cybernetic forests filled with pines and electronics such as the Logplug and Rokplug devices and, of course, the highlight of the Swinging Sixties: the electronic tomato….'

But none of the examples you have given us were actually designed or even rediscovered by landscape architects….. 'Well, maybe that is the very heart of the matter.'

Let's focus on Gross.Max.'s assignment given by the AIR Foundation for the Hofplein line. Rotterdam has of course a rather ambiguous relationship with railway lines. 'What can we say…, the city of Rotterdam has an illustrious track record of using railway lines as a kind of sadomasochistic device for self-mutilation….'

Sorry to interrupt, we all know the story of the havoc created by Rotterdam's first railway viaduct cutting right through its centre, but I hope you are not referring to the most recent proposals for the redevelopment of Central Station? 'No, no…. that would be speaking much too early, and after all we do admire Will Alsop's great talent in designing buildings camouflaged as cheerful Belgian Pralines wrapped in acid-coloured foil.'

In Erasmus's treatise, In Praise of Folly, he says that the crazier a thing is, the more beautiful it is. 'Yes, but that was tongue in cheek…. Most appropriate is the passage in which Erasmus describes the building mania in which today's round buildings have to be turned into square buildings and tomorrow's square buildings into round buildings.'

Let's return to the actual assignment. 'In simple terms we redesigned the former railway viaduct into a raised promenade, linking different elements such as a neighbourhood park and a square and culminating in a glasshouse. This new configuration provides a new network of public open space, which operates on different levels of the city.'

Tell us about the glasshouse. 'The former Hofplein station will become the location for a large glasshouse. The transparent structure is superimposed over the artefacts of the old railway station and will encapsulate a horticultural extravaganza of exotic plants. The minimalist architecture of the glass box is in strong contrast to the organic orgy of flowers it contains. At night the glasshouse is transformed into a light-box with gigantic shadow projections of exotic plants displayed on its outer skin. A dazzling kaleidoscopic image of nature perfected in hybrid flowers, mutant foliage and genetically modified fruits. Anarchic. Nocturnal, amorphous, monstrous and indescribable…. Landscape architecture as skilful, accurate, a magnificent interplay of assembled vegetation under light….'

What will happen inside the glasshouse? 'The glasshouse will act as a hedonistic pleasure zone not unlike the illustrious public winter gardens in Berlin, Paris and Vienna. The arched foundation of the former Hofplein station will become a modern interpretation of the traditional garden grotto. In contrast to the transparency of the glasshouse these catacombs will contain activities which should be better kept in darkness. You know, the word grotesque is derived from the actual garden grotto. There is, of course, a paradox inherent in a glass house. It is a form, yet implicitly it is a desire to eliminate form.'

One of Mies van der Rohe's first projects was a glazed high-rise tower…. 'It is a fascinating thought that the origin of modern architecture is the nineteenth-century glasshouse. Joseph Paxton, who designed the Crystal Palace, was after all a gardener who experimented with glasshouses in order to satisfy the obsessive indulgence of the British upper classes to display the latest discoveries of horticultural eccentricities shipped in from all four corners of Britain's colonial empire. All this sense and sensibility is of course lost on the Dutch who utilized the glasshouse to create a brave new world of high-tech horticulture for mass consumption.'

The whole concept of flowers seems to be of great difficulty for contemporary landscape architects…. 'Our planting manual is a little chapter in a book called **Against Nature** written by the decadent author J.K. Huysmans in 1884.

Hofplein viaduct – Agniesebuurt
Gross.Max. landscape architects

EELCO HOOFTMAN
BRIDGET BAINES
ROS BALLARD

The protagonist of this novel, Des Esseintes, is obsessed by natural flowers which actually do look artificial. We are also greatly moved by a text written by Georges Bataille in 1929 called "The language of flowers". For this particular project we studied many books on orchids. To get the record straight: the first artificially produced orchid hybrid was perfected in England by John Dominy, head gardener at the Veitch nursery, in 1856. Have you ever noticed that much of the trendy architectural jargon such as hybrid, rhizome, cloning etc. is derived from horticultural vocabulary?'

Your fascination with crossing the boundaries of what is natural and artificial reminds me about Walter Benjamin who wrote that in fetishism, sex does away with the boundaries separating the organic world from the inorganic. 'Certain kinds of fat orchids are so shaped that one is tempted to attribute to them the most troubling human perversions.'

Maybe we should clean up our act, after all we are getting carried away a bit…. 'One moment, can I just add that the whole concept of the Hofplein line was escapism for the city-dweller; we are intrigued by the notion that this line was nicknamed the "perfume line" due to its reputation for prostitution. The connection between flowers, perfume and seduction is of course undeniable and reflects upon our attitude towards our proposed glasshouse. In **La fausse maîtresse** Balzac describes a conservatory belonging to the Comtesse Laginska as an immense garden in which the air is laden with perfumes.'

How does the glasshouse idea sit in the wider context of the redevelopment of the Raampoort location? 'This is of course an intertwining knot of great complexity. We quite like the idea that the glasshouse sits as a kind of 'Fremdkorper' in this urban context. From within the glasshouse you will overlook Rotterdam's skyline not unlike the solitary figure in Caspar David Friedrich's painting **Wanderer above the Sea of Mist**. The new TGV shooting along will add to the sublime feeling of this belvedere. The glasshouse is actually positioned within the sight axis of Central Station and will form a mysterious icon seen from the station's elevated walkways as proposed by Will Alsop.'

What about the actual design of the former railway line? 'For us it is important to see the railway viaduct as a linear element comparable for example to the "singels". The singel can be regarded as a romantic transformation of the utilitarian Dutch canal. Our treatment of the former railway line is a similar kind of transformation process. In the proposed design we like, somehow, to reflect on the notion of "frozen speed". In the nineteenth century people were outraged by the possible effect of the speed of trains on the human psyche. In a beautiful book titled **La vie en chemin de fer (Paris 1886)** the Frenchman Benjamin Gastineau describes how 'the railroad has animated everything … The sky has become an active infinity, and nature a dynamic beauty'. We hope some of these feelings will be embedded in our design of the raised promenade; a sensual response to sights, textures, smells, tactile sensations….'

You once wrote: 'Landscape should be convulsive or should not be at all.' I presume this was a reference to Andre Breton? 'The conjunction of stasis and movement is at the heart of the surrealist aesthetic of Convulsive Beauty. Interestingly, in **L'amour fou** Andre Breton explains this aesthetic theory by means of a photograph of an overgrown locomotive after it had been abandoned for many years in a virgin forest….'

Did the railway change the whole space-time relationship? 'Moving out of Rotterdam became a conscious change of scenery, not out of necessity but sheer pleasure. The train provided a kaleidoscopic experience closing the gap in space and time between the city of Rotterdam and the coastal landscape of Scheveningen and Wassenaar. Nature and city became intertwined in the same space and time capsule called the day trip. You see this reflected in the artwork connected to the Hofplein line. The original Hofplein station contained large images of the beach and sea and the viaduct itself has beautiful sculptures representing the flora and fauna along the route, a kind of three-dimensional nature album. Quite extraordinary, we found out that architect Berlage was involved in the interior design of the actual railway carriages!'

The representation of landscape did change accordingly…. 'This change of perspective is very well expressed in, for example, the Panorama Mesdag, a circular view of Scheveningen in 1880. The viewer takes centre stage within the painting, which has an overall length of 114 metres. The effect is dazzling, not unlike more recent inventions of virtual reality….'

The actual construction of the railway line was of course a landscape project in its own right? 'Yes and quite heroic as well. Not only due to the application of reinforced concrete but also the immense effort to make an alignment cutting through the polder. In order to achieve this the railway company commissioned a geological survey up to 16 metres deep over a full length of 17 kilometres. Massive amounts of sand were necessary in order to provide the necessary foundation; as a result sand dunes were excavated in Scheveningen and sand pits such as the Wilgenplas in Schiebroeksepolder were created.'

Can you explain some of your ideas for the neighbourhood park? 'We created a linear park as an extension and complement to the existing square (Ammersooiseplein). The park is simply packed with trees. We chose a combination of white and black poplars, which rise out of a large carpet of ivy. Dotted in this grove of trees are a series of raised pavilions which reflect upon the original signal boxes positioned along the railway viaduct. These structures could be used for all kinds of activities such as neighbourhood committee meetings, youth clubs, nature observation etc. In terms of structure these are simple variations of the freight container, which could be raised and lowered by means of a counterbalance mechanism. Along the full length of the park the railway arches will be utilized and contain activities such as an Internet café, dance school, nursery etc. with glazed facades and open doors towards the park. The transition between the square and the park is formed by a pool of water negotiated by a simple footbridge.'

Besides the trees, the park seems rather empty. 'Maybe. We do however believe in a strong overall atmosphere. We are inspired, for example, by the beautiful grove of plane trees in Girona, and closer to home, the sheer presence of vegetal mass of a "duck-coy" in the void of the Dutch meadow landscape. Too many parks are cluttered with programmatic confetti. If you study all the ethnic groups living in the Agniese neighbourhood we also should respect different use of the park. This Calvinistic idea that you have to do something in a park is maybe outdated. It is very well conceivable that the proper function of a park is not to wind you up, but to wind you down. The highest utility of a garden is its non-utility.'

To create this park you have to demolish a strip of buildings. 'We thought long and hard about this; but the Agniese neighbourhood is very dense and deprived of any major green space. At the end of the day you have to be tough. We do, though, propose a large building block as a full stop at the far end of the park, so the entire park will be stretched between the relatively large-scale DKV-designed building and our proposed high-rise. We like the idea that the new apartment block peeps over the actual railway promenade. This concept is in fact very close to proposals drawn up by the Rotterdam Urban Planning Department [dS+V].'

The garden can be closed at night? 'Indeed. The actual garden wall consists of flexible louvres and the various panels slide or tip up and over and as such allow for a range of variation, from totally enclosed to wide open. The structure is more than a fence; it also forms a canopy and a promenade. The idea of the transparent fence is not unlike the garden fence of "Groenevelts Hofje", the residential courtyard on the other side of the railway viaduct, which provides enclosure but without totally turning its back to the public street due to its transparency and overhanging vegetation.'

Eudokia Square needs a facelift…. 'We agree and propose a large reflecting pool. At the location of the former Bergweg station we propose new steps and an escalator to connect with the raised promenade.'

You also propose a new configuration for Teilingerstraat? 'We believe this street can become one of the most beautiful in Rotterdam. Really what we propose here is very simple; remove the parking from the very centre and create a kind of Ramblas underneath the plane trees. A series of purpose-designed wooden boxes can be utilized as little shops and cafés.'

During this interview I noticed you gazing at me with strange eyes as if you were looking into an immense void…. 'In many of our projects we are interested in the concept of transparency, the layering of imagery. While traditional landscape is often represented by foreground, middle and background we are fascinated by an altogether different depth of field. Like the transparent dresses of the sensuous girls depicted in Egyptian tombs, or the scroll drawings by the great Japanese Zen monk Sesshu, or a winter landscape seen through a frosted window. Having said that, maybe the best way to experience a garden is with your eyes wide shut.'

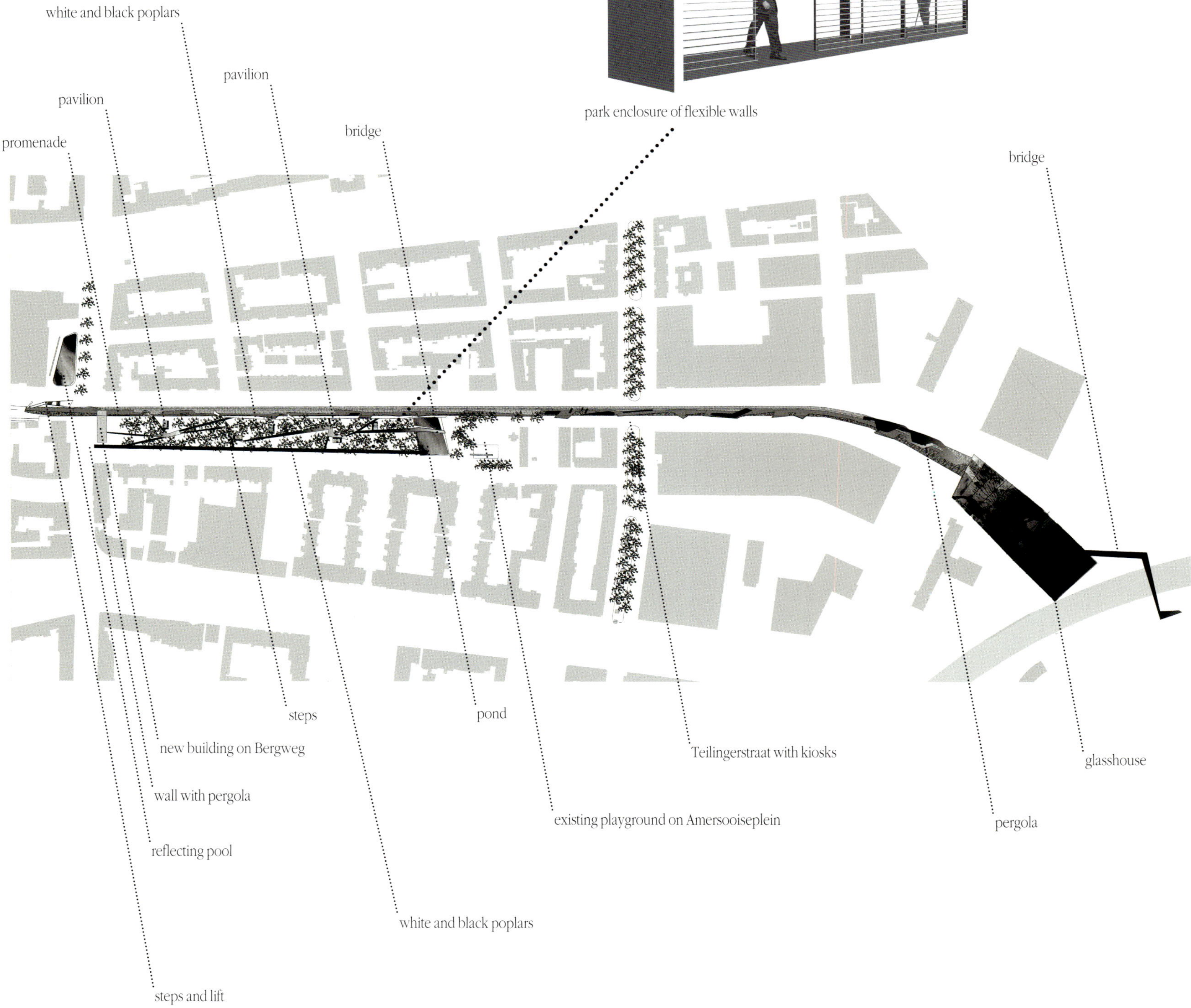

park enclosure of flexible walls

promenade
pavilion
white and black poplars
pavilion
bridge
bridge

steps
pond
Teilingerstraat with kiosks
glasshouse
new building on Bergweg
existing playground on Amersooiseplein
pergola
wall with pergola
reflecting pool
white and black poplars
steps and lift

view of park on Bergweg–Amersooiseplein

A new network of public space emerges in the city

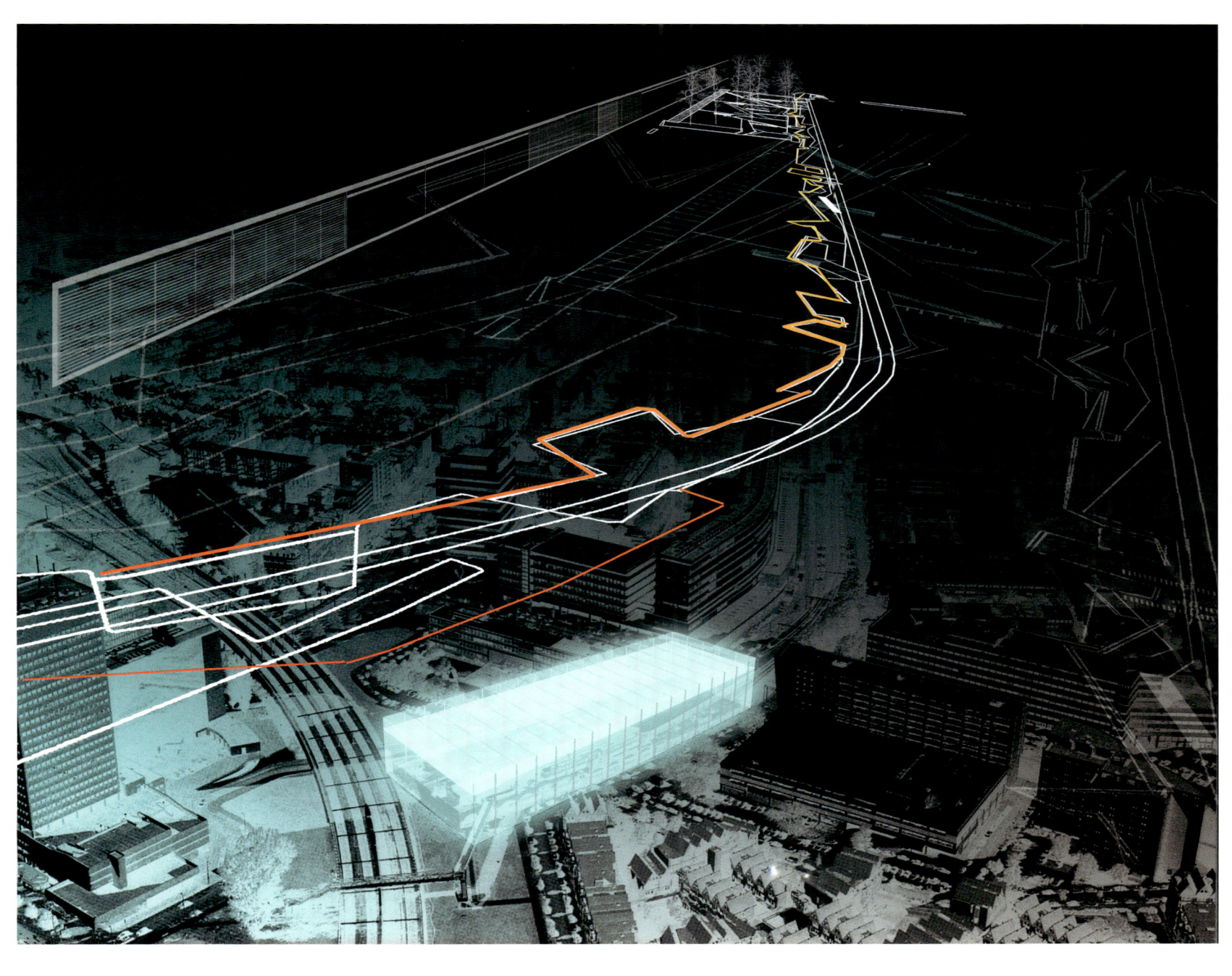

At night the glasshouse is transformed into a light-box with gigantic shadow projections of exotic plants

Interior of glasshouse

...white and black poplars and a series of pavilions which reflect the original signal boxes positioned along the railway viaduct...

view in the park

THE SITE

Located south of the river near Zuidplein, Valkeniersweide (literally 'falconer's meadow') forms part of two garden suburbs, Tuindorp Vreewijk and Tuindorp De Vaan. This elongated park is the easternmost spur of Zuiderpark, which extends across South Rotterdam in a green belt between Waalhaven and Groene Hilledijk. Valkeniersweide is bordered by a hospital and an asylum-seekers' centre (AZC). Cyclists, walkers and dog owners make regular use of the park as a short cut between Vaanweg, Dordtsestraatweg and Groene Hilledijk. Local families, many from immigrant backgrounds, visit the park in fine weather. Here people of all ages hold barbecues, picnic and play football and other games. The residents of the AZC also make frequent use of the park, lending it an international feel. A multicultural project (Vreewijk Vluchtheuvel) has developed the idea of creating in connection with the AZC an enclosed garden in Valkeniersweide, focusing on cultural diversity and the position of refugees and asylum-seekers.

THE BRIEF

There is to be an analysis of specific needs and use forms so as to formulate a proposal for the layout and detailing of Valkeniersweide. The stepping-off point is a development plan for Zuiderpark **(Structuurschets voor het Zuiderpark)** drafted in 1999. The brief calls for a design for a hortus conclusus as a meeting place for many different cultures in Valkeniersweide. It additionally requires a management and maintenance plan for the garden, bearing in mind how the people living in the vicinity might be involved in the park's management and upkeep.

Valkeniersweide in Vreewijk, 2001

photo: Pandion

THE PROPOSAL

As the basis for his design, Louafi studied the structure, function and use of the park, as well as demographic data such as the nationality, age and social status of its users. He believes that the basic layout of Valkeniersweide is satisfactory, and that it only requires the reanimation and redefinition of a number of its spaces. The existing plant growth must be thinned out in order to improve safety, as well as to make the park more congenial throughout the day. Careful pruning of shrubs and trees will serve as 'shock therapy' to create more light and space in the park. In addition, the existing pedestrian and cycle paths will be made more distinctive. The car parking on Dordtsestraatweg alongside Valkeniersweide will be eliminated, giving priority to an improved transition to the park. Louafi has designed different spaces for the variety of park activities. Groene Hilledijk will be transformed into a green stairway with seating overlooking the Moroccan fountain. The hortus conclusus is included in the form of an island to be set in the middle of the widened canal, where a greenhouse and different types of garden will be placed. These will be used and tended by those living at the asylum-seekers' centre and other local groups. The hortus conclusus will thus serve as a meeting place for cultures from all over the world. This new themed garden sets the tone for and lends colour to the issue of revitalizing Zuiderpark.

THE DESIGNER ON THE DESIGN

'The existing content, structures and, above all, firmly rooted habits have defined the new design and its parameters. A place where people of different social status, age and nationality meet, if only as passers-by or casual users – all make use of the space, not just in different ways but also simultaneously. The use forms are oriented around the existing structure, whether these be sports, ball games, cycling, taking a stroll or other forms of recreational activity.

'The task for the redesign of Valkeniersweide entails making an inventory of habits and needs and, at the same time, developing design elements. The purpose of these elements is to encourage better use of the park on the one hand, and to establish some form of identification on the other. A chemistry must arise between the design and the different groups of people that should be understandable for everyone.

'Alongside the customary ground plans, sketches and spatial proposals, traditional gardening tools are included in the design as part of a maintenance plan. The concept of "tools for all" will encourage participation in the proposed maintenance plan. A saw represents thinning out, and improvements to the infrastructure of footpaths and so on are indicated with a spirit level and pliers. New elements to be introduced in the existing layout, such as fountains, the hortus conclusus and a garden theatre, are shown in the overall plan.

'The tools required for the upkeep of the gardens form part of the presentation. Activities such as watering and cutting or rolling lawns are indicated in the appropriate zones. Tools required for the upkeep of the gardens form part of the presentation. Activities such as watering and cutting or rolling lawns are indicated in the appropriate zones.

'Compared with parks in other cities, Valkeniersweide has the advantage of a good soil structure with an established tree population and generously appointed areas of grassland. Our design seeks to reanimate the park's unfulfilled potential to make it more attractive by means of targeted intervention in specific areas. To this end we propose the implementation of three tools, each on a different scale:

Tool 1 – improving the park's spatial structure

'In the southern section in particular there are large areas that are no longer agreeable to use. Undergrowth has grown too dense and the sprawling shrubbery casts a shadow over the rest areas and playing fields. People no longer feel safe in such places at dusk and at night.

Only a radical thinning of trees and bushes will create light and unencumbered space for new activities. The saw is like a shock therapy for the park. It will fundamentally change the park's visual character, at the same time giving it the chance to acquire a new identity, making the park unique. To emphasize this new identity, the stems of trees that have been pruned back are to be painted with a coloured band.

Tool 2 – links

'Apart from the spatial structure, the park's infrastructure can also be improved by laying out new linkages. The park already enjoys a satisfactory network of pathways. There are however frequent conflicts between cyclists and pedestrians due to insufficient differentiation between paths. Intersections and accesses to neighbouring zones of the park could be significantly enhanced. With this in mind, we propose restructuring Dortsestraatweg and the accompanying pathways and pavements as a single surface. This will create a colourful podium tying together the asylum-seekers' centre, the youth club and the park. Parking is forbidden here. Installing water, electricity and telephone facilities will serve to encourage new uses. In the middle of the eastern section of the park the promenade joins a new entrance to the hospital in the form of a grove of linden trees. In the shade of these trees the park visitors can take advantage of a service wall offering such facilities as luggage lockers, telephones with Internet access and a miniature weather station. There will also be a public toilet here. In order to make the park a safe place at night, the main paths will be illuminated.

Tool 3 – selective intervention

'In recent years there has been a fundamental shift in the park's structural usage. If the park was formerly seen largely as decoration for strollers and local residents, Valkeniersweide is now more of a green living room for a wide variety of users. This and a more pronounced conditioning in the park, have given rise to individual spaces with their own use forms. Tool 3 implements additional "magnets" in the park for target groups with their own lifestyles. At the same time, less categorical spaces are to be designed for communal events that provide the opportunity for seeing and being seen.

'In addition to the "garden of the four corners of the world" which, as a hortus conclusus, represents one of the main interventions in the park, we also propose a series of local interventions aimed at enhancing the identity of Valkeniersweide. The entrance on Groene Hilledijk is a garden theatre of grass-covered plateaus that affords an open panorama across the park. Quality space for parents and children is provided by a Moroccan fountain and playground at the foot of the garden theatre. By shifting the dog-walking area to the south side, the eastern central part of the park will be transformed into a broad expanse of lawn for sunbathing and playing, as well as offering plenty of intimate corners for barbecues and picnics in summer. We propose creating in the grassy areas west of Dortsestraatweg, "islands" separated by hedges for a whole variety of potential uses. This is where asylum seekers might set up a café, while another island could shelter a teahouse, or be a place for sunbathing behind the hedge.

The origins of the hortus conclusus

'In the chaotic early Middle Ages, trade had become all but impossible and the urban population was forced to head for the countryside. After centuries of enforced wandering, the first medieval fields, meadows and gardens made their appearance. The church combatted the chaos with strict religious ideas regarding morality and duty: a severe doctrine of atonement and ethics that was to save mankind.

'The work ethic and the ordering of time and space were groundbreaking advances. In view of the limited opportunities for trade the monasteries were almost entirely self-supporting. Orchards, cemeteries, herb gardens, flower gar-

Valkeniersweide
Landscape architect Kamel Louafi

KAMEL LOUAFI
KLAUS OVERMEYER
PETER THOMAS
PATRICK BAIRSTOW
SEBASTIAN HOLTMANN
SABRINA SCHRÖDER
ANJA SCHMIDT
TOM FUCHS

dens, vegetable gardens and cloister-garths were laid out within the monastery walls. These enclosed gardens represented the internalized landscape. By placing work and contemplation on equal footing the garden was elevated above its role as a production unit, to a permitted source of pleasure.

The Garden of the Four Corners of the World
'Since then, the hortus conclusus has become a chameleon among gardens. Today's city-dweller employs a whole variety of methods to design his hortus conclusus as a personal, open-air universe – from terraced-house garden with miniature biotope through to the spontaneously acquired plot of fallow land in the middle of town where vegetables are cultivated. In our opinion the new hortus conclusus in Valkeniersweide needs to satisfy three chief requirements: as a place to gather and meet, a space for individual and nationally diverse needs, and an intimate zone.

'To replace the existing rose garden, which sits in the shade for most of the year, we propose creating in the widened canal an island in the shape of a flower-bulb. This hortus conclusus can easily be identified as a special feature by all groups of users. A simple greenhouse could serve to temporarily house the houseplants of local residents. Or for growing plants for a multi-cultural garden that could then be planted on the island. We do not consider it necessary to design that garden, and restrict ourselves to creating possibilities and preconditions for a space designed, laid out and looked after by the users themselves.

To conclude
'The considerations for redesigning Valkeniersweide allow not only for development of the existing layout and improvement of the infrastructure but also for new spatial allocations for activities such as sports and dog-walking so that these do not interfere with contemplation and relaxation. In this way the park would become a park of quality. To this same end, we propose constructing islands that give added value to the park's use. New paths and seating emphasize this intention. Open spaces do not merely bring greater accessibility but serve to make the park more visually attractive. The emergence of an island whose geometry is reminiscent of a flower-bulb, will enhance the park's identity. It is on this island that people of all ages, social strata, traditions and cultures can meet, and make the island their own. But above all they should be able to enjoy recreation and relaxation here.'

analysis

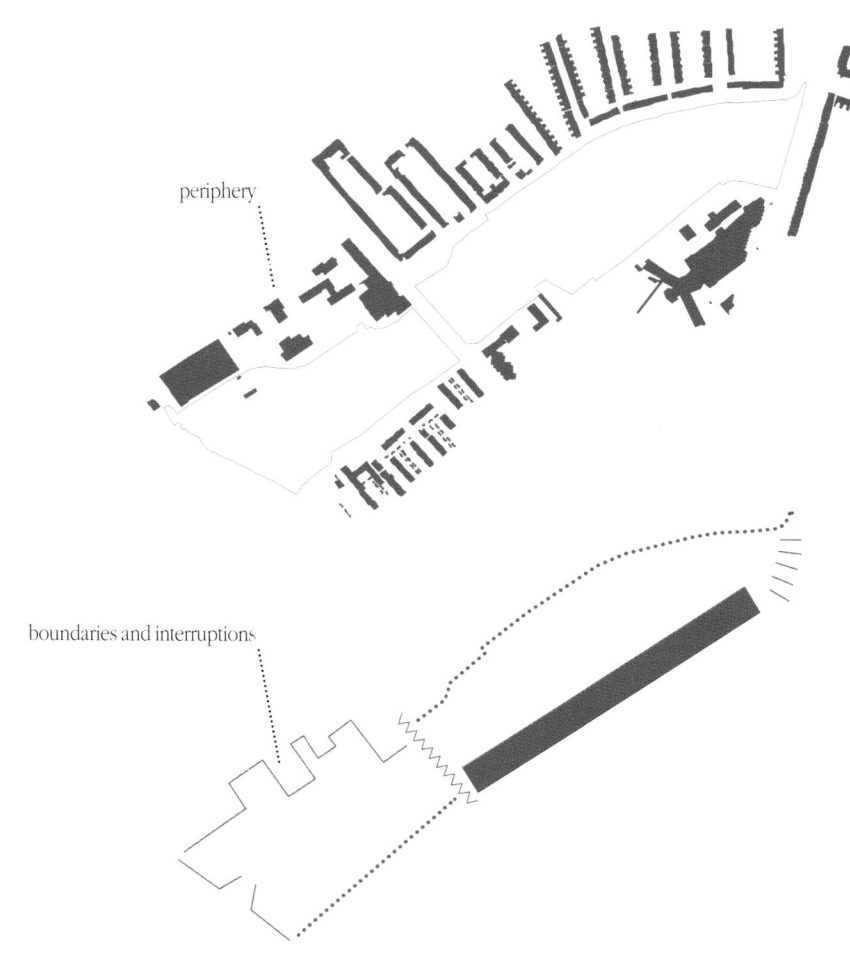

Many use Va
simultaneously and in differe

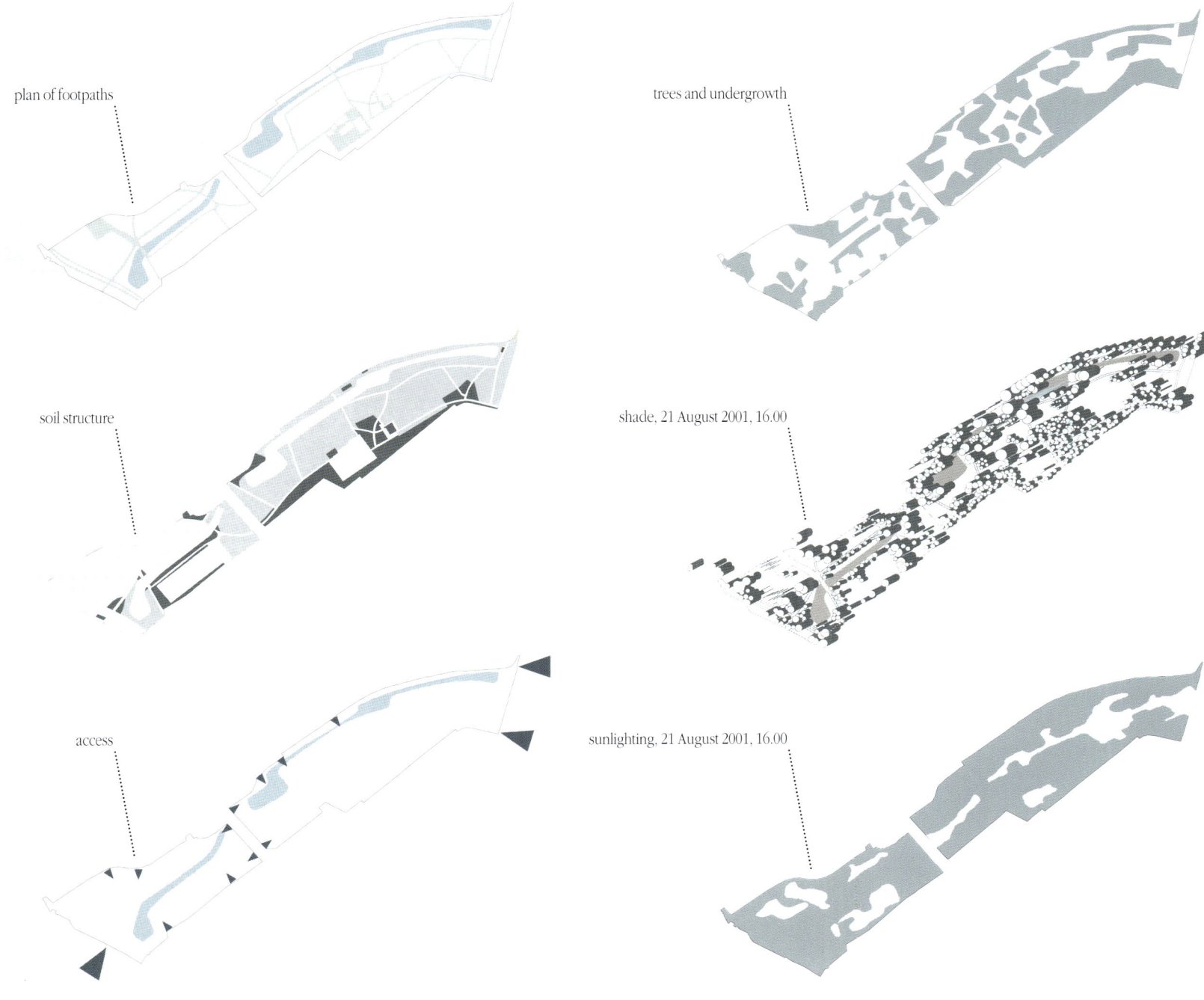

plan of footpaths

trees and undergrowth

soil structure

shade, 21 August 2001, 16.00

access

sunlighting, 21 August 2001, 16.00

eniersweide
t ways

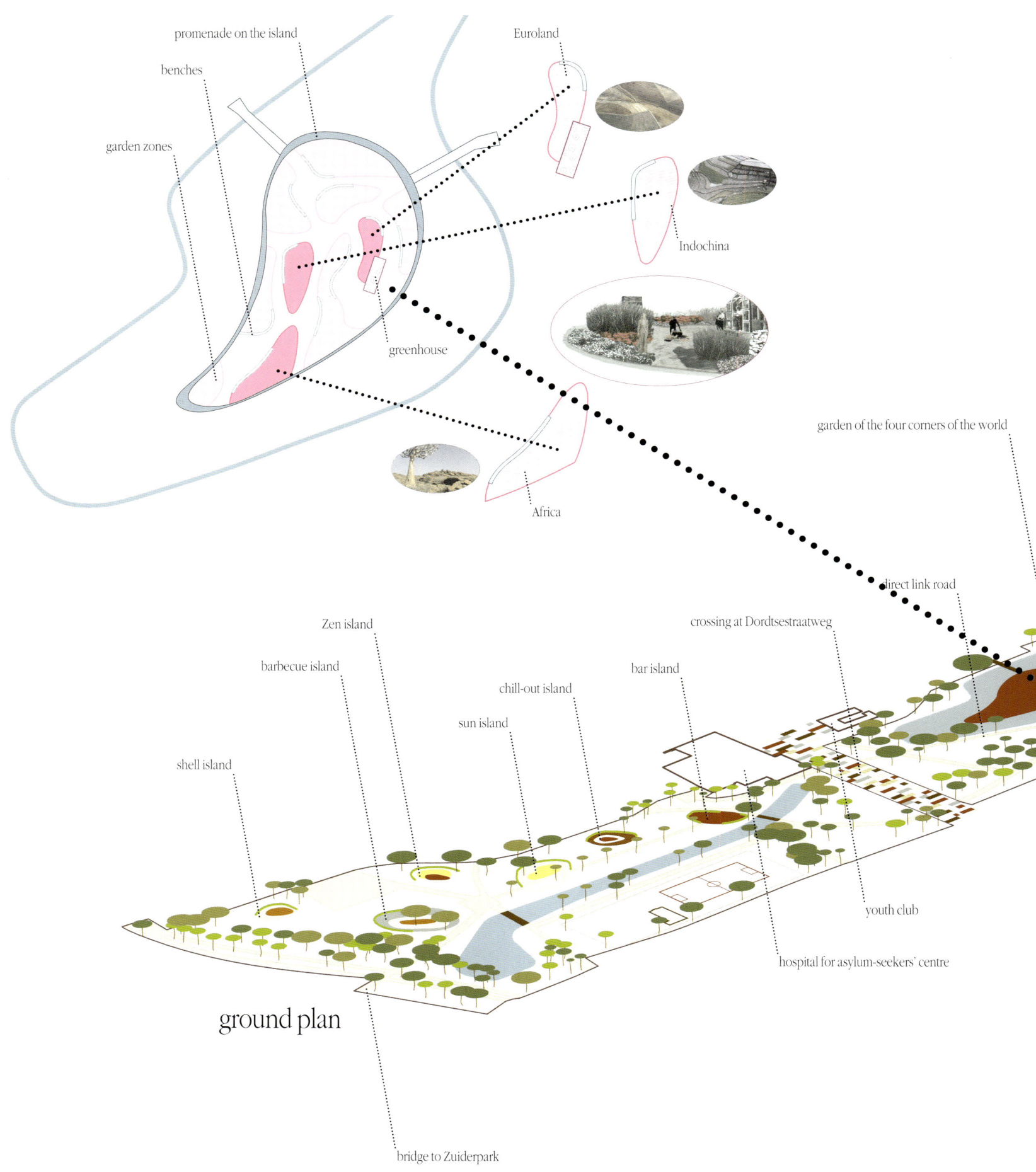

ground plan

the garden of the four corners of the world, a place to gather and meet, a space for individual needs

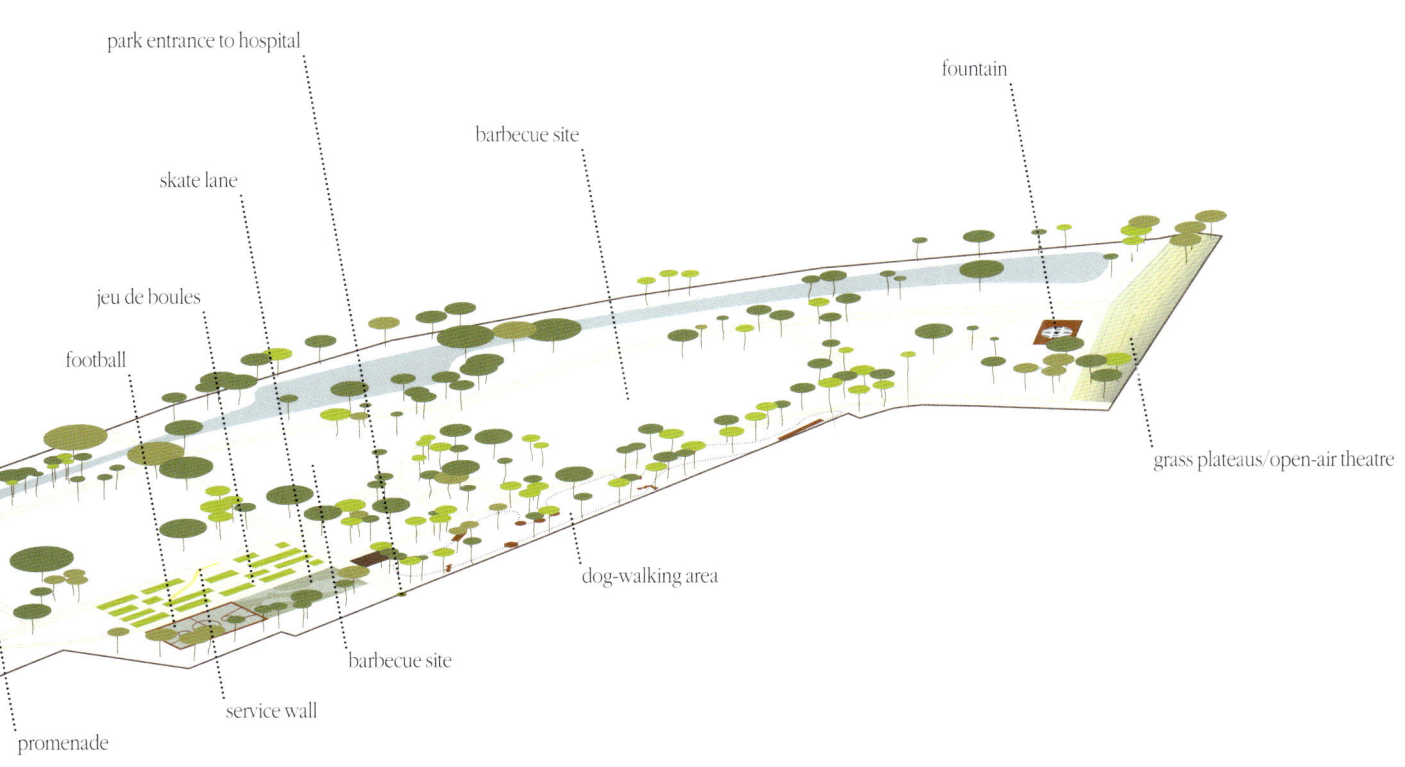

3x March
3x April
3x May
3x June
3x July
3x August
3x September
3x October

1x June
1x July
1x August

Maintenance plan

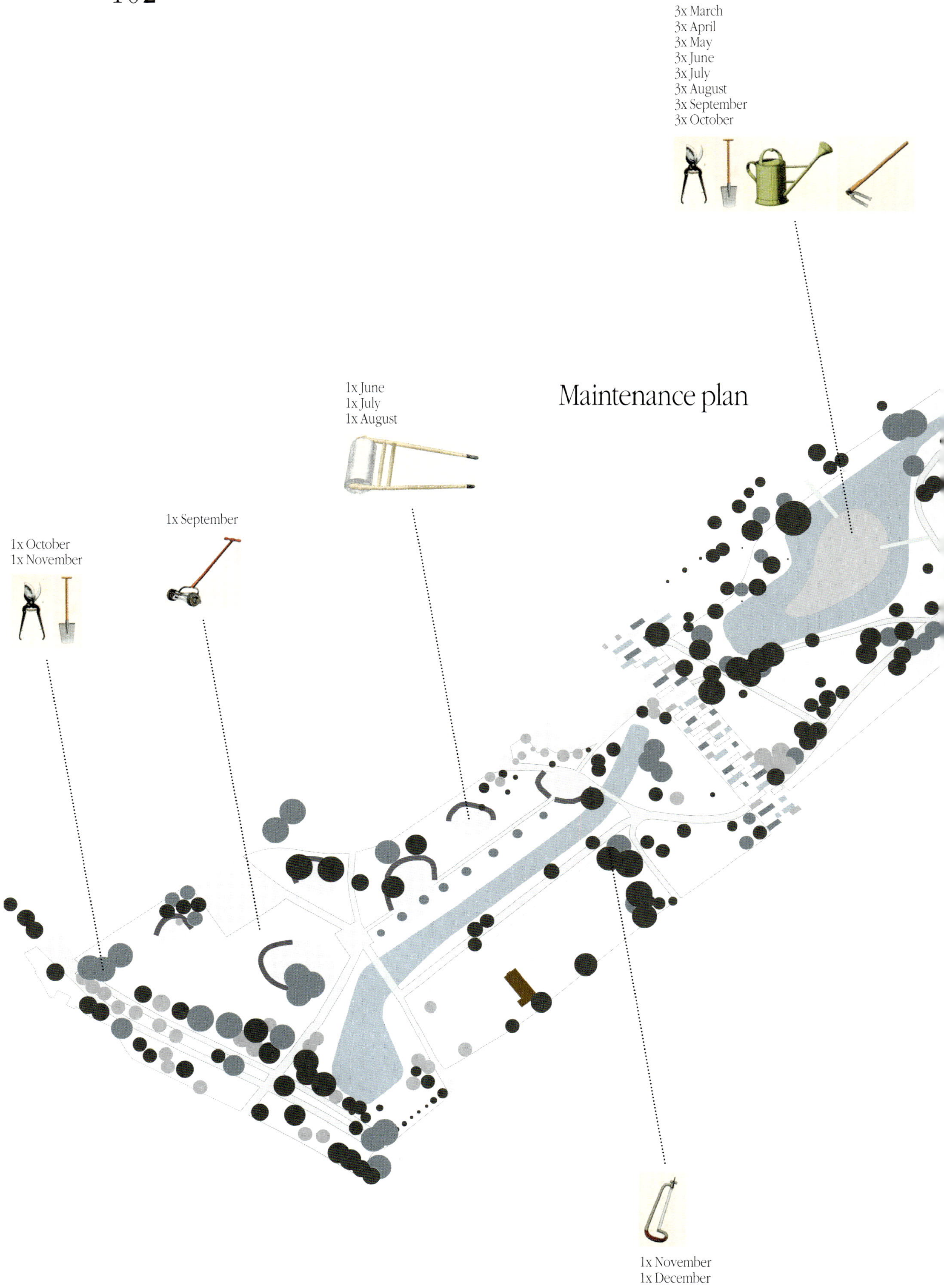

1x September

1x October
1x November

1x November
1x December

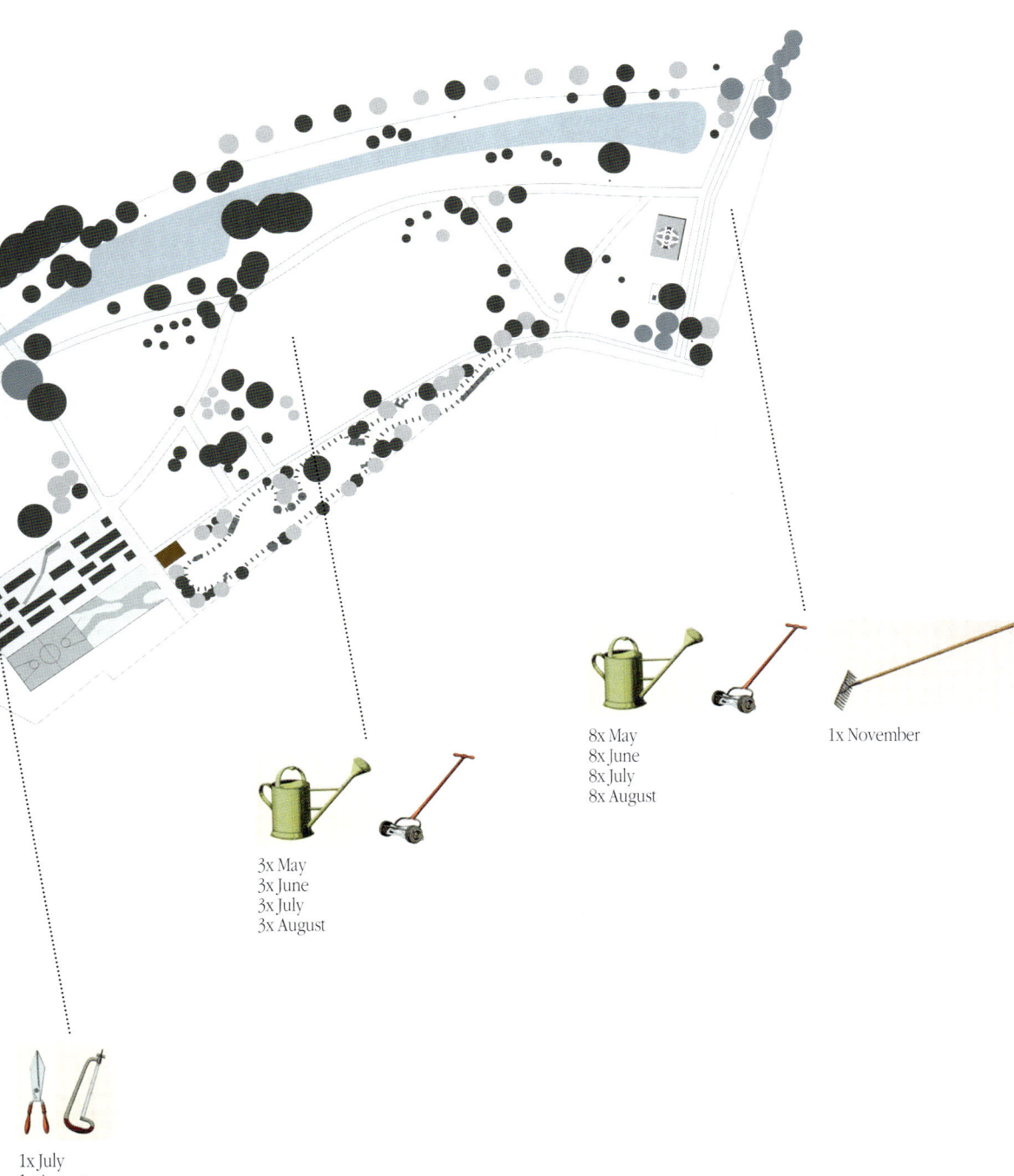

8x May
8x June
8x July
8x August

1x November

3x May
3x June
3x July
3x August

1x July
1x August

THE SITE

Lombardijen is one of three garden suburbs to the south of Rotterdam, the others being Pendrecht and Zuidwijk. The starting point for the design of this post-war urban expansion project was to give form to 'living in green space'. The district is surrounded by a green belt and tree-lined arterial roads. Its seven neighbourhoods are configured like a wreath around the central Spinoza park and the adjacent shopping centre. The district has an essentially verdant resonance. However, in many places it has lost the sense of purpose it once had, a situation for which nobody feels responsible. As a result the Spinoza park, for all its position at the centre of the district, registers as a large anonymous space.

THE BRIEF

How can the introduction of an urban garden imbue the public space in Lombardijen with a special character, differentiating it in future from the other southern garden suburbs? How can this project accommodate the needs of the Spinoza park's users and their diverse age categories?

Spinoza park in Lombardijen, 2001

THE DESIGNER ON THE DESIGN

'The Spinoza park is situated at the centre of Lombardijen, with the main thoroughfares crossing each other alongside and through the park. A post-war district, Lombardijen is spaciously appointed with broad profiles and residential blocks amidst green space. The scenery of mature trees in combination with the generous helping of green gives the district an image of affluence. Yet the green space is monotonous: there is a lack of variety in the visual and physical impact, function, layout and programme. Since the suburb's emergence in the 1950s, the use of the public green space has changed drastically though without the layout being adapted accordingly. The original design was geared to intensive use by large numbers of people. Parks are now increasingly used for individual forms of relaxation and recreation. Because the layout is no longer geared to the use form, the green space has degenerated into an anonymous, almost meaningless residual area for which nobody really feels responsible.

'All kinds of amenities of local function, such as churches and schools, have been ranged around the park's perimeter. A few recreational facilities have been added inside the park: a playground, a hang-out, a horse-riding arena and a half-pipe.

'The Spinoza park lacks a centre of resolute spatial presence. It also lacks distinctive boundaries, and there are no inviting entrances. It is more like a assemblage of green spaces, highly similar in function and in the experiences they offer. Because of the lack of distinctive and varied imagery, the park presents little inducement to spend time there. The serious neglect of park maintenance has resulted in the removal of flowering shrubs, perennials and annuals, and the park has gradually lost its quality as a distinguishing green area in Lombardijen. The three schools that have been built in the park are symptomatic: they have been hermetically sealed by plants and fencing, tucked away in isolation and emphatically inward-looking in a spatial sense, i.e. they are not involved with public life in the park. Although this was not the original intention, the schools have partially privatized and appropriated sections of the park, and thus withdrawn these areas from the public realm. This is also the case with the horse-riding arena and the children's play area. Because of the screen of plants, these places are not perceived as part of the park. Moreover, there are only a few places at a human scale that encourage one to sit there, and they in turn are served by an uninviting system of pathways. For these reasons, the park has become a space to move through rather than spend time in, indeed a space to circumnavigate rather than cross.

'The existing water features play far too subordinate a role here. As a spatial element the uniform water structure lacks connective elasticity, and there is little attraction in the way it is perceived and used because of the limited accessibility. There is no place where the water has real stature. The conclusion is that the current park layout is not an auspicious stepping-off point for creating a valuable and exceptional urban garden. To construct a scintillating urban garden will require making interventions.

'The park's four main routes stem from the most popular circulation movements through it, and are linked to the district's focus on the shopping centre. The park will be furnished with obvious entrances. A "beacon" in the form of an advertising pillar, billboard or artwork will mark the approaches to the four main routes. The water structure will be altered and extended by a centrally situated pool which along with the new urban garden will mark the heart of the park.

'The park design has four components which are spatially interconnected: a sportsfield, a wooded field, a birch grove and a park meadow. These components are to contrast sharply, based on current use of the park and the as yet unexploited potentials of the site. Each component will be distinguished by a specific function, a special object or a place of attraction.

'The sportsfield is the place for games and play activities in the park. Specific activities will be concentrated in the circles: a skate bowl, a basketball court and a toddlers' playground. Its generous dimensions and audacious steepness will make the skate bowl the sensation of Lombardijen. The basketball court will be confined by a sloping wall which will illuminate the court like a half moon in the evenings.

'The toddlers' area is an electronic playground for kids. This interactive play area, composed of screens, sensors, buttons and passwords - false friends of the twenty-first century - is an attraction **pur sang.**

'The wooded field is a new entrance to the park. In the spring it is a riot of colour: over 70 trees in blossom. The poplars currently standing in this portion of the park have seen better days, and are due for replacement. This presents the opportunity to remodel this part from scratch. It is important that it is designed as an obvious park entrance.

'The extended water structure enhances the island-like character of this component and marks out a clear-cut park perimeter. Laying out the wooded field will subtly consolidate the park. The main routes lined with long strips of hedge slice through the grid of blossoming trees in a confrontational gesture.

'The community centre is given a place of its own among the birches. A new path threading through the birch grove links the waterside plaza with the shopping centre. Visually defining this birch grove is a natural covering of **luzula** (woodrush). Groups of overhanging weeping willow to be planted along the waterside path will colour the park at the water.

'The most central green space in the park is the park meadow, which is to contain the new urban garden. A generous pool clearly establishes the presence of water. The plaza on its banks is the new local square: a spot overlooking the water for local festivities and events, and for use by the two adjoining schools. An "island of desire" lies in the park lake: this is a place to be appreciated visually, surrounded by a magical circle of light but inaccessible because surrounded by water. This island is home to the existing marsh cypresses with an undergrowth of ferns.

'The urban garden forms the midpoint of the park, the place where all the major routes in the park converge. The newly profiled routes meet the need to move through the park efficiently and purposefully. Arguably the main reason for crossing the park is to visit the shops. By situating the garden exactly where the main routes intersect, it is always a part of one's route. So it is not merely a place for stopping, but an important point along the way at all hours.

'The garden is designed as a continuous space. It has an open portion oriented towards the lake and a more introverted part surrounded by a tall, broad coulisse hedge with openings. These openings function as windows, offering vistas from various perspectives. The two parts of the garden are internally connected by a curving path with serried terraces for seating.

'Visitors to the park can retreat to the garden and enjoy the beauty of the perennials. The border on the eastern side sports imposing, tall plants which provide shelter for the garden. In addition, the garden projects a powerful mood across the park: casual passers-by experience the special attraction of perennial plants.

'The big terrace overlooking the pool is an invitation to enjoy the garden as the sun sets, giving a view of the illuminated island with its marsh cypresses and ferns. The junction of the three main pathways suggests a site for an art work.

'The planting of the urban garden is informed by an unusual use of perennials. These plants enables one's perception of a place to extend far beyond the purely aesthetic. The selected plants have a natural character. Their combinations recall intense experiences to be had in "real" nature.

'Important reasons for choosing perennials include their manner of growth and the wealth of visual incident, the way they flower, their character and ambience, their significance before

Spinoza park
Piet Oudolf

PIET OUDOLF
in association with
SYLVIE LOUAGIE
CLIMMY SCHNEIDER
MARNIX TAVENIER
TOM DE WITTE

and after flowering, their attractive subsidence into inactivity and the fine winter silhouette. The suitability of perennials for use in the public domain is determined on the grounds of characteristics such as resistance to frost, longevity and manageability, i.e. growth is not overly rampant and the variety does not seed itself excessively. As far as growth is concerned, the main criteria are that the plants should remain sturdy even after heavy showers and that they are insensitive to pests.

'A variety of decorative grasses have been used in the proposed plant combinations, as these are an essential element for achieving natural effects and a dream-like aspect. The garden is attractive throughout the year, thanks in part to the robust plant combinations which will make the cycle of seasons eye-catchingly visible. These combinations of sturdy plants are also more resilient to the effect of litter, dogs off the leash and vandalism.'

four components which are spatially interconnected: a sportsfield, a wooded field, a birch grove and a park meadow including the urban garden

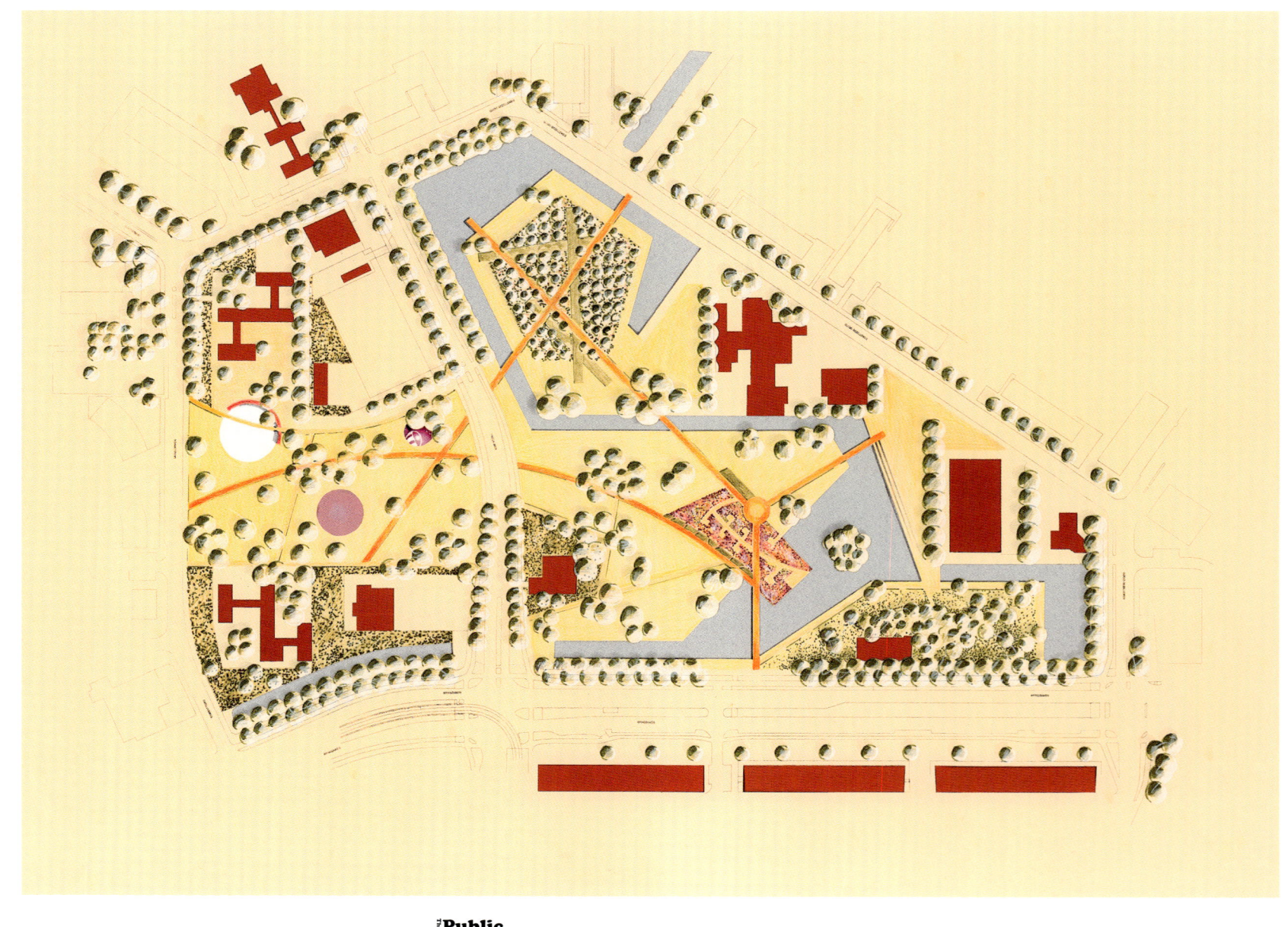

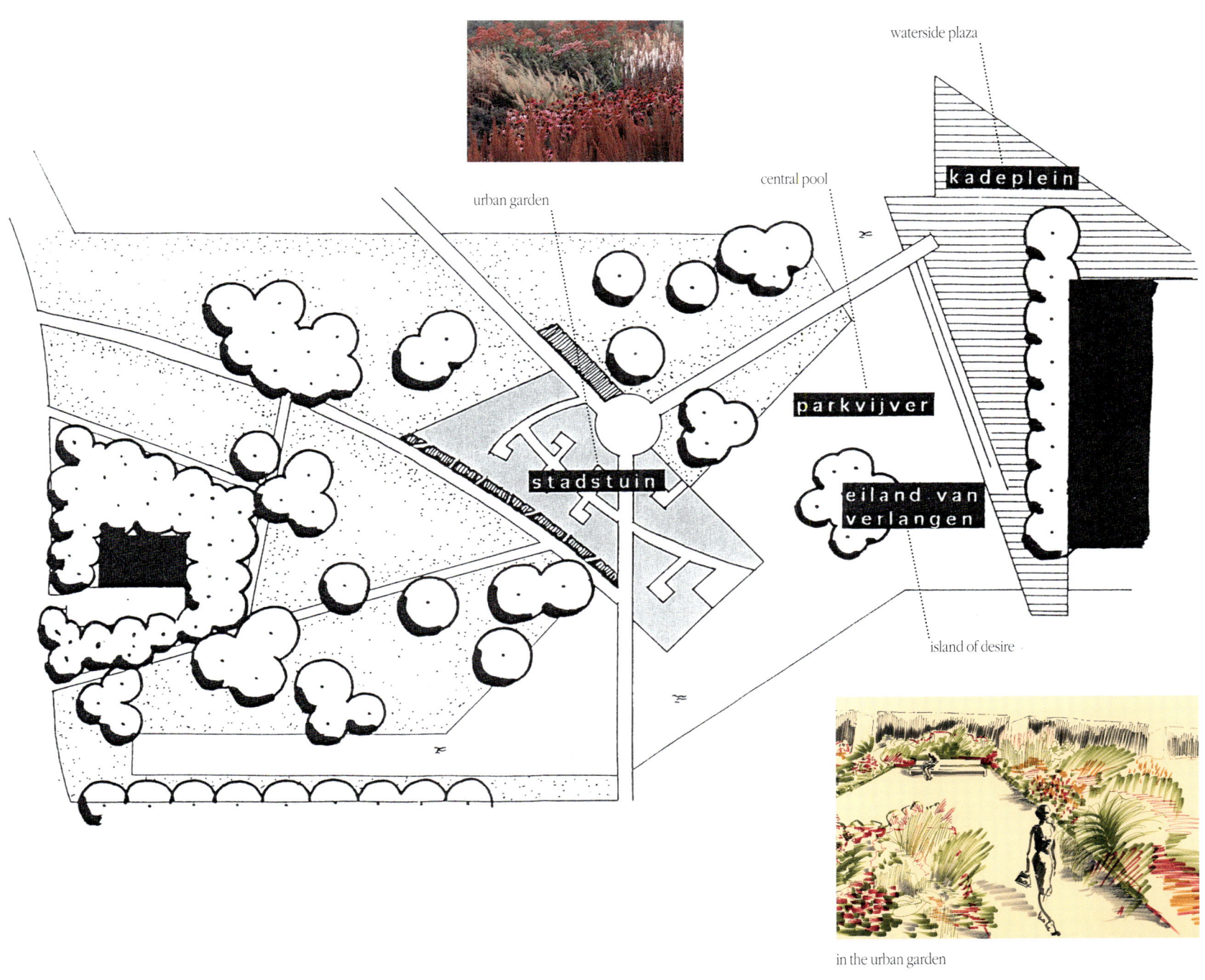

in the urban garden

Here visitors to the park can enjoy the beauty of perennial plants

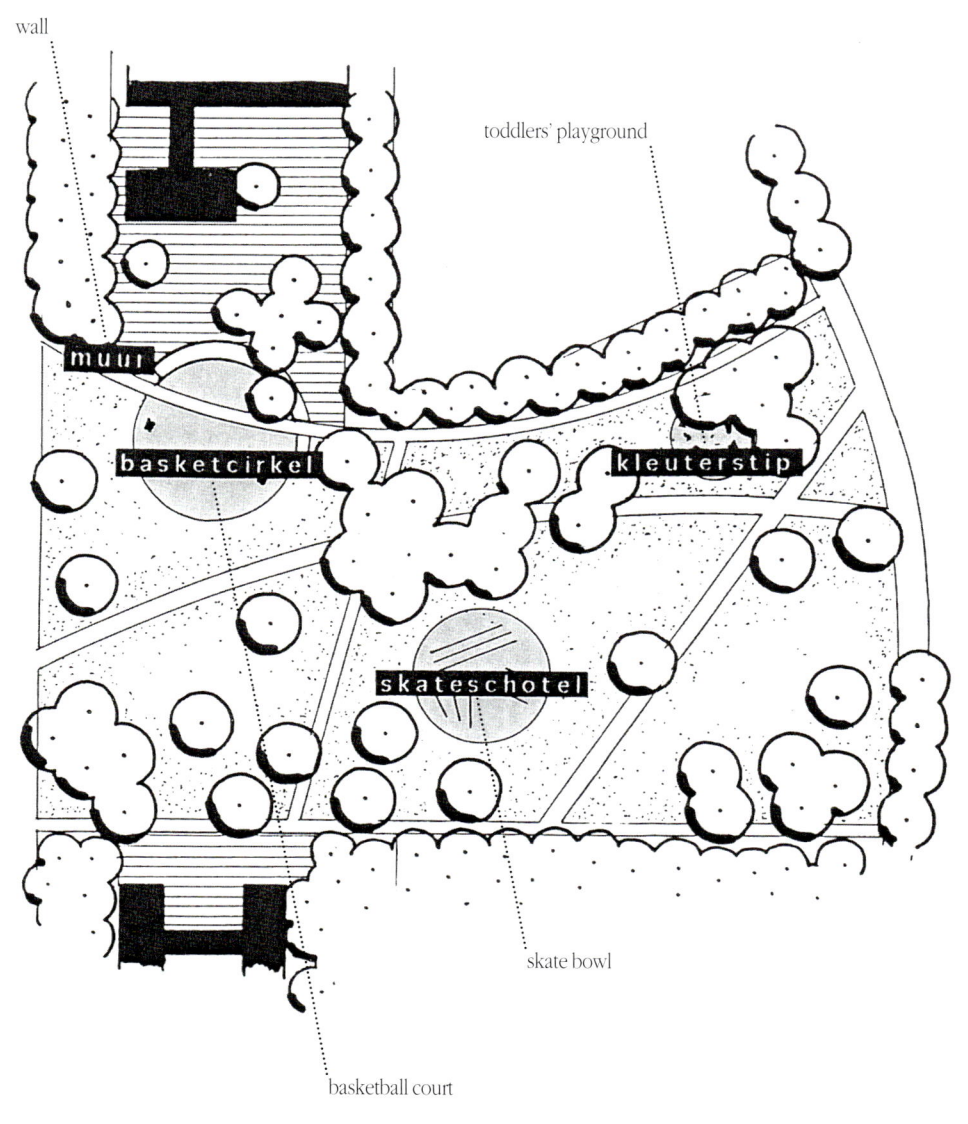

wall
toddlers' playground
muur
basketcirkel
kleuterstip
skateschotel
skate bowl
basketball court

skate bowl

...a sloping wall which will illuminate the court like a half moon in the evenings

In the spring it is a riot of colour: over 70 trees in blossom

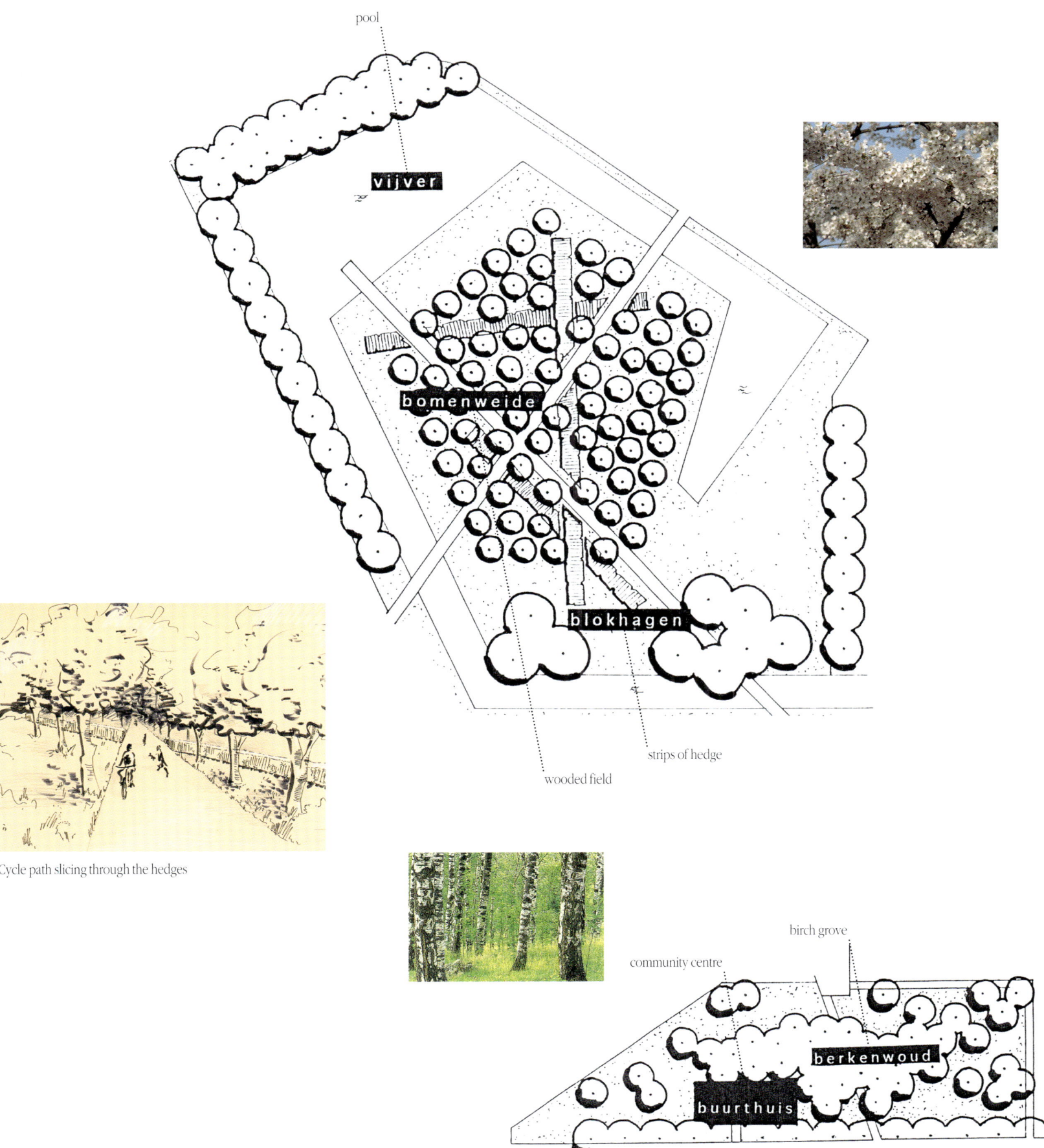

Cycle path slicing through the hedges

plan for planting urban garden

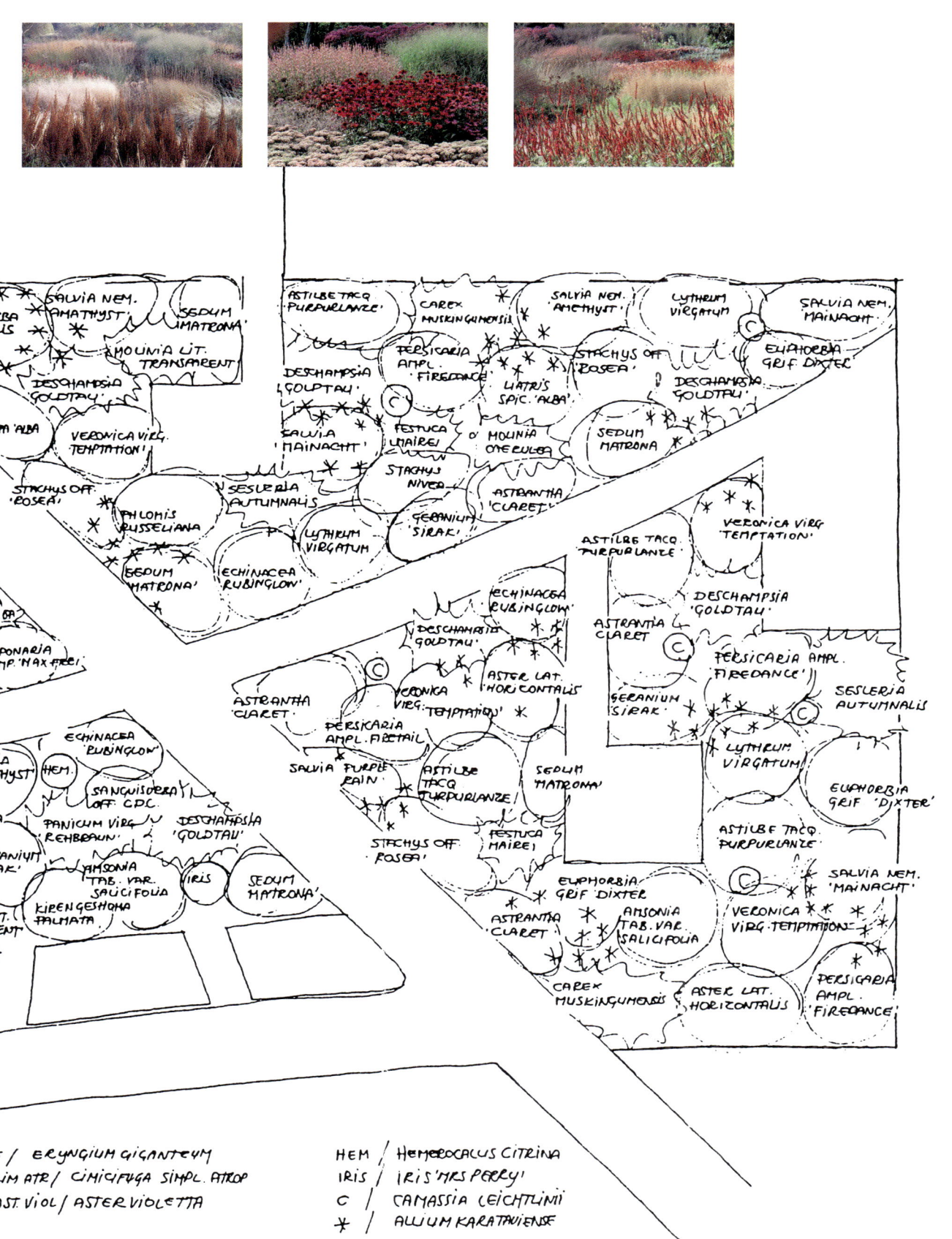

THE SITE

Until the mid-1960s, Rotterdam's residents could walk from the city centre to the banks of the River Maas within a continuous oasis of green. This area, laid out in the 1930s as a parkway, has now disintegrated into fragments of gardens and parks. In the vicinity of Museum Park there are six museums, and Het Park, 'the park on the Maas', is host to large-scale summer festivals. It is exemplary of an area in the Rotterdam region where the visual and performing arts have established an open-air home. The zone attracts people from all over the Netherlands. However, because of the difficulty in crossing the Westzeedijk roadway, these parks lack a good interconnection. One of the park fragments is the so-called 'wild garden', hidden behind fencing at the foot of the Faculty of Medicine of the Erasmus University. In urban planning terms it has the potential to form an important link in the walk through the various gardens in Museum Park and across the Westzeedijk to Het Park.

THE BRIEF

The brief concerns the area between Rochussenstraat and the Maas river, specifically the villa gardens on Jongkindstraat, the rose garden behind the Boijmans Van Beuningen Museum, Museum Park, the wild garden, Schoonoord and Het Park. The different components lack a connection with the surrounding city areas and the river, primarily because of the pedestrian-unfriendly Westzeedijk. So the various parts of the area are in need of improved interconnectivity. Het Park and Museum Park must be logically linked for slow traffic, i.e. pedestrians. The design brief includes an analysis of the route past the villa gardens on Jongkindstraat, the exhibition garden of the Netherlands Architecture Institute (NAi), Museum Park, the wild garden and Het Park. The design must specifically address the route from the bridge across the space between the Natuurmuseum (Natural History Museum) and the Kunsthal, along the on-street parking between the foot of the Westzeedijk and the wild garden via the steps to Het Park, as well as make a proposal for renewing the enclosure of the wild garden and enhancing its accessibility from Museum Park.

The wild garden at the foot of the Erasmus University, 2001

photo: Pandion

THE PROPOSAL

Descombes studied how to improve the pedestrian route past the gardens of Jongkindstraat, through Museum Park, across the Westzeedijk and through Het Park to the Nieuwe Maas river. However, a visit to the area and various discussions made him decide to write a commentary rather than create a design. In his essay he points to the shoddy execution and the poor upkeep, management and use of the area. His analysis of Museum Park in its present state led him to conclude that the intention of the design has only partially been achieved. He criticizes the lack of respect or care for the park. Descombes insists that there should be a better connection between it and Het Park. One solution would be to shift the existing tram stop to the entrance next to the Kunsthal. The hidden garden alongside the Natuurmuseum can indeed form an important link between Museum Park and Het Park, but it is currently in the throes of the recently begun, complex urban transformation and expansion of the Erasmus University and the University Hospital. Descombes also advises moving the entrance to Het Park to Maaskade. Het Park should be given a well-planned extension down as far as the quayside, creating more possibilities for restaurants, cafés and parking.

THE DESIGNER ON THE DESIGN

'I shall follow the linear succession of sites, beginning in the north on Jongkindstraat. First, the problematic state of affairs along the side of the NAi - where there are advertising displays announcing NAi activities, which I see as a good idea - is due to the poor organization of the street between the institute and the "villas". There are at present [ed. autumn 2000] site works on the abutting street, connected with the extension to the Boijmans Van Beuningen Museum. I don't think it is a great idea to change the architecture of the streets at each corner. I therefore suggest the same design should be used for Jongkindstraat and Museum Park. In the plan I have indicated a system of slabs to clarify the walking route towards that park.

'Then we arrive at Museum Park designed by Yves Brunier in association with OMA - a perfect project. Unfortunately not loved, maybe hated, and in any case scandalously lacking in proper maintenance. The beautiful surface of shells near the NAi should be replanted with the trees proposed by Brunier. And the broken wall of mirrors at the main "gate" must be renovated.

'It is strange to hear what people say about the following perfect sequence, namely the large tarmac area for skating, this carpet of painted lines and encrustations of herbs and flowers. It is unique to encounter such concern and space for these kinds of activities in a park. Usually they cause conflict with other users: here the right organization makes it perfectly possible. I was told that it is seen as some kind of offence to the children in the nearby hospital! If I were a sick child lying there, I would certainly enjoy the figures of the players on this huge, horizontal blackboard as much as the trees and tulips. What is terrible here, once again, is the total absence of care and maintenance: a way to make this place repulsive, an abandonment cunningly planned by people who hate this park.

'Then the curved bridge makes a very clever and elegant link with the Kunsthal. It acts as a beautiful and rare promenade among the trees and above the flowers. But once again there are problems of maintenance, this time with the flowerbeds and the benches along the paths.

'The Kunsthal articulates quite perfectly the difference in level between the esplanade of the park and the Westzeedijk dyke-top roadway. This link would certainly work better with a new tram stop in front of the Kunsthal. It is ridiculous to see how people have to walk way back to the existing stop opposite the Erasmus University. There are many examples of tram stops in close succession in our cities.

'The crossing of the dyke is closely bound up with the extension to the Faculty of Medicine. Certainly it is the occasion **par excellence** to establish a new, easy link with the park. This could then be perceived and used as a garden by all the people, patients and students at the hospital. The modifications to be made to the little "water garden" and the improvement of the links with the Kunsthal café's terrace are as much a part of the hospital project. It is a project of such huge dimensions, involving equally huge transformations of the area round about, that I can't imagine myself working like a dwarf in the shadow of this giant.

'My design proposal focuses on the small wild garden at the foot of the Erasmus University's high-rise tower. It will be a garden behind a wall that forms part of the wood. The new enclosure is a metallic structure 10 metres high, with a double wall of square, large-meshed gauze that follows the curve of the existing pond. There will only be greenery growing on the internal wall, while the external one must remain a shining surface. All the bushes outside the new fence will be cut down, save for the few large trees.

'There are two gates in the garden wall and also three large loggias with long benches in the space between the two surfaces. You can walk along the enclosure on a slightly elevated walkway around the pond. Between the ground floor and the hospital's car park entrance and the wild garden, I propose a new screen that plays on the existing structures of the hospital building, such as the columns, terraces, staircases and paving stones. This would take the form of a see-through wall that creates a series of visual effects. From the darkest interior space of the garage the wall will appear as a shining surface, a combination of a smooth, white surface and a shifting, leafy vision of the trees through the translucent structure. Seen from the wild garden, the wall will offer a new intimacy, but will also reveal the movements inside the building because of the distortion of the material.

'The transparent wall is made of TWD (Transparent Warme Dammung), a polycarbonate honeycomb structure, 60 cm wide, protected on both sides by safety glass, with a metallic structure anchored in a concrete base. The wall is 6 metres high and 30 metres long. This part of the project was done in collaboration with the artist Carmen Perrin. She has already realized several works of art for similar walls.

'Regarding Het Park, I would like to express my misgivings about the invasion of cars in the area. However, it seems that tenacious habits are at work here. I would prefer to encroach as little as possible on the deliciously quiet Park Schoonoord with its pond alongside Het Park.

'A possible place for a radical transformation is the park front overlooking the River Maas. The existing unpaved terrace is poorly arranged. I propose extending the park front as far as the river, above the road. This could provide space for an underground car park with shops, services and restaurants, and terraces above. A new entrance to Het Park from the waterfront.'

Museum Park – Het Park
Georges Descombes

GREGORY BUSSIEN
VINCENT MANZONI
AURELIE PARVU
CARMEN PERRIN

Walk along Rochussenstraat-Museum Park-Het Park; additions and modifications

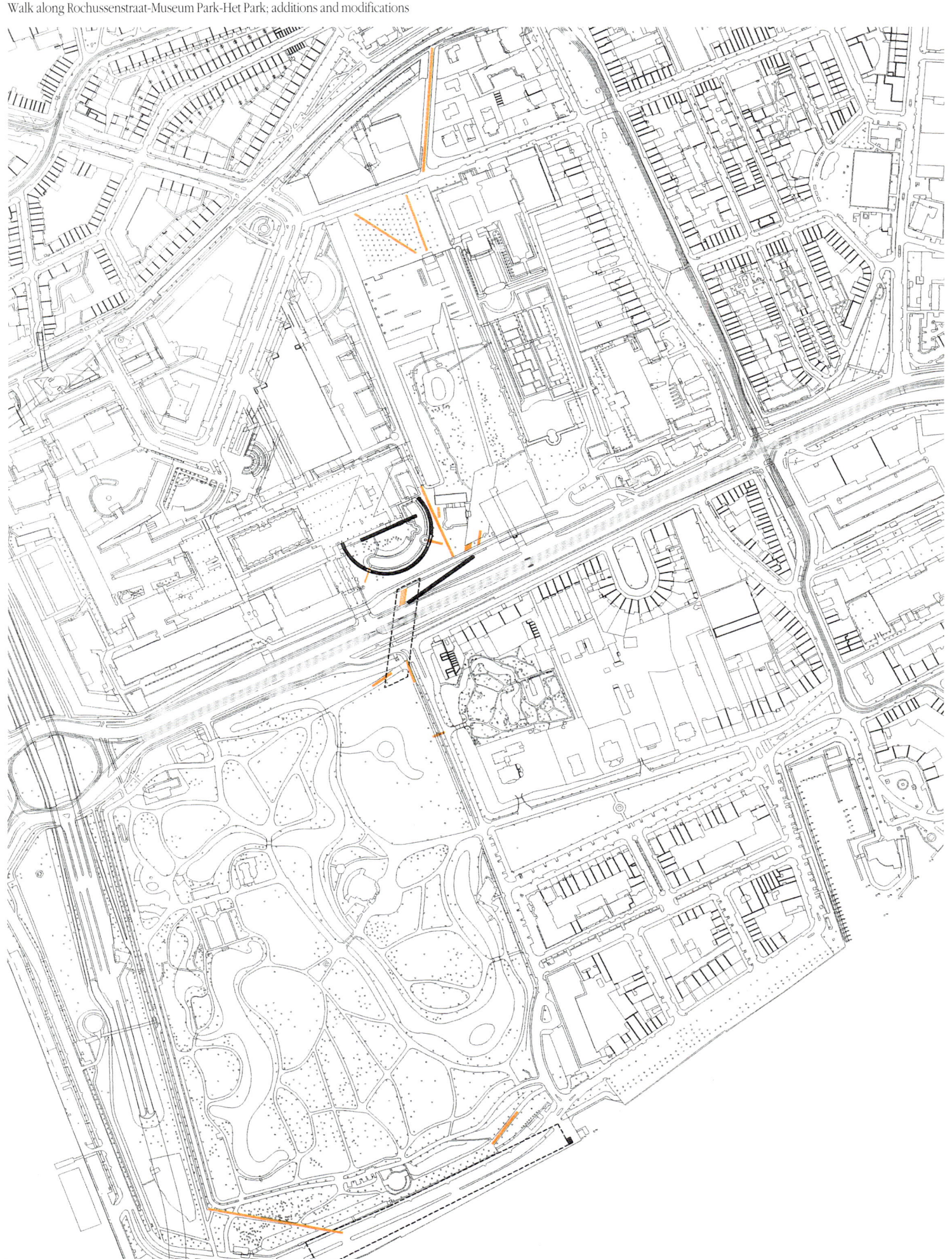

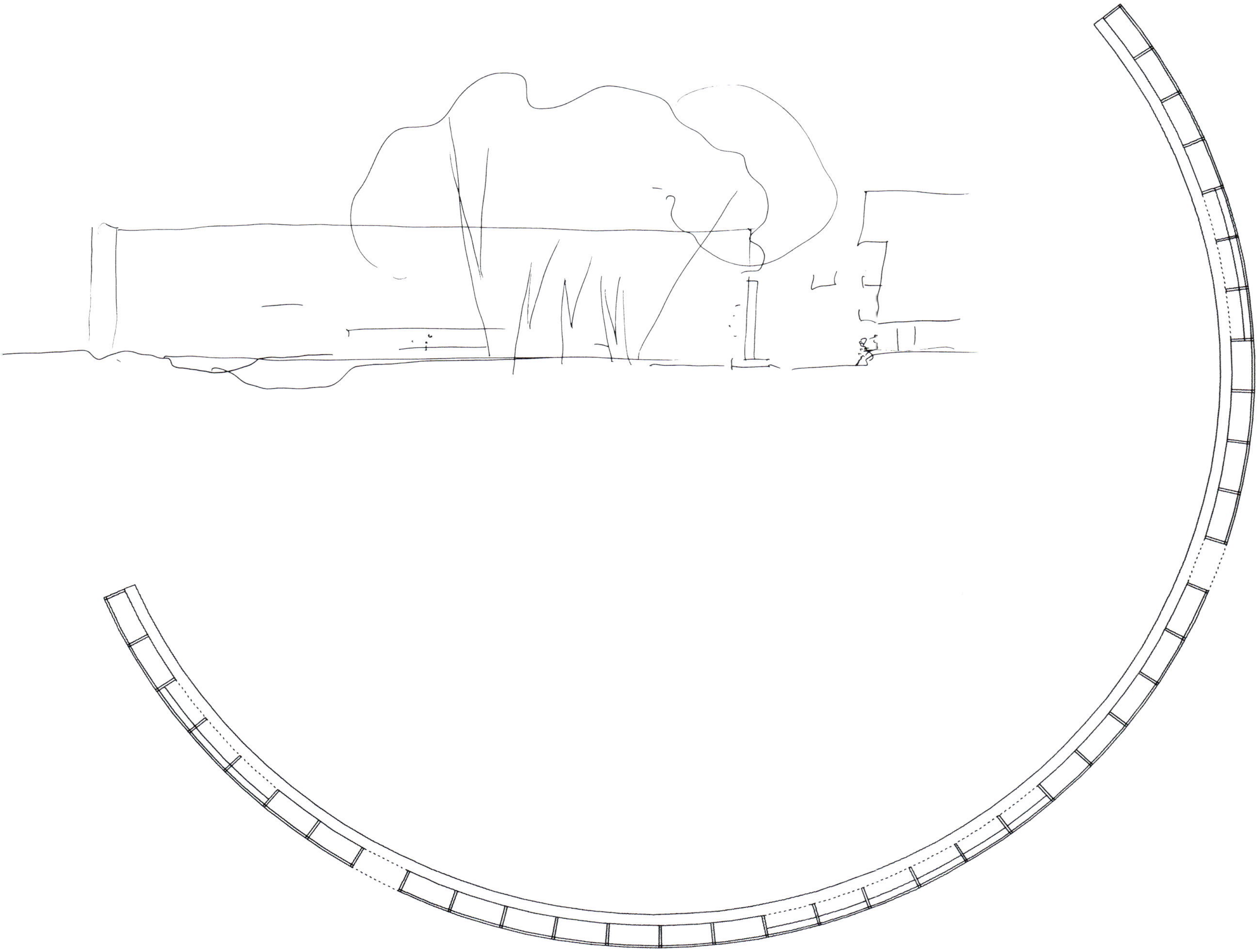

A double transparent garden wall with three loggias with benches

A long garden bench along the garage wall

View of the garden from the garage through the transparent screen

TERESITA FERNÁNDEZ
360º Oasis
Teresita Fernández (b. Miami, USA, 1968) juxtaposes in her work the garden's artificial and natural features. But she is less interested in the garden itself than in the relationship between the public and the environment she has created. An important source of inspiration for her recent works is the artificiality, perfection and atmosphere of the Japanese garden. **360º Oasis** was specially designed for Witte de With. The existing architecture of the exhibition space is divided into two enclosed spaces. The title refers to the smooth and barren landscape of the desert, where an oasis is a welcome interruption, a miniature paradise contained by the vertical lines of the trees that surround the spring, the centre of the oasis. The work in Witte de With also consists of vertical lines, more than 1200 pipes in different shades of green, that enclose an empty calm space. The seemingly infinite row of vertical lines and the intimate but undefined environment turn the installation into a place for contemplation, that at the same time is animated by an optical movement. This cinematic effect created by the viewer moving within all of these vertical lines functions much like a camera shutter: images appear and disappear.

ANTHONY DUNNE & FIONA RABY
Placebo: Compass Room
Anthony Dunne (b. London, UK, 1964) and Fiona Raby (b. Singapore, 1963) have been working together as Dunne & Raby since 1992. Their work – a combination of design and academic research – is concerned with the intersection of industrial design, architectonic design and electronic media. Dunne & Raby are interested in stimulating critical debate about the role and quality of our electronically mediated lives. Their recent research focuses on electromagnetic fields emanating from equipment in the domestic environment. It aims at raising consumer awareness of the proliferation of these fields so as to better their welfare. For 'Hortus Conclusus' they have designed **Placebo: Compass Room,** a space enclosed on three sides with small compasses set in the floor that react to electronic objects. Pink pyramids of foam have been affixed to the walls and ceiling to absorb stray electronic fields. There are also a number of designed products in the Compass Room, which Dunne & Raby group together under the name 'Design Noir': they serve to interfere with electronic signals and induce contradictory and complex emotions. The Tele-jammer prevents mobile phones from working within a range of seven to ten metres. The Truth Phone contains a voice analysis machine and a lie detector.

DENNIS ADAMS
Afwerkplaats for small cars
Adams (b. Design Moines, Iowa, USA, 1948) is best known for work that combines modernist functional design with post-war social critique. In the 1980s, he designed a series of bus shelters for cities in the USA and Europe which carried images and headlines of such contested issues as the Rosenberg trial and Vietnamese refugees. For Schiphol Airport in the Netherlands, Adams designed **Coda** (1995), a house-like structure made of red and white cubes which serves as a meeting point for air travellers. On the inside, one finds a series of pictures of desolate places in the airport grounds. The pictures carry the names of colonial travel destinations: Palembang, Surabaya, Willemstad.

In Witte de With, Adams has designed an enclosed playroom for pre-school children that is based on Rotterdam's 'afwerkplek', a drive-in facility located in an industrial zone at the edge of the city that accommodates prostitution and heroin addiction. A typical product of the Dutch penchant for boxing social problems into a strict spatial order, the 'afwerkplek' includes well-lit sidewalks with rain shelters (for the prostitutes), driving lanes (for the customers), and numbered drive-in cubicles (for the action) beautified with a set of red baskets (for the deposit). By using the existing facility as a model for a playground, Adams transgresses the limits of democratic permissiveness: the prostitution area is absorbed into the symbolic world of children.

MAURA BIAVA
Iride
Meticulously detailed, fictitious female characters are a recurring theme in the work of Maura Biava (b. Reggio nell'Emilia, Italy, 1970). Biava came into contact with acting through performances when she was studying at the academy of art in Milan. In Biava's projects the public can follow the development and the experiences of the characters through series of exhibited drawings, photographs and texts, and via communication over the Internet. Some of the alter egos are granted only a short life, while others are followed for years and develop into fully fledged characters.

In 1998 Biava created 'Iride', a young biology student who asks herself existential questions prompted by her study of plant characteristics. Biava keeps the diary of this fictional character and supplements it with illustrations and drawings. Iride will also be brought to life for the exhibition 'Hortus Conclusus'. Personified by an actress, she spends her time in her garden in a small greenhouse filled with cacti placed on a floating deck in Leuvehaven. Visitors to Witte de With can share their thoughts with Iride using an on-line connection. In Witte de With, visitors can also examine and read her diary.

The Public Garden
Artists' Projects

ZEGER REYERS
Onder-tussen II
Zeger Reyers (b. Voorburg, Netherlands, 1966) is fascinated by growth, accumulation and bricolage. Following his education at the Rotterdam art academy he made **Aardappeleters** (1995; Potato Eaters) and **Goede Voornemens** (1997; Good Intentions) in which he mounted respectively three hundred kilos of potato chips and an enormous pile of tableware on a simple dining-room table. Since then he has focused his attention primarily on organic materials, which he grows in furniture and architecture. He cultivated mussels on iron chairs, grass on pillars, and fungi on children's cots.

The work in this exhibit, titled **Onder-tussen II** (In-between II), is made with oyster mushrooms and subdivided into three phases. In the growth room, mushrooms are cultivated on rubber boots and a whole variety of equipment, such as video recorders, monitors and keyboards. Once they have reached maturity they are brought into the exhibition space to dry, so that they can be placed in their definitive sculptural form in a display case. Reyers prepared a do-it-yourself kit to go with the work. The kit is available at the reception desk.

This is the second oyster mushroom project by Zeger Reyers at Witte de With. **Onder-tussen I** can be viewed through a glass ceiling in Witte de With's restrooms.

CRISTINA IGLESIAS
Untitled (Travel Agency)
Untitled (Travel Agency) has been specially made for a vacant former travel agency in the centre of Rotterdam. The installation incorporates motifs and elements that are already familiar features of the work of Cristina Iglesias (b. San Sebastián (Donostia), Spain, 1956). It is one of a series of recent works that demonstrate the artist's interest in the phenomenon of the city, in the definition of space and in the behaviour of the individual in an environment of anonymity, intimacy and rest as an interruption of urban life. In **Untitled (Travel Agency),** Iglesias represents nature in stilted, static images, which contrast with the noise and the speed of the contemporary city and take the form of a labyrinth or garden. The labyrinth is constructed from screens characterized by organic shapes, and screens with fragments of text from the book **Impressions d'Afrique** (1910) by the French writer Raymond Roussel, in which there are descriptions of parts of an exotic garden and the events that occur there. The work can be previewed in the 'guided tour' on video at Witte de With.

ELMGREEN & DRAGSET
I never promised you a rose garden...
Michael Elmgreen (Denmark, 1961) and Ingar Dragset (Norway, 1969) are interested in architectonic structures. They strive to offer alternatives to accepted architectonic forms using 'Powerless Structures': minimalist spaces, reminiscent of the white cube of the exhibition space. They want to reach beyond the intended function of a building or a public space, and thus create opportunities for other, less obvious activities. For 'Hortus Conclusus', Elmgreen & Dragset designed a small pavilion for the rose garden of the Museum Park in Rotterdam, with the title **Cruising Pavilion / Powerless Structure.** They had already installed this work in 1998 in Marselisborg Park in Denmark. This city park, close to the city of Aarhus, serves in the evening as a meeting place for gays. The Museum Park in Rotterdam also has a decades long history as a cruising area for homosexuals. The white pavilion by Elmgreen & Dragset was meant to create a romantic environment for their nocturnal adventures. It was to be lit by a round skylight and was to have small peepholes (glory holes) in the walls. In the daytime it would also have been possible to use the pavilion for more public activities. Regrettably the proposal was quashed by the parks division of Rotterdam's Department of Public Works. In response to the rejection, Elmgreen & Dragset made this installation.

CILDO MEIRELES
Two Trees III
Two Trees by Cildo Meireles (b. Rio de Janeiro, Brazil, 1948) is a new version of a work exhibited in 1995 in the United States. The work uses both interior and exterior spaces. The first tree in **Two Trees** lies diagonally in the exhibition space, with its leafless top sticking out through the window. A large number of matches are stuck into the base of the trunk. The second tree, also bare, is planted in a small play area close to Witte de With. Green leaves made of paper surround its base. Meireles uses these materials to suggest the transformation of matter: trees into matches and paper, nature into utensils and poetic objects. New work by Cildo Meireles is also on view in the exhibition 'The Garden of Eden' at the Rijksmuseum voor Volkenkunde in Leiden.

Teresita Fernández
360° Oasis, 2001

Anthony Dunne & Fiona Raby
Placebo: Compass Room, 2001

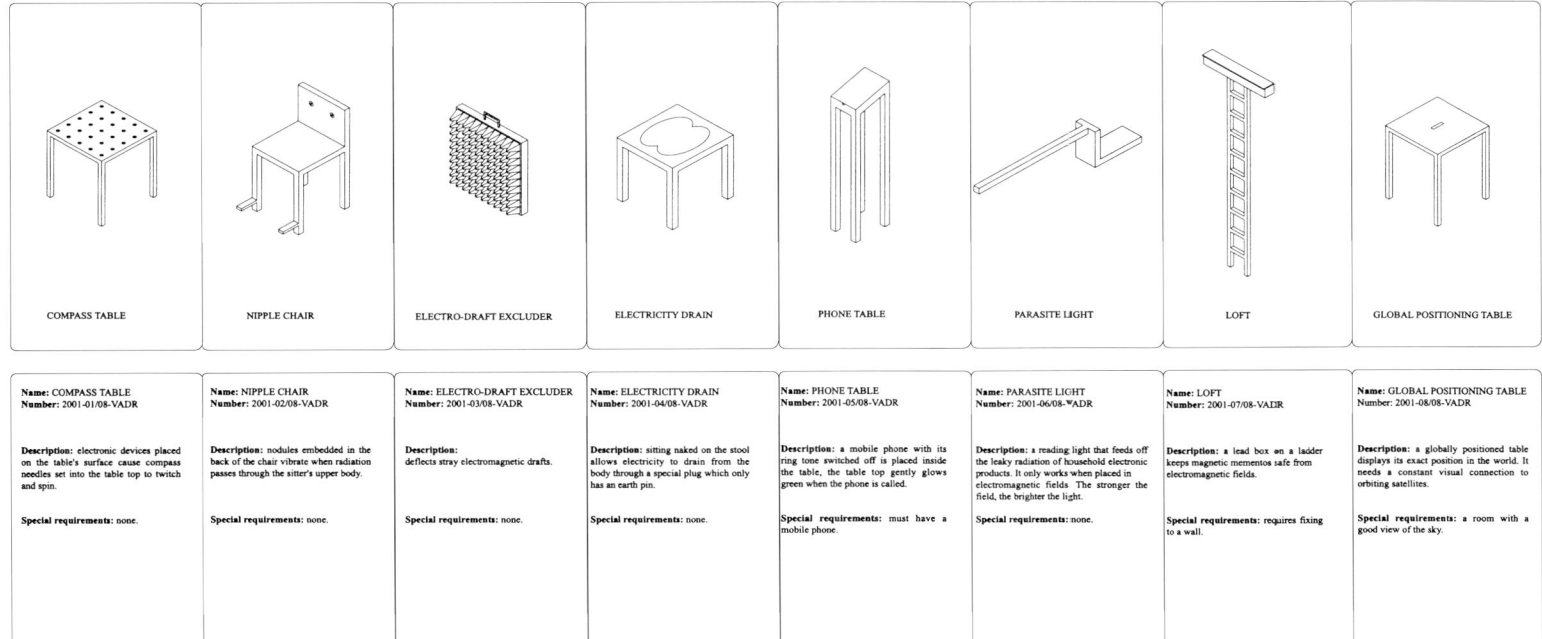

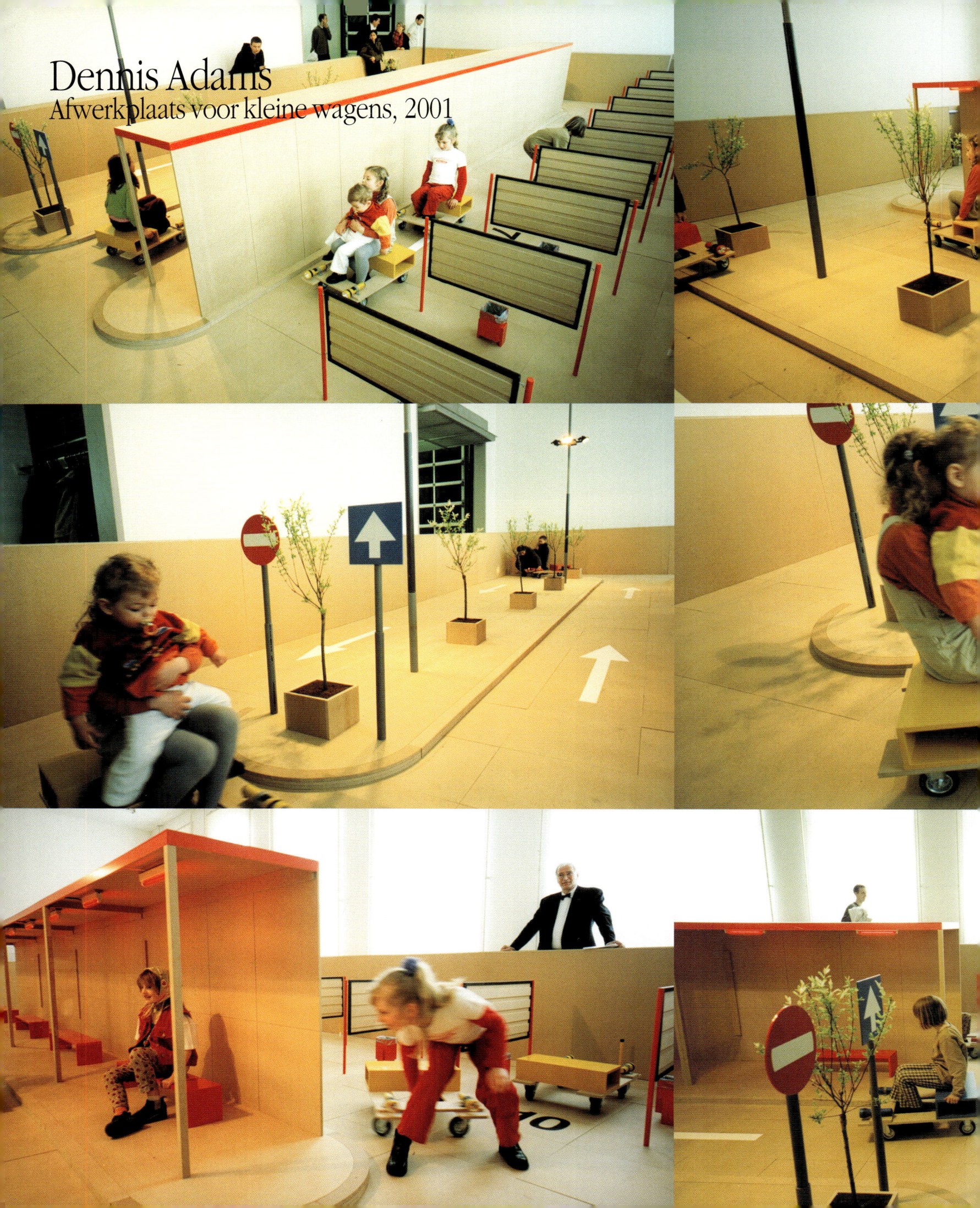

Dennis Adams
Afwerkplaats voor kleine wagens, 2001

Maura Biava
Iride, 2001

Zeger Reyers
Onder-tussen II, 2001

Cristina Iglesias
Untitled (Travel Agency), 2001

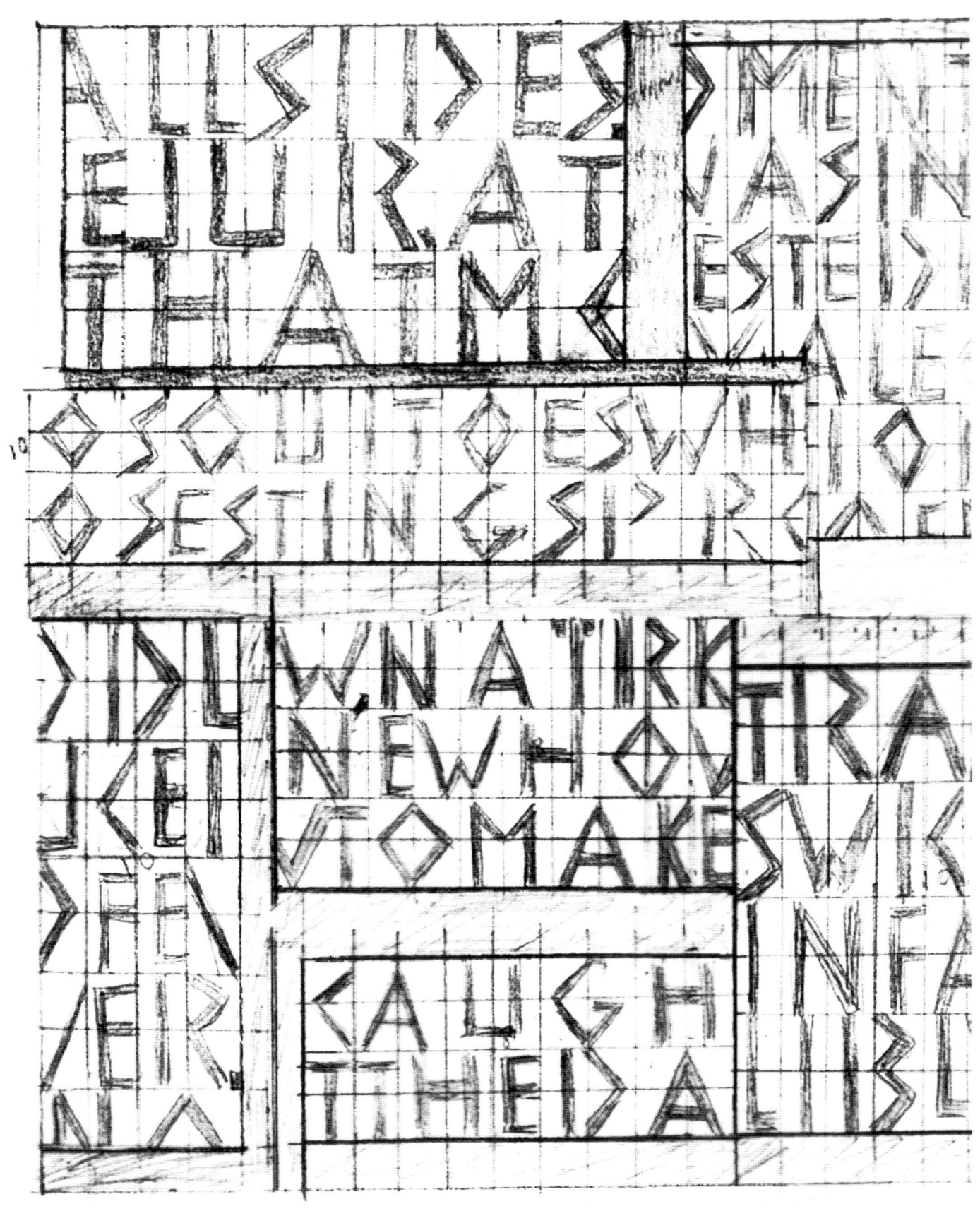

Michael Elmgreen & Ingar Dragset
I never promised you a rose garden..., 2001

HOMOSEXUALS ONLY

I NEVER PROMISED YOU A ROSE GARDEN...

Cildo Meireles
Two Trees III, 2001

138

The Public Garden

The Public Garden
Afterthoughts

1 Lecture given on 11 October 2000 at the opening of the event.
2 Lecture given on 8 February 2001 as part of *Breeze of AIR*.

Nature, Art and the City

TANJA ELSTGEEST

Should you drive to Rotterdam in the spring, on taking the Rotterdam-Overschie exit you pass a railway viaduct above the motorway where a stork has made her nest atop a pylon for the railway's overhead power lines. From her elevated position she gazes down majestically at the weekday commuter traffic. Vrooming cars and speeding trains disturb the peace of the nest, but the eggs will still hatch at this unusual choice of site.

To the left of this slip road lies the Vroesepark. Wander into this city park along the tarmac path and you come across a notice-board emblazoned with the park regulations. Brightly coloured dots indicate the various functions: an area for walking the dog, a playing field, a barbecue area, a fishpond. No unexpected quirks of nature here but a recreational park that has been meticulously planned and laid out.

During the Breeze of AIR event, the nature in the city and the design and use of urban green space were evaluated and innovative ideas devised for the urban public garden. The visual arts played an important part in the event. Like the stork described above, the artists' installations often cropped up unexpectedly, and almost unobtrusively, in the urban scenery. None of the artists chose to offer solutions for problems that had been signalled in Rotterdam's urban green space, nor did they attempt in any way to stand in the shoes of a designer. They likewise avoided making purely decorative works for the city's parks. This common decision, though one arrived at independently, to find a different way to engage with public space does not typify a new tendency within the visual arts, but it does at least deserve brief analysis. Is there still a role for the visual arts in public urban space? How do artists demonstrate their concern with social issues?

Garden design, visual art

Within the framework of Breeze of AIR, the Witte de With centre for contemporary art invited artists to make works that explore the theme of the hortus conclusus, the enclosed garden as a place for repose and contemplation, a locus where culture and nature meet. The AIR Foundation invited designers from the Western and non-Western garden traditions to design for a range of sites public gardens inspired by the typology of the hortus conclusus.

In a lecture delivered by the landscape architect Adriaan Geuze, he illustrated the similarities in visual art and garden design by noting their shared use of visual elements such as composition, palette and play of light. He also noted the similar quest of landscape architects and artists to construct a satisfying representation of nature. Geuze compared the composition and qualities of a selection of famous paintings with the design approach and styles in Japanese and Western garden making.[1] Garden designer Piet Oudolf also gave a lecture about gardening and the art of colour variation using different plant species, the composition of flowerbeds and the beauty of nature.[2]

This comparison of garden design and visual art is opportune. The two disciplines can be analysed and approached autonomously; the comparison becomes more complex, however, when the social and political situation is brought into the equation. In practice, landscape architects have to deal with many pragmatic and financial limitations, legislation and the involvement of government agencies, property developers and private individuals in the decision-making process. Realizing a design for the

[fig. 1]
Lecture given by Adriaan Geuze, 11 October 2000

[fig. 2]
Lecture given by Piet Oudolf, 8 February 2001

public realm is a protracted affair and involves many compromises. Compared with designers, visual artists enjoy a much more independent status, but this too can be easily compromised when an artist ventures to present a work outside the protective walls of the exhibition institute.

The infill of public space

In his book *Moderne Leegte. Over kunst en openbaarheid* (The Modern Void. On art and public space), Camiel van Winkel traces the structure and content of urban space since the 1950s by making an analysis of the collective and psychological concept of space.[3] In his analysis he examines the evolution of the role of the visual arts in this urban space using a sample of urban planning issues and projects. Van Winkel identifies a remarkable development in his analysis of the spatial experience: 'The 1950s were the great hey-day of the open city image – a period when the metaphor of openness and space expressed the central psychological principle for the collective orientation of society in the Netherlands. The "potential of the unfilled space" left its mark on all manner of social issues. In the course of the 1960s, however, there was a revolutionary change of course: the open space of the post-war city quite suddenly came to be regarded as an ugly void. The predominant viewpoint among architects and urbanists shifted towards an excessive programmatic infill and furnishing of the public space, in order to increase the liveability and hospitableness of the urban environment.'[4]

During the concluding symposium of Breeze of AIR 'the potential of the unfilled space' was raised once again, notably by the visual artists. The participating artists were strongly offended by the designers' over-programming of public space with places for play, repose and barbecues, because of its patronizing tone. In the public realm there seems to be little space left over for a personal and creative infill of one's surroundings. Berlin's 'urban golfers', a group of golf enthusiasts who practise their sport on the grassy open spaces of the city's parks and have thus found an alternative for the elitist golf course, were cited as an example.

The artist duo Michael Elmgreen & Ingar Dragset noted that urban planners and most landscape architects base their designs on the behaviour of the 'average citizen'. They wondered which individuals actually conform to this model behaviour. They also argued that the more the function of a place is programmed in advance, the less 'free' space is available for minority groups that may want to use public space for divergent, individually determined ends. That is why the designs of the architectural interventions and structures by Elmgreen & Dragset often refer to the 'white cube'. In recent decades, this originally 'neutral' white architecture has been held up to scrutiny by many artists and imbued with new meanings. However, the way in which Elmgreen & Dragset repeatedly question and employ the 'white cube' is to a degree ironically critical. For the exhibition Breeze of AIR/*Hortus Conclusus* they proposed a small white pavilion with a bench, a round window and a number of 'glory holes'. Originally the idea was to place this pavilion in Museum Park, which has for a number of decades served as a 'cruising area'. At nighttime the pavilion would serve as a meeting place for homosexuals, while during the day it would be a neutral, white aesthetic space for less specific purposes. In this context, the sterility of the white pavilion would refer to the surrounding museums or even the adjacent hospital, but at the same time it would link into the international gay scene, as a counterpart to the 'darkroom'. The work that Dennis Adams created for the exhibition likewise addresses the less idyllic aspects of public space. His original plan was to make a life-size reconstruction of part of the Keileweg *afwerkplaats* (a drive-in facility for prostitution in an industrial zone on the north bank) and place the entire object as a

[3] Camiel van Winkel, *Moderne Leegte. Over kunst en openbaarheid* (Nijmegen: SUN Publishers, 1999).
[4] Ibid., p. 7.
[5] *Metropolis M* no. 4, August/September 2001, p. 22.

[fig. 3]
**Elmgreen & Dragset,
I never promised you a rose garden**

[fig. 4]
View from Witte de With

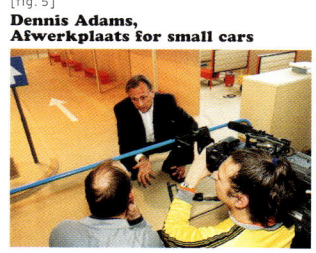
[fig. 5]
**Dennis Adams,
Afwerkplaats for small cars**

monumental artwork in the centre of the city.

Rotterdam City Council turned down the planning applications for the projects by Adams and Elmgreen & Dragset. Adams' proposal was disallowed due to 'the political sensitivity of a (second) zone for prostitution and the possibly undesirable consequences for the public order'. In addition, installing the work would apparently have resulted in a lack of space for other events being held during that period. Elmgreen & Dragset's offering was censured on the advice of the Parks Division of the Public Works Department, on account of 'structural damage to the trees, shrubs and lawn' and because it would 'attract additional litter, which would involve extra costs and negatively affect the beauty of the park'. Both Elmgreen & Dragset and Dennis Adams eventually realized installations in the exhibition space of Witte de With that were in part a response to the rejection of their original ideas.

The artists succeeded in touching the sensitive nerve of 'public order' in a culturally critical manner with works that brought the fringes of society into view. In the reactions to their proposals and the discussions during the event, the desire for urban green space that is as pleasant and as recreational as possible was made clear time and again. Public art is also expected to fulfil these criteria. In response to this, most of the artists eventually chose to realize their work within the walls of Witte de With. They used it to pose cultural-critical questions about the boundaries and potentialities of the use of public space. None, except for Zeger Reyers and Cildo Meireles, made proposals that related to nature. As Adriaan van der Staay has noted elsewhere in this publication, they seem more absorbed 'by the inner workings of the human mind, the technical solution to questions of privacy and quiet, than by a dialogue with a living, growing or dying nature.'

A new escapism

In his article 'Margaras Unlimited Art', Siebe Thissen discusses the urge of today's artists to circumvent the control society and search for alternatives for regulated geographical space.[5] He writes: 'The age-old desire for autonomy is primarily a craving for space: free space, one's own space, creative space. The contemporary artist lays claim to that space, seeking out new autonomous zones like a true space invader.' In this introduction, Thissen refers to artists who are looking for alternative routes through the urban landscape and make this the subject of their work. He describes a new kind of escapism that transcends the ideals of the 1970s and no longer claims to be independent of commerce, media and state, though it does seek to give everyday reality an infill of its own.

A like playful and creative freedom seems to be the driving force in the work of Zeger Reyers. Over the last few years he has specialized in cultivating oyster mushrooms on everyday objects. Like a true gardener he scatters the spores, monitors the growth of the mushrooms, and knows the right moment to pick them for drying so that their beauty is retained. In his installations, the mushrooms seem to slowly but ineluctably take possession of the things around us. He juxtaposes the transience of the product with the (albeit artificial) immortality of nature. Reyer's specialism is a delineation but at the same time an enrichment. With his eye for detail, he uses his works to teach the viewer to see the beauty of nature in unexpected places, and examines the relation between nature, product and decay.

A literal escapism can be detected in the works that Maura Biava and Cristina Iglesias made for the exhibition. Iglesias chose a vacant shop premises as the site for her work and created an artificial garden which referred in form and meaning to part of Raymond Roussel's *Impressions d'Afrique* (1910). Her work was a labyrinthine construction of openwork screens and curving partition walls decorated with plant

[fig. 6]
Zeger Reyers,
Onder-tussen II

[fig. 7]
Zeger Reyers,
closing symposium 15-16 June 2001

[fig. 8]
Cildo Meireles,
Two Trees III

[fig. 9]
Lecture given by Maura Biava,
19 April 2001

[fig. 10]
Cristina Iglesias,
Untitled (Travel Agency)

motifs. Imbued with an Oriental ambience, it presented a transparent aesthetic within an enclosed space, while its viewers remained in visual contact with the Rotterdam street scene via the shop window and through the screens. The installation was a temporary point of repose, so characteristic of the eccentric notion of the hortus conclusus.

Biava, on the other hand, made a more contemporary reading of the hortus conclusus, in which the garden was symbolized by an industrial cacophony of ships and machinery in the harbour basin of Leuvehaven. For Biava, the buildings around the inner harbour represented the characteristic enclosure of the hortus conclusus. The social encounter meant to take place in the garden was a virtual one. As a metaphor for the Dutch garden, she used a small greenhouse floating on a raft in the harbour alongside the ships. For a few afternoons each week, the greenhouse was inhabited by 'Iride', a fictional female character already brought to life in earlier works by Biava. It was possible to chat with Iride from a second part of Biava's installation in Witte de With thanks to an Internet connection, and thus exchange ideas with her about the relation between nature, humankind and the human environment.

A more individualistic take on urban space was expressed in the contribution by the designer duo Anthony Dunne & Fiona Raby. They found themselves absorbed by more or less enclosed areas that subdivide and control the urban space invisibly: the 'cells' of mobile telephone networks and electromagnetic fields generated by electrical appliances. In their designs for AIR they strove to make such fields and cells palpable for the public. For them, the idea of 'withdrawing' and 'temporarily shutting oneself off from the outside world', implicit in the theme of the hortus conclusus, is encapsulated in the use of a mobile phone in public space, or in listening to a walkman and seeing the city pass by to a new beat. For Dunne & Raby the contemporary hortus conclusus was an invisible and temporary space that one could move in and out of.

Placebo: Compass Room exhibited in Witte de With was a final addition to their series of furniture pieces entitled Placebo. Dunne & Raby designed this range of furniture to make people aware of the mass of electrical fields in the daily environment. The furniture indicates where these fields are present in our homes by means of colour changes, little compasses or sound. Although the *Placebo* series – in Latin 'placebo' literally means 'I shall be pleasing' – is designed 'to please', the objects are a medicine without effect, the furniture indicating the presence of the electrical fields but not dispersing them. Because the furniture makes an invisible world visible, pleasure can quickly switch to paranoia.

The hortus conclusus as metaphor

During the Breeze of AIR/*Hortus Conclusus* event, Marres, the centre for visual arts in Maastricht, staged together with Joke Robaard the project *No Hortus is Conclusus*. This project also consisted of lectures, presentations and an exhibition. The proceedings were conducted within the high-walled garden at the rear of the eighteenth-century building behind the art centre. This is how Marres described the project: 'The hortus conclusus is a paradox, and partly for this reason – as Gerrit Komrij stated in 'Over de noodzaak van tuinieren' [On the necessity of gardening] – it is a suitable means of expression if one is trying to establish some link between cultural values and a social structure that is in a process of transition. At the present time, marked by such far-reaching developments as information technology and genetic technology, the visual arts seek to develop meanings and forms that provide insight into the changes in our environment and the communities in which we live. The garden, as a place for fantasy, repose and encounter, offers a fertile framework for these

[6.] Frederique Bergholz, press release, Marres centre for the visual arts, Maastricht, 2001.

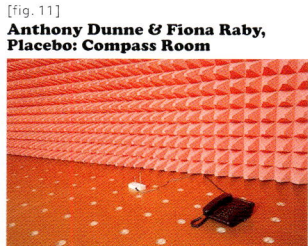

[fig. 11]
Anthony Dunne & Fiona Raby, Placebo: Compass Room

[fig. 12]
Lecture given by Fiona Raby, 11 January 2001

[fig. 13]
Teresita Fernández, 360° Oasis

endeavours.'⁶

The garden with its fertile stratification of meanings was used as a framework to temporarily isolate complex structures and relationships. As the title suggests, the protective framework was immediately broken down in this project. In a literal sense, because Joke Robaard placed ladders against the high walls that surround the garden at Marres so that the public could look over the walls, but also more symbolically in that the public, speakers and artists in the garden gathered together with their own stories, ideas and social networks. In addition, as part of her work, Joke Robaard visited the neighbours of the Marres garden: a Montessori junior school, a student house and a religious hospice. Along with the art centre, these communities are symbolic of the various stages of life, or the 'different species in a habitat'.

The artists involved in *No Hortus is Conclusus* and Breeze of AIR/*Hortus Conclusus* approached the idea of the boundaries of the enclosed garden from a whole variety of angles. Whereas the Marres artists sought a means of approaching the external from within the walled garden and sometimes literally tried to reach out over its walls, the artists involved in Breeze of AIR/*Hortus Conclusus* tended to demarcate their territory and protect it from all the complexities that constitute the urban environment.

This was the approach adopted by Teresita Fernández in her work *360° Oasis*, an empty space surrounded by an artificial bamboo forest in three shades of green, all fitted perfectly into the exhibition space. The work isolated the viewer and only occasionally allowed a glimpse of the outside world when the viewer moved past the layers of vertical tubes, like a shutter of a camera momentarily opening and closing so that you begin to doubt your own eyes. Fernández metes out her colours, forms and images with great precision and in this work she is not afraid of leaving space empty.

In *Two Trees*, Cildo Meireles poetically addresses the complex relationship between culture and nature. Meireles had two condemned trees in Rotterdam sawn down and transported whole to the Witte de Withstraat. One was set up with its crown sticking out of the window of the exhibition space. The other was placed in a small playground close by Witte de With. The sawn-off base of the tree in the exhibition space was then stuffed with thousands of red matches, while paper leaves were scattered daily under its counterpart in the playground. This work by Meireles captures the relationship between the tree and its products. He also questions the meaning and role of nature as culture in urban space. Can this tree without leaves, transplanted by the artist, be called 'nature'? Can a tree that is specially cultivated in order to withstand polluted groundwater and poor soil conditions be termed 'nature'? Can we talk about 'nature' in urban space, or is everything 'culture'?

According to Camiel van Winkel, retaining the void in the public space of the city is an outdated tactic, and also no longer possible. I agree with him: it would be overly romantic to idealize fields of grass and open space as the ultimate freedom where creativity can flourish spontaneously. At the same time, for me it seems to have become just as meaningless to fill in every last centimetre of public space with all manner of activities, functions and products derived from the entertainment and consumer industries. The artworks realized within the framework of Breeze of AIR/*Hortus Conclusus* turned out to be either modest additions to the urban realm or autonomous installations in the exhibition space. The artists – even in the context of *Rotterdam 2001, Cultural Capital of Europe,* for which an enormous number of activities and events were organized in the city – clearly felt disinclined to add new objects to the urban environment. They were more interested in using their work to pose cultural-critical questions about nature, art and the city, less to elicit answers than to prompt the public to reconsider or re-examine the public spaces in their city.

MARC TREIB

Park, Garden, Rotterdam

The public garden in the city has historically served two primary purposes: it has established the presence of nature within a world constructed around it, and provided a setting for recreation and amusement. The first purpose tended to be solitary and passive, the second social and active. Without question, urban parks and planted gardens have additional significance for society, but these two generalizations – individual/passive and social/active – offer a basis from which to review the nine projects developed for the Breeze of AIR programme.

Geographer Yi-Fu Tuan has directed our attention to the changing attitudes toward land and nature in his classic study *Topophilia*.[1] Our views today of nature and wilderness, he tells us, are not those of our predecessors; nor will they be those of our successors. To a city built to high density with only negligible amounts of natural areas, the importance of a sizable open space such as New York's Central Park has been uncontested [fig. 1]. But even in lower density communities, parks are always regarded as amenities. Frederick Law Olmsted, one of the park's principal designers, intended Central Park to provide *passive* nature, a place for individual and tranquil group restoration, a communing with urban nature for those who could not escape to the true wilderness.[2] The park was thus cast as an antidote to the city, its opposite in form and intended effect. But social, cultural and recreational activities crept into the park nonetheless, like a serpent into the Garden of Eden.[3] Over time, even neighbourhood parks became more a collection of sportsfields than quiet respites for contemplation. To the local communities, multi-use open space was deemed more valuable than planted areas without formal activities.

Landscape writings from the 1980s on have questioned the nature of the park under contemporary conditions.[4] Curiously, the discussion focuses on what the park for the twenty-first century will be, without really identifying the shortcomings of the contemporary park. The rhetoric behind the design of Parc de la Villette in Paris, for example, describes ideas for the future park and the formalistic means by which the design will be realized.[5] Although interesting as architecture, as a park *today*, La Villette's lawns and trees are relatively uninteresting, if benign [figs 2, 3]. Remove the buildings (well-termed 'follies') and there is little landscape of any consequence.[6] Some few years later, the Parc André Citroën opened on the opposite side of Paris. Built on the site of a former automotive factory, this fourteen hectare green space by the Seine offered many of the amenities one expected of a park: lawn, water features and a surfeit of plantings that rivalled a botanical garden [figs 4, 5]. What it did *not* offer was the informality, simple bosks with earthen floors, or even shade so characteristic of the traditional Parisian park [fig. 6]. These two parks – magnificent in their state sponsorship as cultural vehicles – bracket two sides of the thinking on designed urban green space.[7]

The American architect Louis Kahn, in a discussion with students, once suggested that there were two primary types of places. The first were those to get away, to escape from somewhere else [fig. 7]. For example, we might seek a library or a lobby to flee the constrictions of a dormitory room. Or the smells and colours of a garden to counter the sensory deprivation of a high-rise office work space. In these examples, the main attraction of the place is that it *reacts* to some other place that is regarded as being of lesser quality.[8]

[fig. 1]
**Central Park, New York, New York. 1853+.
Olmsted & Vaux.**

[fig. 2]
**Parc de la Villette, Paris, France. 1988.
Bernard Tschumi.**

Landscape as lawn, rows of trees, and little else.

[fig. 3]
**Bamboo Garden, Parc de la Villette, Paris, France. 1988.
Alexandre Chemetoff.**

The exposed infrastructure traversing the site melds with the stands of bamboo in this garden set well below ground level.

---

[1] Among the most interesting sections of Tuan's thesis is his discussion of paradise in various cultures spread across space and time. Paradise, he explains, was normally conceived as the opposite of normal life: for example, a place warm and secure for those from cold climates, lushly planted with abundant water for desert peoples. *Topophilia: A Study of Environmental Perception, Attitudes, and Values* (Englewood Cliffs, NJ: Prentice-Hall, 1974). Art historian Barbara Novak explored the changing idea of the picturesque in American art, and demonstrated how the existence of real terror in the landscape (the majesty of mountains and the furore of storms) modified the idea of the sublime – adapted from the British, who had lived in a more benign landscape. *Nature and Culture: American Landscape and Painting 1825-1875* (New York: Oxford University Press, 1980)

[2] The volume of literature on Olmsted is extensive, covering the full range of this multi-talented personage. For Central Park see: Elizabeth Barlow, *Frederick Law Olmsted's New York* (New York: Frederick Praeger, 1972); for Olmsted's own thoughts see: Frederick Law Olmsted, Jr. and Theodora Kimball (eds) *Forty Years of Landscape Architecture: Central Park as a Work of Art and as a Great Municipal Enterprise, 1853-1895* (New York: G.P. Putnam's Sons, 1928). Extensively renovated and managed through a public-private partnership, Central Park's recent history is also of considerable interest. For that story see: Elizabeth Barlow Rogers, *Rebuilding Central Park: A Management and Restoration Plan* (Cambridge, Mass: The MIT Press, 1987). For changing views on wilderness see Max Oelschlaeger, *The Idea of Wilderness* (New Haven: Yale University Press, 1991).

[3] Olmsted only intended pure (created) nature in the park and loathed the idea of a cultural institution like the art museum disturbing the pastoral feeling. We are fortunate that Olmsted's vision was not rigorously maintained; the same laxity that allowed sportsfields in the park also permitted the intrusion of the Metropolitan Museum of Art, one of the world's greatest art institutions.

[4] A series of conferences has produced publications most of which have stressed what the park would be like in the future. Like science fiction films, few of them asked about the years between the present and the future. Today's park would not retain its validity tomorrow, they claimed. And yet few of them – there **were** certain exceptions – stated just what those shortcomings were, nor asked how we could revive our treasury of existing parks. A sample of the literature: Martin Knuijt, Hans Ophuis and Peter van Saane (eds), *Modern Park Design: Recent Trends* (Bussum: Thoth Publishers, 1995); Deborah Karasov and Steve Waryan (eds), *The Once and Future Park* (New York: Princeton Architectural Press and Walker Art Center, 1993); a broader vision is offered by Lodewijk Baljon, *Designing Parks* (Amsterdam: Architectura & Natura Press, 1992), although it centres discussion on a single project, the competition for the Parc de la Villette. Parc de la Villette.

[5] See Marianne Barzilay, Catherine Hayward and Lucette Lombard-Valentino, *L'Invention du parc* (Paris: Graphite Editions, 1984).

[6] The counter argument, of course, is that the follies are critical to the design as a park. This tends to be the architect's view of landscape design, i.e., that it is as a constructed field.

[7] The park, designed by a team including Gilles Clément, Patrick Berger, Jean-Paul Viguier and François Jodry, opened in September 1992. In this brief discussion I must omit any reference to true natural preserves such as state or national parks which are **managed**, rather than **designed**, landscapes.

[8] He said, 'I think a boys' club is a **from** place. It is not a **to** place but a **from** place. It is a place which in spirit must be **from where** you go, not **where** you go.' Louis I. Kahn, *Talks to Students* (Houston: Rice University School of Architecture, 1969), p. 11.

[9] Bagatelle, in the Bois de Boulogne on the edge of Paris, was laid out in 1780 by Thomas Blaikie, and became part of the greater public parkland in the mid-nineteenth century. Early in the twentieth century it was lightly formalized by J.C.N. Forestier – who also added an iris garden and other plantings – to accommodate the intrusions of a greater number of visitors. See Dorothée Imbert, *The Modernist Garden in France* (New Haven: Yale University Press, 1993), pp. 12, 14.

[10] See Marc Treib, 'Aspects of Regionality and the

Kahn's second category of place was going to spaces, places created as a destination in themselves. These tend to be more the monuments that society constructs: the cathedral, the city hall; the stadium; the auditorium for musical or theatrical performance [fig. 8]. They tend to be collective spaces rather than private ones, places we choose either for their ability to draw many people together for an event, or as fantastic places in themselves. A world's fair, for example, will draw an audience to its pavilions but the event also invites people to join the crowd.

This binary division is just too simple, however, and most of the places we design serve both purposes to varying degrees. The cathedral or the world's fair provides escape as well as spiritual uplift or excitement, for example. Or a café could be seen as a place of retreat as well as a destination in itself. So, I think it best to consider our outdoor space proposals in light of *both* of these aspects rather than one or the other. This might be one of the ways that landscape architecture distinguishes itself from architecture, that is, that spaces are not so easily characterized as having a simple, singular purpose.

Apply these categorizations to urban exterior space and the problems compound. For one, several landscape spaces conceived for Breeze of AIR more squarely address a third function, primarily or in part. This third function comprises *transitional* spaces through which we move rather than stay [figs 9, 10]. The Lijnbaan gardens and the Hofplein viaduct, for example, fundamentally perform in this way: spaces to *go through*, important as the connections between other sites. They link, but they are also important in themselves, as might a glass-covered galleria [fig. 11]. Spaces of this type must be regarded in connection to those to which and from which they extend, and should not be evaluated solely as distinct places.

A second set of issues concerns the definitions of the terms *garden* and *park*. Although debate has raged for many years now, there is no single satisfactory answer. Instead, definitions tend to be relative. We could say that gardens are private and parks are public, that is, attempting definition by social purpose [fig. 12]. But do we not call some urban landscapes 'public gardens'? And what of former gardens, like Bagatelle in Paris, that were once private gardens but are today public parks [fig. 13]?**9** The landscape has remained more or less the same; only the classification modified with the change in use. Thus, defining by functional purpose alone is not satisfactory.

Perhaps scale provides a workable classification: a garden is small; a park is large [fig. 14]. This doesn't sound very precise either, but it may not be as poor as it first seems. But we have pocket parks of course – the same size as gardens – and we have some very large gardens that are used as parks [figs 14, 15]. So here too, we encounter limits.

Could we try to use 'greenness' to distinguish garden and park? Gardens have flowers and plants and carefully made paths, with multitudes of colours and textures, with radical seasonal change [fig. 16]. Parks have trees and grass and play equipment, less emphasis on colour and texture, with more space to be used [fig. 17]. This adds to our range of considerations, but remains less than complete.

In terms of examining the Breeze of AIR programme, perhaps, distinguishing park and garden is not critical. Whether the Lijnbaan gardens are really a park perhaps does not affect their use – or does it [fig. 18]? To some degree, a name suggests how we should read and interpret a place; language does prejudice our perception. Because of language we arrive at the space expecting a certain form of space or experience which may or may not exist.

The garden, in my thinking, is *a defined zone of modified ecological process*

[fig. 4]
**Parc André-Citroën, Paris, France. 1993.
Gilles Clément, Patrick Berger, Jean-Paul Viguier and François Jodry.**

The central lawn reveals a lack of shade.

[fig. 5]
**Parc André-Citroën, Paris, France. 1993.
Gilles Clément, Patrick Berger, Jean-Paul Viguier and François Jodry.**

The theme gardens are more intimate, and more intricate in their planting.

[fig. 6]
Luxembourg Gardens, Paris, France.

A classic French park, relying on bosks of horse chestnut trees, gravel and movable chairs.

[fig. 7]
Beachfront hillside, San Francisco, California.

A classic 'going away from' space, adjusted for the wind and sun.

[fig. 8]
Italy area, EPCOT Center, Disneyworld, Orlando, Florida.

A 'going to' place – but also an escape to 'Venice'.

that may be created for functional or aesthetic purposes.[10] Gardens require a sense of limits, conveying an impression that the course of natural processes has been adjusted in some way [fig. 19]. We don't regard nature as a garden very often, except poetically,[11] but we can be fooled into thinking that constructed gardens are actually natural.[12] This also applies to the park, of course, except that sense of boundary may not be as strong and activities may be more significant. Trees and hedges, not only walls, may determine the physical limits. The bosk, the allée and even natural clumps, define spaces within the landscape as well as spaces within the city.

One additional consideration: What is the purpose of vegetation in the city? Broadly taken, landscape can serve us in three ways:

It can be a subject in itself (i.e., brilliantly flowering trees) [fig. 20].

It can serve as a buffer (softening the meeting of buildings or uses) [fig. 21].

It can serve as a link (planting instead of architectural elements) to create spaces or connect structures [fig. 22].

How designers use these varies to a large degree, not only due to personal design thinking, but also influenced by municipal budgets for construction and maintenance.

With this shaky foundation established, let us turn to the nine proposals for Rotterdam's open spaces. My intention is not to critique the proposals as might a jurist, arguing that this is good and this is not, but instead to look at some of the concepts and approaches behind them.

At one end, we have the proposals to *reform* two parks, adjusting large-scale spaces to better accord with their uses and users. The projects for the Spinoza park by Piet Oudolf, and by Kamel Louafi for Valkeniersweide, both mark how uses of Dutch parks have evolved, by introducing ideas foreign to historical precedents. The zones within the Louafi proposal are intended as 'living rooms' for different cultures, acknowledging that park spaces are appropriated in different ways.[13] Realistic schemes such as these accept the extant conditions, reforming plantings and water areas in correlation to the evolved social patterns. These are more interventions than radically new designs, keeping what is good and adjusting what requires improvement. The Oudolf plan is bolder in its stance, displacing the existing pattern with a scheme formed by geometry and new pathways, some of which lead to specific places and others to nowhere in particular. At its heart is a richly planted garden that beautifully layers shrubs and grasses to create a place always changing.

Interestingly, both designers have continued the Dutch practice of zoning the park, assigning distinct areas for play, gardens, contemplation, water, and sitting. A second approach might carefully conflate uses by embedding one *within* another. To use an analogy: yellow and blue interact to produce green. Or placing blue *within* yellow could produce a checkerboard of blue and yellow, or a target-like form of concentric blue and yellow rings. In each case, a new relationship between parts results. Perhaps, both proposals would benefit from a stronger mix of activity zones and more complex transitions between them.[14]

Although differing radically in their assertiveness and materials, parallels mark the gardens for the Boijmans Van Beuningen Museum by Charles Correa and for the rooftop of Las Palmas by Kazuyo Sejima & Ryue Nishizawa. Behind both stands the classic idea of the garden. One, a true hortus conclusus that first considers its enclosure; the other, an architectural device of pure acrylic that interweaves the *karesansui* dry gardens of the Japanese Zen tradition with the *shakkei* of the seventeenth-century stroll garden.[15] Correa's scheme is quiet, precise and seemingly static. It addresses the beautifully-detailed brick walls, softening the edges with rows of trees that seasonally vary to softly animate the court throughout the year. The spiral foun-

Modern(ist) Garden in California', in Therese O'Malley and Marc Treib (eds), *Regional Garden Design in the United States* (Washington, D.C.: Dumbarton Oaks, 1995), pp. 5-42.

11. Unless in phrases such as 'God's garden' or other metaphors.

12. Even at the scale of the park this is true: many New Yorkers think that Central Park is a piece of natural land preserved from development, when in fact, all of it was designed and built. French geographer Augustin Berques requires two aspects as critical to making a place (**milieu**): 'The first, is that the production of "landscape", whether urban, suburban, or rural, is not simply a question of environment (or environmentalism) but the **mediation** of the landscape;' second, that landscapes 'are a combination of object and subject, of the place made and the place-maker or place-user'. Cited in John Dixon Hunt, *Greater Perfections* (Philadelphia: University of Pennsylvania Press, 2000), p. 8.

13. Breeze of AIR / Hortus Conclusus, International Symposium Programme Book (Rotterdam: Breeze of AIR, 2001), p. 48.

14. Here we could learn from music, thinking of rhythms, overlappings and transitions – as opposed to just putting one thing next to the other without too much regard for their interaction.

15. Intended primarily as objects of contemplation, the dry gardens (karesansui) were essentially static and meant to be viewed, normally from an adjacent veranda, rather than physically entered. The technique of shakkei (usually translated as 'borrowed scenery') attempts to establish formal correspondence between elements of the immediate foreground with those in the background, thereby incorporating distant landscape as a part of the garden. See Teiji Itoh, *Space and Illusion in the Japanese Garden* (New York: Weatherhill and Tokyo: Tankosha, 1973) and Marc Treib and Ron Herman, *A Guide to the Gardens of Kyoto* (Tokyo: Shufunotomo, 1980), pp. 30-31.

16. In some ways the Las Palmas project is a child of the viewing piece on the roof of the Dia Foundation in New York by Dan Graham. Its circular glazed enclosure draws the surroundings of lower New York City into its viewing plane using complex patterns of reflection and refraction. See Martin Küttering and Roland Nachtigäller (eds), *Dan Graham: Two-way Mirror Pavilions, 1989-1996* (Nordhorn: Städtische Galerie Nordhorn, 1996), especially pp. 40-43.

17. It is interesting, I think, that five of the proposals included glass houses in some way. In the park schemes these were minor highlights; in the Quadrat proposal it was the major element of the design. What is the fascination with the glasshouse? Is the glass house the ultimate modernist structure, with a de-materialized structure and surface, an ambiguity that is both there and not there? Is it the sense of transparent limits that the glass house offers, a hortus conclusus and unrestricted at the same time?

[fig. 9]
Louisiana Art Museum, Humlebaek, Denmark. 1958+. Jørgen Bo and Vilhelm Wohlert.

A corridor that is a transitional architectural space and a destination in itself.

[fig. 10]
Chenonceaux, France.

The approach allée, a transitional landscape space that is also a destination in itself.

[fig. 11]
GUM Department Store, Moscow, Russia. 1893. Alexander Pomerantsev.

A transit space that is also a destination – especially in winter.

[fig. 12]
Galvez garden, Mexico City, Mexico. 1955. Luis Barragán.

The intimate scale of the walled garden.

[fig. 13]
Rose garden, Bagatelle, near Paris, France. 1780. Thomas Blaikie.

Refurbished by J.C.N. Forestier, early 20th century. Once a garden, now a park.

tain entices the visitor to achieve the centre before re-emerging anew. By contrast, in the Sejima-Nishizawa proposal the rooftop yields an enclosed, yet transparent, space that views the Rotterdam cityscape refracted, reflected and distorted. The city becomes the subject of contemplation in a pure space conceived as its opposite.[16]

Despite these parallels, however, the schemes differ considerably in their manner, focus and force. Although the Boijmans Van Beuningen space is highly confined, the Correa scheme is essentially centrifugal, moving from the centre outwards, dispelling vitality. The Sejima-Nishizawa project, although transparent, is essentially centripetal, drawing the surroundings inward to the centre of the space.

Atelier Quadrat's proposal for the Central Station area is the most difficult to explain and to evaluate. This is especially true given the standing development plans for the area around and over the station that will accompany the construction of the TGV line. The Quadrat proposal is neither a park nor a garden alone, but some hybrid of types, perhaps more urban than landscape design. Taking advantage of the underground railway lines, a flat green fronts the station, its use left unspecific to solicit multiple interpretations. Accompanying this open area are two glass houses: one destined for birds, the other for monkeys. The curiosity of the idea diminishes on learning that the station now occupies the land that once hosted the Rotterdam Zoo.

More open to question is the shift in type from a transit landscape to one recast as a destination. Unlike an airport, where travellers may wait for hours between flights, the turnover at railroad stations is normally rapid. On the other hand, railroad stations are notorious these days not only for their unattractive surroundings, but also for giving travellers only limited places to wait for trains. Perhaps in this situation, the confrontation of ape and human is the ideal social encounter. One could imagine the magical light quality of a glass structure filled with birds and primates, and the tropical plants that might accompany them.[17]

The glass house also figures prominently in the Hofplein viaduct proposal by Gross.Max. Their scheme preserves the existing viaduct structure as an elevated green promenade, with access by several stairs along its length. Why should we climb and walk on an upper level rather than stick to the streets? Because the increased elevation provides new views and new relations to the cityscape. Removed from traffic and the interruption of traffic lights and crossings, we walk on a continuous belt of green with trees setting the cadence of the stroll.

At either end of the viaduct, Gross.Max. propose constructed termini. A ground level park replaces existing housing at the west end. Although the organization unfortunately stymies development as a non-linear design, its enclosure serves to buffer park users from street traffic and the surroundings. A glasshouse contributes the corresponding focal point. The interior plantings are intended to recall the vital market gardens in Westland, dramatically displayed at night when the glass box is illuminated. As a totality, the proposal sensibly acknowledges the viaduct as essentially a transition space, anchored by elements at either end, and develops it accordingly.

Transition also directs the Georges Descombes design proposal surrounding Museum Park, potentially integrating a zone that starts at the Netherlands Architecture Institute and ends at the south shore of Het Park – an important urban connection, today almost completely invisible to citizens and visitors alike.[18] Descombes cites the lack of maintenance in Museum Park as the root of the problem, and asserts that one should reinvigorate the Yves Brunier design rather than superimpose something new upon it. This may be true. But certainly there are elements of the scheme which never worked well – at least not in the way the park design was realized after the designer's death, and which could be improved.

[fig. 14]
Paley Park, New York, New York. 1967. Zion & Breen.

The classic pocket park: small surface area, large effect.

[fig. 15]
Sceaux, outside Paris, France. Circa 1680+. André Le Nôtre.

Once a aristocratic garden/park, now a public park.

[fig. 16]
St James's Park, London, England.

The classic social park, with chairs tracing the movement of the sun.

[fig. 17]
The Whale fountain play area, Pinocchio Park, Collodi, Italy. 1972. Pietro Porcinai.

[fig. 18]
Lijnbaan Gardens, Rotterdam, Netherlands. 1950s.

Using the park.

As a designer, Descombes always uses an intelligent and very light hand. He suggests that even a gesture as simple as moving the tram stop may completely recast the problem of crossing Westzeedijk. Why not, Descombes asks, connect the path with the hidden and all but inaccessible water garden, now a part of the hospital? Descombes sketches out a route that could take us from point to point, from one destination to another. But this route could be a vital destination in itself, as some intriguing path along the sea or through the mountains.

The gardens for the Lijnbaan housing comprise a composite landscape type that couples the station area with urban districts to the southeast. While in certain ways the North and South gardens comprise a pair, in other ways they are quite distinct. The South Garden serves greater foot traffic, used by many people on their way to and from the station and other parts of the city. A path cuts through the space more or less diagonally, overlaying the movement of transit upon the prevailing equilibrium. The North Garden, in contrast, serves as a refuge for residents of the slab blocks, but also as a resting point for people in the neighbourhood, shoppers and visitors. The North Garden is taken as a pocket removed from the flow of heavy through circulation.[19] More recently, both of these gardens have been troubled with drug problems, the homeless, and yes, even *hondenpoep*.

The Hargreaves Associates design looks to reform and reinforce rather than to demolish and invent completely anew. It is an insightful approach that addresses social problems more than formal issues. The North Garden is granted greater tranquillity; the surrounding buildings are resurfaced and the planting adjusted. Shifting the position of the vegetation lining the South Garden increases the visual permeability of the space and discourages transient sleeping; paths are reshaped, and new plantings contribute vegetal richness. The number of formal ideas are restricted but each is employed discerningly and with considerable skill. The two proposed gardens demonstrate that one does not need to radically alter an existing landscape to improve its function and aesthetics. As the Japanese say: 'At times a whisper can be heard when a shout cannot.'

The composite design for the Arboretum Trompenburg, by West 8/Adriaan Geuze, addressed the need for a second entrance to the arboretum far from its principal gateway. A tower at one end of the L-shaped canal announces admittance to this beautiful though under-visited garden. Questions of announcement and entrance were important functional issues, but the true design task, as the designer conceived it, was to create an Erasmian garden for our era: a garden within a noisy urban context in which one contemplates nature, life and a heightened sense of aesthetics that could be called art.

The project develops from a pergola-covered canal, upon which one travels by small boat to a tranquil pavilion. There one encounters the garden, with its evocation of evolution, vegetation past and perhaps future. It is a place of withdrawal for thought and maybe reading. Wisterias subsume the pergola: one can imagine floating smoothly beneath a lavender river in springtime, or a crusty pattern of branches in winter; or perhaps one might skate there in winter. The intentions are well communicated by the developed state of the design and the completeness of the presentation, although the sense of the context surrounding the garden is incomplete.

The four projects we could call gardens – the Lijnbaan gardens; Arboretum Trompenburg's Erasmian garden, the Boijmans Van Beuningen Museum courtyard, and the rooftop of Las Palmas – raise questions about the role and identity of gardens today.

Are they primarily social vehicles that aid and adjust collective behaviour?

18. While it is difficult to grasp the essence of the design from a verbal statement and few sketches alone, this design task could be the most important of the entire **Breeze** project.
19. I wonder whether some of the social problems that now trouble the North Garden could be helped by a second diagonal path that might encourage more people to pass through. Perhaps the additional use is not desired, however.
20. On the California garden see Thomas Church, *Gardens are for People* (New York: Reinhold, 1950), Garrett Eckbo, *The Art of Home Landscaping* (New York: McGraw-Hill, 1956), Marc Treib and Dorothée Imbert, *Garrett Eckbo: Modern Landscapes for Living* (Berkeley: University of California Press, 1997) and David Streatfield, *California Gardens: Creating a New Eden* (New York: Abbeville, 1994).

[fig. 19]
Patio of the Oranges, Seville, Spain. 16th century.

Public, yet intimate in scale.

[fig. 20]
Cemetery, Harvard, Massachusetts.

The characteristic brilliant autumn colour of New England.

[fig. 21]
Queen Square, Bath, England. 1728-36. John Wood the Elder.

Vines cover the building and soften the effect of the architectural elements.

[fig. 22]
Baseball Bat Clipped Shrubs, Los Angeles, California.

Topiary replaces construction.

[fig. 23]
Versailles, France. 1660s+. André Le Nôtre.

Garden as expression of power.

Are they about providing places to go to, places to escape the more difficult social and environmental aspects of daily life?

Could we call for yet a third role for the garden, that of a cultural expression for today?

Throughout history, landscape design has embodied and expressed the values of a culture: at times the power of the state, at times the aesthetics of those at a distance from power [figs 23, 24]. It is no different today. In the past, the French gave us the garden for the monarchy; in this century California provided a model borrowed internationally for the suburban back yard [fig. 25].[20] What are the purposes served by the garden and park in today's Rotterdam? What role can the city play in realizing landscapes with resonance far beyond the borders of the Netherlands? What can these nine design teams offer the city socially, functionally, environmentally and as cultural expressions for the twenty-first century? The Breeze of AIR programme has mapped out some provocative directions to be followed. The prospects are interesting.

[fig. 24]
Joju-in, Kyoto, Japan. 17th century. Kobori Enshu.

Garden as rejection of power.

[fig. 25]
Donnell garden, Sonoma, California. 1948. Thomas Church.

The classic California garden, more about living than looking.

TURGUT CANSEVER
Afterthoughts from Istanbul

Breeze of AIR was an exemplary event that could well be copied in Turkey and elsewhere. Due to the collaboration between Architecture International Rotterdam (AIR) and Rotterdam City Council, a number of social problems were raised for discussion. In addition, the event was educative, and broadened perspectives. As an attempt to find answers for concrete locations requiring design, Breeze of AIR was directly focused on the development of contemporary society. The garden served as a reference point for studying how people relate to the planet and to nature. Internationally renowned garden designers were offered the opportunity to develop nine garden projects that could make Rotterdam considerably more colourful. The nine projects highlight the different approaches and standpoints of the designers. An important aspect here is the way that socio-cultural solutions, economic policy and non-Western ideas were communicated to the city's inhabitants. Moreover, it is unusual in that Rotterdam's residents were able to learn about the resulting design proposals. I would like to congratulate the AIR Foundation and the City of Rotterdam on this, and I hope that Rotterdam City Council will in fact implement the garden projects that were designed for Breeze of AIR.

An important conclusion is that the economic, social and moral questions unearthed by this project must be approached holistically. For this it is necessary to develop rudimentary knowledge by bringing age-old knowledge up to date. In order to find out how today's problems have arisen, it is not sufficient to look at history as something specific to one geographical area in one particular period, but rather as a component of an evolutionary development. Only when people appreciate that history offers a treasure trove of wisdom that is repeatedly forgotten and then rediscovered, and honestly confront the negative aspects of everyday successes, can they broaden their horizons.

The notion that intellectuals take the lead in this and Joe Public follows, must be abandoned. This can be done by finding a way in which to share high-quality knowledge with the citizens.

After a brief evaluation of the designs for the various sites, I shall propose a new approach to the design and management of urban gardens, one that is inspired by the historic gardens of the Ottoman city.

Valkeniersweide

Immigrants living in the neighbourhood regularly go walking in this park in Rotterdam-Zuid. The design made by Louafi provides space for a diversity of activities and thus shows a great deal of respect for the multifarious cultural backgrounds of the users. I consider this a step in the right direction, because an ever-increasing variety of cultures are represented in our cities. Significantly, the design has improved the structure of the landscape. I feel that this project would also give people the sense that they can linger in peace and quiet. Parks should not merely be functional, but should have the resonance of an art work through high-quality design.

Spinoza park

Oudolf's design brings more unity to the layout of the park and creates an interesting environment where a body of spaces is accessed by a new network of paths. The lively design employs new, eye-catching elements to lend the existing, somewhat anaemic

[fig. 1]
Working visit to Rotterdam by Turgut Cansever, 13 June 2001

[fig. 2]
Visit to courtyard in Bloemhof
Layout developed in deliberation with women of non-Dutch extraction

[fig. 3]
Working visit by Turgut Cansever
Renewal of Gildebuurt, Charlois

surroundings a stronger identity as well as satisfying the functional requirements. The present functionalistic arrangement of the park will be complemented with a dynamic entity of clipped hedges, clustered trees and borders of flowers and plants. The design for this park, wedged as it is between the shopping centre, characterless post-war residential blocks and schools, redeems the surroundings from the prevailing monotony.

Hofplein viaduct

The introduction of three new elements makes the project intriguing on various scales. Two long, narrow buildings at the head of the square (Agnieseplein) will be demolished to make space for a new neighbourhood park, enclosed by the railway viaduct and a wall. The high rail viaduct will be transformed into a boulevard at city scale. The designers propose a glass pavilion with exotic plants on the former site of the station, a reference to the glasshouse horticulture in the Westland market gardening area. The brightly coloured exotic flowers and plants in the greenhouse, the climbing equipment and the trees in the park are design elements that add up to a highly impressive project. When the conservatory is illuminated at night, it will transmute into a mysterious object. The design exudes an aura of boundless enthusiasm.

Lijnbaan gardens

These compact city gardens, walled in between blocks of flats, are still redolent of the collectivist spirit of post-World War II reconstruction. I find the proposal to transform these gardens into beautiful, inviting places extremely positive, though I do hope that they will have a greater variety of functions than simply serving as a way through or a place to take time out on a bench. Hargreaves' proposal to establish direct access to these gardens from the ground-floor apartments is therefore very valuable. The use of these urban gardens could be increased, were they to include a café or a clubhouse in the ground floors of the surrounding buildings. The introduction of more water and the thinning of shrubs will give the project a more distinctive character.

Museum Park – Het Park

I agree with Descombes' observations on the poor maintenance and miserable state of Museum Park. In his plan he proposes improving the structure of pedestrian routes through the area across the dyke (Westzeedijk). He approaches the problem with due deference for the design of his predecessors. He understands that his intentions can be accomplished with minimal intervention and that this does, in fact, achieve satisfying results.

Central Station area

The proposal by Atelier Quadrat will turn Central Station into much more than just an arrivals and departures terminal. In order to simultaneously transform the station into a meeting-point where people can pleasantly spend time, the railway tracks and platforms are to be relocated underground. Establishing a public or semi-public space at street level is, in my opinion, an effective measure. Aside from the question of whether the flamingo pool would be a success, I believe that the monkey-house and the aquarium would make no contribution to the site as a meeting place. They would more likely reduce the ambience of a tranquil urban garden where people can meet and talk, into little more than a circus attraction.

[fig. 4]
Visit to Millinxbuurt

Mijnsherenplein

[fig. 5]
**Left to right:
Tugut Cansever, Nadia Mabrouk, Sibel Eskici, Feyza Cansever and Fevzi Karaca**

[fig. 6]
**Left to right:
Sibel Eskici, Turgut Cansever, Fevzi Karaca**

[fig. 7]
Playground in Slaghekstraat, Bloemhof

Boijmans Van Beuningen Museum

Correa proposes placing an Indian water feature at the centre of the inner courtyard. Around this he has set out a circle of trees, thus creating a second space. In the garden design of Turkish-Persian and Indo-Turkish cultures, not to mention other Islamic countries, the central element of water is regarded as a dynamic and spiritual object. The water spiral will be at ground level. Visitors from an occidental background might therefore fail to grasp the intrinsic value of this object. If the intended effect is not perceived consciously, I fear that its value will be levelled out to that of a purely ornamental feature.

Rooftop of Las Palmas

At the time of the design Las Palmas was to be converted into a centre for visual culture. The Japanese designers propose a covered rooftop garden where visitors, escaping the scurry and stress of work, would be able to find peace and contemplate a distorted image of the outside world. They would not be able to see or consider the outside world as it really is. In my opinion, it is not right to deny people a view of reality and the beauty of the real world.

Arboretum Trompenburg

Trompenburg is a place where peace and quiet holds sway. Visitors can paddle along the waterways through pergolas bedecked with wisteria in small boats. The elegant enclosed garden alongside the pavilion catches the eye. It explores the theme of life and death; the fossilized trees represent death and the fast-growing plants vitality. This project is provocative and dramatically confronts visitors with mortality. I would personally opt for flowering plants, which bud and die in line with the seasons, so as to allude to death in a more elegant and more forceful manner.

A new approach

The various briefs and the diversity of individual approaches adopted by the designers cannot make it easy for Rotterdam City Council to come to a decision. Establishing common goals is, therefore, a prerequisite so that general conditions can be borne in mind when implementing the projects. It is important that the increasingly heterogenous population is involved in the design process as well as with the management and upkeep of gardens and parks.[1] Inadequate budgets for the construction and management of public urban gardens constitute the biggest stumbling block for their revitalization. For this reason there should be an attempt to devolve gardens or sections of gardens to private individuals or groups, so that maintenance can be carried out by the owners. In addition, the limited budgets for upkeep must be borne in mind in the design and organization of larger gardens.

Ottoman gardens

The Ottoman gardens, which regrettably disappeared from the Turkish cityscape more than seventy years ago, can serve as a model for the contemporary urban garden.

As in other medieval Islamic, Western and Asiatic towns, the intricate network of streets in the Ottoman cities was constructed in accordance with the topography. Each family could build its house on irregularly shaped plots without interference from the authorities. The gardens lay hidden between the houses behind garden walls so as to safeguard privacy. Each family created its own paradise. All elements of the garden were treated with respect and valued as a divine gift. In the gardens, families and their guests enjoyed the beauty of life, of which the garden was an inextricable

---

[1] According to the estimates of the Habitat Conference held by the United Nations in 1996, the world population will grow from 6 billion to 10 billion within 30 to 50 years, while the total urban population will increase from 1.2 billion to 8 billion. Urbanization will become one of the most serious social problems due to increasing emigration from poor to wealthy countries. The large number of immigrants already living in Rotterdam indicates that the city will be party to this process.

[fig. 8]
Playground in Slaghekstraat

[fig. 9]
Pimpernelstraat in Bloemhof

Satellite dishes for telecasts from the country of origin

[fig. 10]
Visit to the mosque on Afrikaanderplein

Prayer room and meeting rooms in a former school building

part. People spent the summer months in the shade of fruit trees, where they could enjoy the cooling effect of the ponds. The sound of water had a calming influence. In the garden people talked about flower beds, the pattern of pathways, the season in which flowers could best be cultivated, which flowers could be planted alongside one another, and about the properties of the soil where perennials such as rose bushes would thrive. Such ideas were founded on knowledge passed from generation to generation, and followed the example of the better appointed gardens. That is how many families continued the venerable garden culture.

In the hilly landscape of Istanbul the houses were built on slopes. The view to be had from them represented a window on eternity. As in other Ottoman cities, such as Bursa, the architecture of Istanbul formed a unified entity with the varied world of gardens. Tree branches and rose bushes hung over the garden walls and adorned the facades of the houses. People could enjoy this nature at every turn, and along with the ornamental, coloured frontages it was the central feature of the street scene. The square stood in the centre of the neighbourhood, paved with solid, hardwearing natural stone, and could be reached from every direction. A library and a mosque overlooked the square. After a visit to one of these buildings you sat in the shadow of a centuries-old plane-tree, drank tea and took part in the discussions.

The inner courtyards of schools and monasteries were another important aspect of the Ottoman city. The centrally placed pond was a symbol of cleanliness and purity. A tall, dark-green cypress adorned the courtyard along with another variety of tree. Sparse flowerbeds were planted tastefully. These were examples of minimalist garden architecture.

The presence of a pond was also important for the large courtyards of mosques. Here too they planted one or more cypresses and, say, a monumental plane-tree. Because cypresses represent eternity, they added to the spirituality of the courtyards. The gardens of the mosques were separated from daily life by walls. Windows in the garden wall represented the belief in the boundlessness of creation. In this sense, daily life was simultaneously divided from and at one with the spiritual world. Before and after prayers, people sat on rugs or reed mats and joined in discussions about religious and social issues.

Other examples of public green space in Ottoman cities were the cemeteries and kitchen gardens. In the cemeteries there were white, marble monuments like abstract sculptures in the shadow of dense arbours of dark-green cypresses. The kitchen gardens, for the cultivation of vegetables, were owned by collectives and used as public walking areas with a special status.

During the Ottoman Empire, many low-lying parks were established along the banks of the river in Istanbul, surrounded by woods and reachable by boat. These were pleasant and popular spots for picnics and music-making.

Sadly there is no trace left of these beautiful places. The great fire that devastated Istanbul in 1919 marked the beginning of their demise. When Le Corbusier left Istanbul by ship during the fire, he wrote: 'With its wooden houses painted deep red in the shadow of wide awnings, all those windows with their balconies arching forward that decorate the ornamental facades, and the silhouettes of the domes and the countless minarets with their fantastic forms on the hills of this city; it brings to mind a magnificent Persian carpet stretching down to the ocean like a sea of flowers.'

In conclusion, the beauty of this city too was achieved through the efforts of individuals and the beneficence of simple but noble people across the years.

[fig. 11]
Working visit by Cansever, 13 June 2001

Renovated houses on Kokerplein, Slaghekbuurt

[fig. 12]
Working visit by Cansever

The new Kokerplein, Slaghekbuurt

[fig. 13]
Working visit by Cansever

KEN WORPOLE

Urban Parks in Europe: topology and geometry, economics and aesthetics

[1] Eric Luiten and Ivan Nio pointed this out many times in the course of the conference proceedings.

The role which the park or public garden plays in the modern city, is not just an issue for Rotterdam, or indeed the Netherlands alone. In many cities throughout the world, politicians, environmentalists, urban planners, landscape architects and citizens' groups are trying to find a new role and function for urban green space. Unfortunately, they are often wanting to travel in different directions. The politicians are worried about the costs (especially the long-term maintenance costs), the environmentalists want everything to revert to nature or be converted to urban agriculture, the planners are concerned with fulfilling legal requirements for the exact quantity of open space, the landscape architects and designers want to experiment with new materials and public art, and citizens' groups want somewhere safe for the children to play and where older people can meet and walk their dogs without having to travel too far. One principle which seems to be emerging from parks policy in the UK is that in future *the solutions to these dilemmas will always be site-specific and negotiated and decided locally.* There are no universal solutions anymore.

Many of the problems which have arisen for urban green spaces in recent years have resulted from the fact that the design and maintenance of the public park has increasingly moved from a locally-managed horticultural tradition to a rationalized, mass-production form of provision and maintenance. In recent research on open space provision in London, in which I was involved, the study team looked at how other cities in Europe assess the need for open space. We discovered that the majority still plan for green space as an issue of quantity, not quality. It is easy to measure quantity of course, and therefore to fulfil the targets which politicians and planners love; but the same is not true of quality. This is where economics meet aesthetics, which is always a difficult rendezvous.

The same quantitative standard has now existed in the UK since 1925, requiring all cities where possible to provide 6 acres (2.42 hectares) of green open space per 1000 people. As long as the city is providing this quantity, then many politicians feel that they are delivering their programme. But this rationalist mode of planning is no longer suitable for modern cities which have changed enormously in terms of social demographics, ethnicity, lifestyles and continued individualization.[1] The mass production of landscape is no longer appropriate in a diverse and multi-cultural society, and issues of quality and context are now much more important. One must therefore look to more local, site-specific, solutions to the planning and management of green space, based on a respect for the needs and interests of the people who use these spaces, and have to live with them all year round.

By way of preparing for the closing Breeze of AIR conference the three invited visiting critics spent two days travelling round Rotterdam visiting many of the sites under discussion. On one day we travelled by bus, and on the other day by bicycle: naturally the bicycle was a much better means of understanding the topography and social character of the district than the bus, because the bicycle journey always took you slowly through the streets and communities surrounding the parks, and made one more aware of the social and demographic context. This made me realize that planners should not be allowed to travel by car, though in Britain they nearly always do, and everybody suffers as a result. As some of the following photographs taken from these visits reveal, it is possible to see how the rationalist trend in management and maintenance has allowed certain parks in the city to become rather dull and meaningless places, which is particularly surprising in a city as energetic and responsive to change as Rotterdam.

Take, for example, the two parks close by the Lijnbaan: the Lijnbaanhoven. One assumes that when the apartments were built and the gardens established, the residents regarded these as the 'front' gardens of their flats, for the use of their children to play, as well as to admire from their windows. It was probably assumed that in spatial terms they 'belonged' to or were 'owned' by the people living in the apartments, and that wider public use was a secondary matter. Today, many of the people in the flats have grown older and no longer have children at home, and over the years these gardens have become the 'back' gardens of the neighbourhood. The residents just exercise their dogs in these parks, and no longer feel they have a special relationship to them, and the spaces are often used today by homeless people and drug users, and have become a kind of 'no man's land'.

The symbolic status of these two gardens as 'back gardens' can be seen from the photographs which show that this is where businesses and the city council locate their waste containers, in the same way that many people put their rubbish bins out the back [fig. 1]. Another photograph shows that the person maintaining these gardens is not actually a gardener by skill or profession, but a street cleaner: so one can see that these places have lost their horticultural status and have become part of the everyday urban street space [fig. 2].

On the other hand, this is not the case with the apartment block at the junction of Westzeedijk and Kievitslaan which overlooks Het Park, and which still gains its status and prestige from its position overlooking the park. The name of the building, 'Parkflat', proclaims with pride its privileged relationship to Het Park, which is no doubt how the relationship between the flats and the gardens at Lijnbaanhoven used to be, and could be again.

We can represent these general trends schematically as follows:

Public garden or 'Hortus Conclusus'	Modern urban green space
The 'front gardens' of the city	The 'back gardens' of the city
Maintained by gardeners	Maintained by street cleaners
Craft tradition	Mass production
Local topography	Universal design
Emphasis on quality	Emphasis on quantity
Multi-functional	Mono-functional
Spiritual and moral renewal	Physical recreation and play
Seasonal rhythms	Urban rhythms
Consecrated space	Democratic space

Across Europe, the response to this dilemma of the future of urban green space seems at present to be taking two directions (though we should always be wary of making too simple classifications). Towards the Mediterranean the emphasis in urban planning is on modern design and architectonic values, most famously in the 150 new public spaces developed in Barcelona in the 1990s, as well as the recent modernist parks of Paris such as Parc de la Villette, Parc André-Citröen, Parc Bercy, among others. The recent Second European Biennial on Landscape Architecture held in Barcelona in April 2001, was called *Jardins insurgents* or 'Gardens in Arms', clearly emphasizing the uncompromising and militant nature of the design values now inherent in modern urban landscaping. In such programmes the emphasis is on the role that the new parks play in urban regeneration and increasing land values, while emphasizing modern design aesthetics and cosmopolitan urbanity. In the UK the report commissioned by the government from the Urban Task Force led by the distinguished architect, Lord Richard Rogers, *Towards an Urban Renaissance* (1999), was very much more about the architectural and design quality of urban space badly needed in British cities, and said very little about environmentalism or ecology.

Towards the Baltic, by contrast, there is less emphasis on design and more on ecology: so there has been a strengthening of the green infrastructure of the city, on riverside and canal walks, on city farms, ecology gardens, allotment colonies, and establishing a more responsive approach in the whole of city planning to the unique deep structure of the local topography. One of the pioneers in creating such a 'green structure' approach to urban planning was the city of Stockholm, under the leadership of Holger Bloom and Erik Glemme between 1930 and 1970, notably in the Norr

[fig. 1]
Rubbish containers at the entrance to Lijnbaanhoven, June 2001

[fig. 2]
Road sweeper June 2001

Malarstrand linear waterside park, a 4-kilometre-long narrow linear park running alongside Lake Malaren from the city centre to the west. No wider than 12 metres in many places, the waterside park contained a softly curving footpath, seating of many different kinds, boat landings, sculptures, ponds, play areas, a café and some garden bowers for rest and relaxation. For landscape historian Thorbjorn Anderson: 'It is the masterpiece of all Stockholm parks from the period. It was constructed on what had been, practically speaking, wasteland, and in this respect the park and its designer refuted [the assertion] about the impossibility of recreating naturelike settings in the city.'[2]

The same difference of emphasis can also be seen in the landscaping or design of cemeteries in Europe, which also provide a very important 'hortus conclusus' in the historic city. Those in the more southern countries prefer to create architectonic cities of marble and stone, such as Père Lachaise in Paris, whereas in the more northerly countries there is greater emphasis on the redemptive qualities of the garden or woodland cemetery, most famously of course in the early twentieth-century design of the Stockholm Woodland Cemetery by Gunnar Asplund and Sigurd Lewerentz. Closer to home, Rotterdam's Crooswijk Cemetery provides a very fine example of a garden cemetery with very high landscaping and horticultural values: I doubt if there is a cemetery in the UK which has been designed and maintained to such a high standard [fig. 3]. This difference between the 'garden cemeteries' and the 'cemeteries of stone' to be found in northern and southern Europe is captured expressively in David Robinson's book of photographs, *Beautiful Death: Art of the Cemetery*.[3]

These important differences of emphasis were already noted nearly a decade ago by the Dutch commentator Gerrit Smienk at an earlier Dutch seminar on landscape design:

'Architects, urban designers and landscape architects do not seem to feel at ease when confronted with each other. A dialogue between representatives of the ecological, historical and modern movements has yet to begin. The various countries from northern and southern Europe do have entirely different backgrounds and no common language, even if English is universally understood.'[4]

It was this precise and eloquent formulation which in fact was the starting point for my own recent book, *Here Comes the Sun: Architecture and Public Space in 20th Century European Culture*, which explores the diverging cultural histories of landscape and architecture in northern and southern European urban settings, particularly in the planning of urban life and leisure outdoors.[5] The Norwegian architectural critic, Christian Norberg-Schulz, has expressed this polarity more philosophically:

'We have suggested that northern space is primarily a clearing rather than a comprehensive Euclidean whole. A clearing, however, presupposed a context within which it opens, and this we have characterized as a space of moods. This implies that northern space is not geometric but topological.'[6]

This tension between ecology and design – or topology and Euclidean geometry – was always close to the surface at the Breeze of AIR conference. Erik de Jong argued, for example, that gardening is a performance culture, not a design culture, and has more to do with theatre, mise-en-scène, character and setting, than with the dominance of the plan. Of course many cities in the world try to embrace both concepts of urban green space. While most people think of New York as principally the home of the unique Central Park (which is fortunate enough to be able to secure very large amounts of corporate sponsorship to underwrite its enormous annual maintenance costs), the city is also home to the 'Green Guerrillas', who take over abandoned or vacant lots and turn them into allotments and community gardens.

[fig. 3]
Crooswijk Cemetery, Rotterdam

[2.] Thorbjorn Anderson, 'Erik Glemme and the Stockholm Park System', in Marc Treib (ed.), *Modern Landscape Architecture*, Cambridge, MA, 1993
[3.] David Robinson, *Beautiful Death: Art of the Cemetery*, Penguin Studio, London 1996
[4.] Gerrit Smienk, in Martin Knuijt et al. (eds), *Modern Park Design: Recent Trends*, Bussum, Netherlands, 1995
[5.] Ken Worpole, *Here Comes the Sun: Architecture and Public Space in 20th Century European Culture*, London 2000
[6.] Christian Norberg-Schulz, *Nightlands: Nordic Building*, MIT Press, Cambridge, MA, 1996
[7.] Eric Luiten and Frank de Josselin de Jong, 'From garden city to city garden', in *Breeze of AIR, de ontwerpopdracht*, Stichting AIR (unpublished).

However, neither topology nor geometry alone is enough to guarantee the success of a new green space, urban park or public garden: the human element must also be given equal priority. And here we cannot allow the general trend of social change to go unremarked. My original field of study was in literary history and theory, where it is a commonplace that literature began as stories told about the Gods, then came dramas and poems about the intrigues of the Kings, then sagas about the great warriors and nobles, then novels concerning the life of the bourgeoisie, then next came the fiction of the working classes, until more recently literature has concentrated on the anti-hero and the outcasts of society. As each new social formation emerged centre-stage, so literature corresponded accordingly, both in form and content. As we know, the great parks started as royal hunting grounds, then the picturesque landscaped garden was developed to meet the needs of the large country-house owning classes; the mid-nineteenth century saw the development of the great civic parks in towns and cities for middle-class elevation and display (the Burgerpark), followed in the twentieth century by the development of the recreational park (the Volkspark) for popular sport and leisure. Today, many parks in Europe, including Rotterdam, have become sanctuaries for homeless people, or immigrants and asylum-seekers, who feel a particular attachment to them because their present community attachments are so weak, and the public park gives them perhaps the first sense of civic belonging [figs 4, 5].

In Britain many new immigrant communities have become particularly interested in acquiring allotment gardens, where they can grow their own food (as many of them come from farming or rural backgrounds) and they also feel safer in these more highly regulated environments. Ecological spaces such as allotments and leisure gardens, wildlife centres and community gardens, are also less costly to maintain because this work is usually done by the individuals and communities themselves. I have visited a number of leisure gardens (*volkstuinen*) in Amsterdam, The Hague and Rotterdam, and all of them are maintained to a very high standard – not a blade of grass is out of place – because people feel a very strong sense of ownership [fig. 6]. At the other extreme, a modernist urban landscape such as Museum Park in Rotterdam, is very expensive to maintain, and yet if it is not maintained to a high quality it can quickly fail – as has been the case.

This issue therefore is not just a matter of aesthetics or politics as to whether one favours a more ecological approach to urban green space or a design approach: both come with very different costs and maintenance regimes attached. As Eric Luiten and Frank de Josselin de Jong pointed out,[7] the average costs of laying out parks and gardens in the Netherlands varies from 7 to 25 Euros per square metre, whereas Barcelona has spent up to 135 Euros per square metre on its new urban spaces, while Parisian parks such as La Villette cost up to 450 Euros per square metre in initial investment. These latter sums are large public investments geared to enhancing the global image and international competitiveness of the cities in question, as much as they are designed to meet local environmental and community needs and concerns. In Rotterdam only Schouwburgplein has approached this level of public spending. We might assume from such great differences in investment that 'form follows funding': modern architectonic design is expensive to undertake and can require very high maintenance costs. Here, as was pointed out many times at the conference, questions of scale are always crucial. Most cities need investment at both ends of the scale, whether in the relatively low-maintenance green corridors and networks which bind the city's green structure together, or in the highly designed 'flagship' city parks and gathering places which may well secure international attention and acclaim.

It goes without saying that any urban parks strategy will always give a high priori-

[fig. 4]
Het Oude Westen local park, Rotterdam, June 2001

[fig. 5]
Heemraadsplein, Rotterdam, June 2001

[fig. 6]
Allotment garden, Rotterdam

ty to the provision of play spaces and neighbourhood parks, something for which the Netherlands enjoys an international reputation, and clearly evident in the trips we made throughout Rotterdam. I personally have always admired the Dutch architect, Aldo van Eyck, especially for establishing the civic programme which created over 700 playgrounds in Amsterdam after the Second World War as the most effective means of rebuilding neighbourhoods and communities devastated by war. Whatever social and demographic changes occur, children will always need to explore and engage with others in the familiar territory of their local streets, neighbourhoods and parks [fig. 7].

However, the ability to provide parks, play areas and green spaces of so many different kinds is going to require a revolution in public management and funding policy. In a cosmopolitan city with many lifestyles and cultures, 'one-size-fits-all' management regimes simply will not work. Parks and leisure gardens, playgrounds and riverside walks can never flourish as part of the street maintenance programme, and require specialist skills and timetables to look after them. This calls for a more decentralized, flexible style of management on the part of the municipal authorities. Both industry and commerce have in recent years developed the concept of 'flexible specialization' to describe the production processes which have replaced the age of mass production, and this is what is now required in urban parks policy.

Finally, it is now clear in the UK at least, that the funding for parks and open spaces has suffered in recent years, as municipal politicians and managers have chosen to prioritize investment in indoor leisure. Indoor leisure seems more glamorous, younger and sexier: the cult of individual fitness has replaced the culture of public health and well-being. But in the long term such policies are not sustainable. If cities neglect the quality of their outdoor public spaces, parks and street networks, which is where the majority of the people find much of their sense of democracy and civic confidence (as well as their general physical well-being), then society will be further divided and the public sphere diminished. The rewards of the exercise machine and private swimming pool are no substitute for the pleasures of the street, the park or the evening stroll outdoors.

[1.] For a more extended discussion of the hortus conclusus, see the essay 'The Enclosed Garden' by Adriaan van der Staay.
[2.] An urban sociological study was done into three design sites within the framework of *Breeze of AIR*: Ivan Nio and Marloes Wevers, *De stadstuin verkend. Een onderzoek naar het gebruik en de betekenis van de Lijnbaanhoven, de Valkeniersweide en het Spinozapark* (Amsterdam 2001).
[3.] Gerrie Andela, 'Van de wieg tot het graf in het groen' in Arnold Reijndorp and Hanneke van der Ven (eds), *Een reuze vooruitgang. Utopie en praktijk in de Zuidelijke Tuinsteden van Rotterdam* (Rotterdam: 010 Publishers, 1994).
[4.] Herbert Gans, *People and Plans. Essays on Urban Problems and Solutions* (New York: Basic Books, 1968).

[fig. 7]
Parkflat, the park adds status and prestige to the nearby housing

IVAN NIO
The Urban Garden as Public Space

The theme of Breeze of AIR was the cultural significance of the hortus conclusus in today's city.[1] As a cultural task, the public urban garden has a sociological dimension besides those pertaining to cultural history, landscape architecture and urban politics. The importance of the urban garden as a metaphor for city culture and as a blueprint for public space was explored at nine sites in Rotterdam. Until now there has been little research into the use and meaning of green public space in the postwar city. The reflections on public space, founded on a long tradition of urban sociological research, are essentially focused on the city centre. The variations in type, situation, ownership, management and the degree of publicness of the design sites meant that Breeze of AIR was also an exploration of how urban gardens can reinforce the meaning of a range of public spaces. For a number of sites the brief was closely bound up with changes in use.[2] Positioning the hortus conclusus in a contemporary context raises a number of dilemmas related to the conjunction of design and layout on the one hand and use and meaning on the other.

The Spinoza park in the district of Lombardijen is a site that is illustrative of the continually evolving relationship between urban culture and the design of green public space. In the 1950s the green space in Lombardijen was established hierarchically in the form of private gardens, communal gardens, neighbourhood gardens, green belts and a central park. Each patch of green was meant for a specific target group. The young were a prime concern when laying out the Spinoza park. Here the concentric arrangement of residential areas with services and amenities at their centre and neighbourhoods all around, was intended to foster a sense of community, in accordance with the 'neighbourhood' concept. The entire centre had to form 'a natural meeting point for the district's inhabitants, where the combination of shopping public and youngsters at play could enliven it throughout the day'.[3] However, the actual use of the Spinoza park diverges acutely from these original intentions. The shopping centre and the park fail to constitute any kind of unified whole. In day-to-day use, the park is sooner a green barrier that must be negotiated in order to reach the amenities in the centre from the southern neighbourhoods. The park functions as a shortcut. Although used intensively as a way through, the park generally has a desolate air about it.

The question is, what possibilities does the urban garden typology hold for establishing a new relationship between socio-cultural changes in the city and the form and layout of public green space, without once again lapsing into spatial determinism? A design is never capable of uniformly influencing human behaviour. The sociologist Herbert Gans once expressed this phenomenon as the discrepancy between potential and effective space. A particular layout may well be a condition for encouraging the desired use of public space, but it is in no sense a guarantee that people will actually behave in that way.[4] The fact that Lombardijen's central park is not used as intended is only partially related to changes made to its ultimate layout. The Spinoza park's lack of meaning as a space for informal activity is primarily the result of social changes over the last two decades, such as the ageing population, the trend to individualization, cultural diversification and increasing mobility. The collective space in Lombardijen has lost its meaning as a social platform for the organic community. More than before, the expectations for public green space, as well as the meanings attached to it, are more closely bound up with the major differences between its users.

Between encounter and avoidance

Breeze of AIR has sought to revive the concept of the urban garden in terms of changes in Rotterdam's social demography and the use of leisure time in the city. In Vreewijk (Valkeniersweide), Agniesebuurt (Hofplein viaduct), Lombardijen (Spinoza park) and also at the Lijnbaan flats (Lijnbaan gardens), the once so homogeneous population has become more culturally diverse, and these districts and neighbourhoods, sociologically speaking, have therefore become urbanized. In the Spinoza park, Valkeniersweide and the Lijnbaan gardens, the communal has been supplanted by a more urbane publicness.

There has been an influx of new residents: first-time tenants and others moving up the housing ladder, including those of foreign extraction or immigrants (with the exception of the Lijnbaan flats). This cultural diversification has resulted in a great variety of lifestyles. After a period when the population was ageing, the average age is now seen to be dropping. In some neighbourhoods, the number of children – primarily of immigrant descent – is increasing again. These processes of diversification and rejuvenation are visible to varying degrees: whereas Agniesebuurt has already undergone radical changes and Vreewijk has also seen an influx of immigrant residents in recent years, Lombardijen now stands at the threshold of this transformation process.

The use of public green space by different groups has brought a proliferation of meanings. The diversity of lifestyles makes new demands on the design, layout and management of public green space. Specifically, it requires more differentiation among public green spaces, as well as a new relationship between form and use. For many indigenous residents, use of the green space in the immediate vicinity of the home has decreased because of a decline in the average number of people per household, an enlargement of the radius of activity owing to increased physical mobility, and a stronger focus on the home itself. They not only make less use of it, but use it differently: protracted recreation has been superseded by less time-consuming activities such as jogging, walking the dog, or just walking [figs 1, 2, 4]. On the other hand, the elderly, children and people with limited budgets still seem strongly attracted on the whole to the local green space.

Immigrants also often attach great value to the public space in their living environment, but their use of it may differ from that of the original residents. Research into the recreational behaviour of Turks and Moroccans shows that immigrants spend a relatively large share of their free time in city parks.[5] Immigrant families regularly visit parks and recreation areas with relatives and friends for picnics, barbecues or informal sport activities. For foreign women in particular, who often have a restricted radius of activity and limited financial means, the role of local public green space for meeting others is an important one [fig. 3]. The women often combine business with pleasure: they bring their children to a playground and make use of this opportunity to meet and talk. For Valkeniersweide, the influx of new residents has diversified its use and so the meaning of the space is no longer clear-cut. Spending time in Valkeniersweide now means spending time among people with another way of life and background, people who use the space in other ways. The various affective and functional relationships with the park result in a wide range of definitions of public space, and thus in different and sometimes conflicting claims to it. The presence of groups of young people can be perceived as a threat by older visitors. A section of the park dominated by men constitutes a hindrance for immigrant women who want to sit there undisturbed. Dogs off the leash annoy picnicking families with children, while the litter left behind irritates native Dutch residents.

The multiformity of meanings gives rise to a need for distance among all these groups. In a multicultural district, the brief for the urban garden therefore lies in that area of tension between encounter and avoidance. However, the use forms and the other cultural meanings attributed by immigrants to public green space do not necessarily have to conflict with those of the original residents. Alongside the partial theming and programming of public space, another task is to examine the conditions for flexible and simultaneous use by different groups.

The involvement and identification of the various groups of users with green public space can be enhanced by a design that is better attuned to the various ways of spending leisure time and to the varied perceptions of nature. This might be achieved by ensuring that there is adequate and comfortable seating close to play areas, the present lack of which is regarded particularly by immigrant women as a shortcom-

[5] Margrit Jókövi, *Recreatie van Turken, Marokkanen en Surinamers in Rotterdam en Amsterdam. Een verkenning van het vrijetijdsgedrag en van de effecten van de etnische cultuur op de vrijetijdsbesteding* (Wageningen: Alterra, 2000); Steunpunt Wonen, *Een wereldpark op Zuid. Gesprekken met bewoners over het Zuiderpark* (Rotterdam 2000).

[6] In general this exchange between different social worlds is the basis of the social importance of public space as public domain. See further: Ries van der Wouden (ed.), *De stad op straat. De openbare ruimte in perspectief* (The Hague: Sociaal Cultureel Planbureau, 1999); Maarten Hajer and Arnold Reijndorp, *In search of new public domain*, trans. Andrew May (Rotterdam: NAi Publishers, 2001).

[7] Liz Greenhalgh and Ken Worpole, *Park Life. Urban Parks and Social Renewal* (London: Comedia/Demos, 1995).

[8] Lyn Lofland, *A World of Strangers. Order and Action in Urban Public Space* (New York: Basic Books, 1973).

[fig. 1]
Spinoza park

[fig. 2]
Path through Spinoza park to shopping centre

[fig. 3]
New Rotterdammers in Valkeniersweide

[fig. 4]
Walking the dog in Valkeniersweide

ing. In many parks there is also a demand for water taps or fountains, barbecuing facilities and sanitation.

The enclosed garden can serve as an inspirational concept for renewing the programming of public green space. This involves more than just attending to specific lifestyles and use forms in the park. In Vreewijk, Agniesebuurt and Lombardijen in particular, the role of the hortus conclusus is caught between the relatively unprogrammed space of the park and the monofunctional and monothematic idea of the garden. What kind of garden would be most suitable? The notion of the enclosed garden presupposes a place for reflection, relaxation, peace and quiet: the garden as a contemplative space. Alongside the garden as contemplative space (*hortus contemplationis*), the tradition of the *hortus ludi,* the garden for music, dancing, drinking and pleasure, could also be imbued with a new lease of life. In keeping with the increasing diversification of society, the demand for green space is characterized by a whole array of expectations and desires. There is a demand for spaces for contemplation as well as for picnicking, gardening and playing. Herb gardens, play areas and vegetable gardens also deserve putting on the agenda alongside the contemplative garden. One of the dilemmas facing the urban garden has to do with the discrepancy between gardens for looking at and gardens for using.

Open and closed

While the park functions as an ambivalent, anonymous space for a multicultural public the garden has a more specific meaning, as space with a particular ambience, for a particular activity or group of people. The garden has a more semi-public character than the park. Which is why the closed garden is also a metaphor for the privatization of public space. Access to the garden is literally or symbolically restricted. The interesting thing here is that the garden concept straddles the threshold between private and public domains. The garden can add a more private aspect to a park designed with the communal in mind. Thanks to the mechanics of social exclusion the privatization of public space usually has a negative connotation in the discourse on the public realm. Indeed, urban sociologists emphasize the need for flexibility and free access to parks. They make a distinction between parks and commercial public spaces such as shopping centres in that a great deal of freedom prevails in parks: users can ascribe their own definitions and use their creativity to appropriate park space. What is more, parks constitute public domains where different social groups are able to interact.[6]

One dilemma that the enclosed garden presents is its semi-public character. Yet there are urban gardens in all shapes and sizes, everything from private to public: 'squares' in London that are only open to the residents, parks in Paris that are locked in the evening, privately managed parks such as Bryant Park in New York, and parks subject to practically no regulations in Dutch cities. Some form of behaviour control in the guise of layout or management can be important for the smooth functioning of public spaces. 'Public parks need a paradigm of controlled freedom, but not one that mimics the consumerist model,' is how Greenhalgh and Worpole phrased it in a study of parks in Great Britain.[7] Regulation is acceptable if it improves the quality of life in the city. By approaching green spaces from the perspective of the urban garden, Breeze of AIR has transformed the dilemma of openness versus seclusion into a theme. The programming, design and management of the urban garden were studied for each site to strike the best balance between 'publicness' and privacy.

The way public green space is used shows that there is no easy distinction to be made between public and private space. Groups of people often appropriate public space informally as a meeting place, angling pool, football pitch, picnic area or hangout. Encounters in public space usually occur on the basis of a common lifestyle, age or ethnic origin. Where encounters are primarily between relative strangers, social scientists follow Lyn Lofland in using terms like colonization, spatial ordering and locational transformation of public space.[8] But unlike the parochial domains of private clubs, cafés and entertainment complexes, which cater to the wishes and behavioural conventions of specific categories of public, park visitors are generally open to the presence of other groups. One can observe others in the park. This can result in greater tolerance. The social value of the park as public domain rests on the fact that parochial domains in public green space are flexible and not closed by nature. The different groups can always look past the boundaries of their and other domains, resulting in a confrontation between lifestyles, ages and ethnicities. The park's integrative qualities are primarily at the level of seeing and being seen, rather than involving actual encounters between strangers. The public and parochial forms of spatial use are usually not spatially separate but can overlap. Reintroducing the urban garden lays bare this area of tension. In culturally diverse city districts, the urban garden as public domain can be utilized for the shared use of one and the same space as well as for positioning different spheres and activities alongside each other.

Establishing domains, or claiming them, can also lead to undesirable monopolization of space, as with the Lijnbaan gardens. The use of the Lijnbaan gardens is extremely varied – from a place to eat lunch for the shopping public to a refuge for the homeless – and these public spaces also serve as major pedestrian routes [figs 5,6]. But residents and visitors can also find the sometimes-dominant presence of groups of youngsters and drug addicts a nuisance and feel unsafe. Redesign might be an effective solution, in order to transform the Lijnbaan gardens into urban 'pocket parks' comparable with Bryant Park in New York. In the 1980s, this park was faced with an even greater drug-related problem than are the Lijnbaan gardens now. Bryant Park was transformed. Not by closing it off but by making it more accessible and attractive. According to the sociologist William Whyte, who was involved with the redesign of the park as a consultant, it was in fact extensive use of the park that was the issue rather than the drug dealers. According to Whyte, making the space attractive for as many people as possible is the most effectively means of counteracting the negative effect of the presence of undesirable users.[9] Since the transformation, Bryant Park has become one of the most visited places in the centre of New York. Not only has it been made more accessible and better organized, it now boasts additional amenities including a kiosk, a public toilet and countless movable park chairs.

Sharon Zukin has commented on the flipside of the rearrangement of Bryant Park. In her view, the design, the permanent surveillance and the extra facilities – 'domestication by cappuccino' – have affected the public character of the park, effectively turning it into a privatized space for the middle classes.[10] Perhaps Zukin's criticism is exaggerated. However, the Lijnbaan gardens must deal with a similar dilemma: how to reduce the nuisance and the sense of a lack of safety without restricting public access and openness. Enclosing and perhaps even closing off the gardens with a fence might keep out the urban nomads and passers-by, but there is more to be said for making these urban gardens into publicly accessible pocket parks, without having to deny access to more marginal users such as the homeless.

Between government and private parties

A hortus conclusus with special plants is labour- and maintenance-intensive. An important condition for the eventual success of the public urban garden is that someone or some organization assumes responsibility for its creation and upkeep. In the first instance, the management of green spaces is the responsibility of government. However, thanks to cutbacks in maintenance budgets, municipal councils have failed miserably in the regular management and maintenance of green public space. In many districts a 'green mush' has evolved, lacking in identity and quality as a place to stop and relax. Vulnerable designs, including Rotterdam's Museum Park, have not received the attention they need. As well as having put the management of parks back on the agenda, the theme of the maintenance-intensive urban garden also broaches the topic of new clients and new forms of management and upkeep. The aim of Breeze of AIR was to arouse the interest of various parties in garden design, so that its renewal would not be decided by government or government-controlled organizations alone. Using the smallest sliver of public space, the urban garden – as 'hortupuncture' – has once again raised the whole question of the makability of the city and urban culture.

[fig. 5] **Vagrants in Joost Banckertsplaats**

[fig. 6] **Lunching in Joost Banckertsplaats**

[9] William Thompson, *The Rebirth of New York City's Bryant Park* (Washington DC: Spacemaker Press, 1997); William H. Whyte, *City. Rediscovering the Center* (New York: Doubleday, 1988).
[10] Sharon Zukin, *The Cultures of Cities* (Cambridge, Mass.: Blackwell, 1995).
[11] Rob van Engelsdorp Gastelaars, 'Het verdwijnen van de leefwereld, de opkomst van het woondomein; collectief ervaren territoriale binding op laag niveau in Nederland' in W. Derksen and W. Salet, *Bouwen aan het Binnenlands Bestuur* (The Hague: Sdu, 1996).

In getting urban gardens implemented, account must be taken of the increasing number of new players operating in the field of spatial planning alongside government. It is not just the government and the public sector (schools and colleges, hospitals and museums) but also residents, housing associations, developers and other private parties who are potentially interesting clients and managers of urban gardens. By involving these private parties and the general public, the support for garden making can be increased considerably. Indeed, private individuals and other interested parties can use the semi-public garden to present themselves in the urban arena. The privately or collectively developed and maintained garden can thus reinforce involvement with the city or the immediate vicinity.

In recent years, private parties have at times already created noteworthy urban gardens, such as the public garden of the Interpolis insurance company in Tilburg. The design locations of Breeze of AIR that most obviously lend themselves to new-style clients and new forms of management are Arboretum Trompenburg, the courtyard of the Boijmans Van Beuningen Museum [fig. 7], the rooftop of the former workshop building Las Palmas [fig. 8], the wild garden of the Erasmus University [fig. 9], and the future Central Station area. Urban gardens can also gain new forms of management if these are places of significance in everyday life such as school gardens, playgrounds, yards, courtyard gardens and residential green space. All the design locations touch on the theme of the new clients and managers. New forms of management would also be a possibility for Valkeniersweide, the Spinoza park and the Lijnbaan gardens.

Devolving plots to the care of residents could reduce the actual area of communal open green spaces in the post-war districts. Fencing and hedges could be employed to more clearly mark the transition between public and private. Formalizing the space in this fashion can give rise to both privately and collectively managed gardens.

That leaves the question of how residents can share responsibility for the management of urban gardens, and whether or not this requires more institutionalized frameworks. In the longer term, the management will have to be properly regulated. In addition to the government and residents, there is a role here for corporations and other letting agents. Residents' associations could also maintain semi-public urban gardens. The collective garden would then be financed and managed by the community.

At a number of locations in the Netherlands, in inner-city environments as well as in the suburbs, residential parks with collective gardens have already been realized as an alternative for the single-family dwelling with private garden. The search for new forms of collective gardens ties in with the recent reappraisal of the residential park as a living environment.

The dilemma facing the urban garden is deciding on the degree of openness. In which cases can and must the public character be retained? According to the social geographer Rob van Engelsdorp Gastelaars, an increasing number of people are interested in establishing a domain in and around the home that is subject to their own rules and co-managed with others living locally. They regard these domains as necessary buffer zones for the protection of their personal property, status and cultural identity.[11] Public-private management constructs might offer a solution to the question of how to safeguard the public nature of urban gardens, in residential areas as well as in gardens established and maintained by private organizations. The urban garden not only lends itself to various forms of collective and private patronage, but also to hybrid management constructs in which either government and residents or corporations and associations participate.

[fig. 7]
Courtyard of Boijmans Van Beuningen

[fig. 8]
Roof of the former workshop building Las Palmas

[fig. 9]
The wild garden of the Erasmus University

Networks versus places

The meaning of the hortus conclusus within the context of modern-day Rotterdam is different to that in the old town centres of Leiden, Amsterdam, Groningen or Delft. With the exception of such oases in densely built nineteenth-century neighbourhoods as Het Oude Westen local park and Jacobustuin [fig. 10] near Endrachtsplein, public space in the city has in recent years primarily been tackled from the perspective of keeping it empty. Using the concept of the garden makes it possible to devise another angle on public space. The garden is a concept for creating specific places that are distinguishable from the recently reprofiled parks, squares and shopping streets through their green and secluded aspect. Besides serving as a model for the creation of closed-off spaces, the hortus conclusus can also be used to reinforce the cohesion of public space: the urban garden can be employed to urbanize collective and private domains. The semi-public garden offers a means of integrating into the system of public spaces, such privatized spaces as foyers, lobbies and shopping centres. This is why Breeze of AIR also explored the meaning and form of a garden in the area of Rotterdam's forthcoming Central Station. An urban garden can make an key contribution to the station's status as a place to voluntarily or involuntarily spend time and as a component of public life in the city.

If we are to use the concept of the hortus conclusus to gain a new perspective on the city, then it is important to bear in mind the increase in scale, rise in mobility and globalization of culture. Alongside a reconsideration of the garden in the bustle of the compact city, Breeze of AIR looked at the meaning of the garden in the network city of limitless spaces. Nowadays, transport and communication networks constitute part of the untamed nature beyond the bounds of the enclosed garden. Again, amidst the whirl of the city, the enclosed garden – with its focus on deceleration and meditation – is an answer to the acceleration of networks and communication via these networks. The garden is then a hiatus in the network flows and so forms a counterpoint in the network city. Demarcating the hortus conclusus also presents the opportunity to make meaningful places of 'non-places' and undefined spaces [fig. 11, 12]. The concept of the enclosed garden can be applied as a form of opposition, a form of resistance against the forces of uniformity: the 'space of flows' (the world-encompassing space of rapid communication) of Manuel Castells.[12]

According to Castells, a 'space of places' develops in reaction to the 'space of flows', leading to a reassertion of the identity of localities. The principle of the urban garden can perhaps be used to isolate the 'space of flows' by making places with a clearly defined boundary and identity, in the 'green mush' of the post-war districts as well as at infrastructural hubs such as Central Station, and amidst the dynamic of visual culture, commerce, work and recreation, as for example with the Lijnbaan gardens and the rooftop of Las Palmas. If situated at mobility hubs or major attractions, the urban garden can facilitate new and interesting confrontations between the local and the global, between the world of repose and inertia on the one hand and the high-speed world on the other. By implanting the hortus conclusus in the network city, it is possible to create modern-day interpretations of the walled garden. The introduction of the urban garden, therefore, implies an investigation into the importance of form, programme and management when designing meaningful places at network city scale.

[12] Manuel Castells, *The Rise of the Network Society. The Information Age: Economy, Society and Culture, Volume 1* (Cambridge, Mass.: Blackwell, 1996).

[fig. 10]
Communal garden on Jacobusstraat in the city centre

[fig. 11]
Garden behind a noise baffle at a traffic intersection

[fig. 12]
Kitchen garden along the highway

ERIK DE JONG
Prelude to a new understanding of garden design

1

A discussion about the hortus conclusus is like an Erasmian colloquium: a discourse on the position and significance of garden and landscape architecture in our society. The hortus conclusus is nothing more nor less than a symbol for the commingling of nature and culture. It stands for seclusion as an essential space for life and experience. As a practical and philosophical premiss, the hortus conclusus represents the garden, the park and the landscape in its limited scope and, at the same time, the world that comes together and is revealed there.

2

Our culture in the Netherlands is pre-eminently an urban culture, and from that perspective the history of the city tends to be described from the larger scale of planning and at the smaller scale of street and building. Historians have found it difficult to see city and landscape as actors of equal worth, and also rarely notice how there have been attempts to give a place to landscape and nature as essential components of the urban fabric since the dawn of our urban planning tradition. For many, urban space is street and square rather than park or garden, and the discussion about public space more a question of art and 'cladding' than of the quality and artistic value of 'green' design. The recent discussion about the future of the urban park in the Netherlands reveals just how long this issue has been ignored. Creativity, newsworthiness and glamour are more readily associated with *grands projets,* which must be able to convey a generous dose of civic pride, transformation and renewal. Garden and park have long borne the stigma that they must be self-explanatory and unwaveringly propagate the immutable values of nature. That there is little expectation that a park or garden would be representative of artistic and/or historical values is evidenced by their minimal upkeep and maintenance: 'Nature speaks for itself.'

This is the price of a long modernist tradition in the historiography of architecture and urban planning: garden and landscape architecture – sibling art forms – are treated like orphans. Because it is taught almost nowhere, we seem to have forgotten how rich the Dutch tradition in garden and landscape architecture actually is, rooted in the medieval hortus conclusus and still evident in countless urban courtyards. It is a history which shows that since the end of the 16th century the Netherlands as regards garden and landscape design had belonged to the 'avant-garde', enjoying a modern and trend-setting position in Europe through a combination of engineering skill, horticulture and artistic design. To some degree, the dominant position occupied by urbanism and architecture in the modernist tradition still stands in the way of an interdisciplinary discourse, perhaps not so much in the design professions themselves but certainly outside them, say among municipal and provincial administrations, with a few exceptions.

3

The garden in the Netherlands had never before been the subject of such a wide-ranging project as Breeze of AIR: a veritable overture of ideas, observations and reflections. It demonstrated the vitality and richness of this theme: as a theme for artists and designers, as a crucial factor in the debate on public space, as a vital component in the discussion about the meaning and quality of urban life and an ecological and sustainable environment. But it also revealed at times a lack of ease, and deficiencies in conceptualization and execution, as if we today had lost our capacity to work with this theme. Furthermore, the hortus conclusus, which is so closely entwined with architecture and urban development, posed new questions about the social and anthropological significance of public space. We still know far too little about how it is used and perceived by different sections of the population, immigrant or indigenous, meaning that renovation, regeneration, redesign and new design can only roughly estimate either the historical significance or current and future needs. For those who are concerned with garden and landscape in a professional capacity (administrators, implementers, designers, academics) there are crucial research, management and design tasks in all these domains. The hortus conclusus could well become a linking element in the diffuse city, because it is where both private and public are brought out to full effect.

4

Unlike any other form of design, garden and landscape architecture are integral in character, naturally inclusive rather than exclusive. This does not merely apply on the scale of Rotterdam, but also on the larger scale of the Randstad conurbation. The discussion about the 'Green Heart' concerns the creation, or preservation, of an urban park landscape, a large-scale landscape reserve where design, ecology, water management and recreation should go hand-in-hand with the needs of the urban agglomeration. In that sense, spaces large and small are part of a general planning problem which must do its best to facilitate the symbiosis of nature, landscape and culture. The discourse on spatial design could find inspiration in the tradition of the hortus conclusus in the knowledge that borders are never far away here in the Netherlands, while at the same time the space is open, varied, international even.

5

Now the Netherlands may have a government architect, but it lacks a government landscape architect, never mind an 'urban green space task force', as in Britain, engaged with upholding the quality of garden, park and landscape. Perhaps it is a good thing that the landscape here is spared such governmental interference. This means, though, that the initiative to promote research, establish guidelines, spur discussion, defend the cultural values of garden and landscape design, and encourage and oversee the quality of decisions and their execution at all levels, must rest with others. There are opportunities to do this within the cultural planning strategy currently on the rise, providing that the design history of garden and landscape is considered a factor of importance that sits alongside architecture, archaeology and historical geography. After all, it will be a new generation of designers (architects, urbanists, garden and landscape architects) that will have to give form and content to the new tasks, and these possess practically no historical awareness of processes, meanings, lines of development, cohesion or objects. Garden, park and designed landscape will thus have to become part of a broadly defined cultural assignment in city and countryside.

The ambit of this task must be regarded as something much more comprehensive than design culture. Form and design need content, and most particularly use and experience. Garden, park and landscape define our sense of relaxation, freedom and individuality, and also our sense of involvement and tradition, perhaps to an even greater extent than does architecture. Garden and park are as much a component of social processes, of customs, expectations, ideals and projections, of narratives, experiences and identifications. For many of us, the garden, of which there are thousands alongside, behind or in front of houses, villas and other buildings across the Netherlands, is much more a process than an object: one is continually busy with it. Gardening is habitual action. And this garden culture, sitting astride the fence between public and private, between commerce and individuality, holds many lessons for the public domain, lessons about process, the state of incompleteness, about growth and change, participation and identification, about everyday activities and daydreams. The Netherlands could gain a new term comparable to 'urban gardening' in the United States. It speaks volumes that it is mainly private organizations and foundations that defend green space. For them the green space of the hortus conclusus is an everyday fact of great worth. 9000 visitors to an open gardens weekend is a good measure of that worth, and should also serve as a gauge for policy. One of the main achievements of Breeze of AIR has been to raise our awareness that the strategy with regard to the political discourse demands a great deal more attention from us.

6

This is why it is necessary for garden and park to be integrated in a comprehensive cultural policy: not merely a subdivision of the government's Nature and Environmental Services. The hortus conclusus teaches us that what counts is the symbiosis of nature and design, of landscape and culture. Why is there no ruling that would give investors the choice of assigning two per cent of construction costs to a garden (public or semi-public), a park or a patio? Why is it only art that enjoys this prerogative in public space? Why does the Dutch National Lottery sponsor ecological nature but not the regeneration of parks and gardens, as it does in the UK? How might architects be encouraged to design more inner spaces for new 'horti conclusi'? Can we devise ways to make garden maintenance part of the management of buildings?

7

The hortus conclusus straddles the borders of the private and public realms. It can be a back garden, or a park, a yard, a courtyard or pavement garden, a cul-de-sac, an urban watercourse, an allotment or roof terrace, a windowsill, a patio or conservatory, a garden within a garden of every possible size, shape and constitution. It can be applied to existing gardens and parks in need of a new approach in design, planting, layout, use. This demands a sensitivity that balances the historical with new possibilities. As a 'performing art', garden and park beg reinterpretation, but then proceeding from the existing material. This may lead to preservation of its current state, sometimes to renovation or to a complete 're-staging' of the place as such. But because of their variety of uses and the changes this brings about, garden and park can take the form of a subtle palimpsest, to be peeled back layer by layer before starting afresh, and that demands creativity, insight and originality.

New designs can embrace myriad possibilities: from complex to simple, from ambiguous to monotonous, from low to high maintenance, from natural to artificial. The hortus conclusus is both a *topographía* (an experience connected to time and place) and a *topothesía* (a place of imagination and memory). As always, simplicity is a virtue here too: then the hortus conclusus can be wholly and naturally present.

8

In all of this, considerations about maintenance and flexible management must be foremost in the minds of both client and designer: without a clear picture it is doomed to fail in the long term. A park and gardens policy must weigh up all these possibilities in terms of the desired gradients and variety, natural and cultural values and, on the larger scale of the urban landscape, diversity in use. Differentiation in design, use and management is imperative. Lightweight programmes ensure flexibility: existing parks and gardens often have to satisfy all too many requirements. The education and involvement of their users must be the cornerstones of this process. The Rotterdam urban planner Pieter Verhagen regarded the *volkstuin* or personal allotment as the prototype of garden culture: like the hortus conclusus it is private yet public, with freedom of enjoyment yet subject to rules, there you can be your own man and at the same time part of a social process.

The hortus conclusus, as the Breeze of AIR event demonstrated, is ready for a new lease of life: it can be opened in order to be closed, and closed in order to be opened. The designs by artists, architects, and garden and landscape architects presented a veritable powder keg of ideas. Alongside practical solutions for existing problems and sites, the material collected demonstrated the extent to which the hortus conclusus is a metaphor for desires, dreams and memories, for form, colour and poetry, for harmony between nature and culture. And even should the hortus not exist, it lives in our desires and we seek out a hortus of images and words.

That is why the hortus conclusus is indeed a performing art: along with activities such as visiting the theatre, listening to music, enjoying sports and dining in company, it constantly regenerates the sensibilities of users from different cultures and gives shape to their desires and habits. The hortus conclusus is not static but in flux, continually reinterpreting itself. Its power is that it can be experienced and used by different cultures in different ways. This requires a new approach in planning and management, at least if we want it to be a component of garden culture: the hortus conclusus can be a dynamic instrument in multicultural politics.

Breeze of AIR has taught us that the future of the hortus conclusus still requires the enlightened visions of patrons, private institutions, government agencies and individuals who couple a public garden culture with a high level of idealism. Above all, the hortus needs sponsors. There are enough designers and users who belie what in the 1930s was called 'the death of garden design'. The need for the hortus conclusus is more urgent than ever before, and not just in the Netherlands. The root of this desire may lie in our awareness of a new responsibility for how we must inhabit this earth, collectively and individually, in town and country. This utopian ideal, again, is an essential characteristic of the world of the hortus conclusus.

AIR - A BRIEF CHRONOLOGY

Architecture International Rotterdam (AIR) fuels the discourse on architectural and urbanistic developments in the contemporary city, communicates the perspectives of designers to administrators, clients and the public, and promotes quality in architecture and urban design. The AIR Foundation is critical and informative, engaging in verbal battle on the architectural, urbanistic and landscape-architectural fronts while striving to heighten public and professional interest in these disciplines.

1979: Keurmeestersproject

In 1979 the Architecture arm of the Rotterdam Arts Council took the initiative to organize an architectural-urbanistic festival whose theme was 'The image of the city'. This so-called Keurmeestersproject sought to establish a link with the international architectural discourse, and involved a number of leading spokespersons from the world of Dutch architecture. Three architectural critics – Stanislaus von Moos (Switzerland), Kenneth Frampton (USA) and Francisco Dal Co (Italy) – were invited to select from a shortlist of twenty Rotterdam buildings what they considered to be the three best and the three worst. Their findings were presented at a public debate.

1982: Kop van Zuid

Oswald Mathias Ungers (Germany), Josef Kleihues (Germany), Derek Walker (United Kingdom) and Aldo Rossi (Italy) were invited to submit designs for the port and industrial zones on the south bank of the River Maas, the so-called Kop van Zuid. They were also asked to examine the meaning of the area in the context of the city as a whole. This approach was imitated in urban design practice, which until then had usually failed to look beyond the project itself. This event was a trendsetter, calling as it did for the deliberate deployment of architecture's seductive qualities (image-making) to open up new perspectives and bring architecture to the attention of a wider public. The results as well as the public debate had an impact on the eventual plans for the area. Rotterdam dropped the original proposals to use this ground as an overspill area for surrounding urban renewal districts.

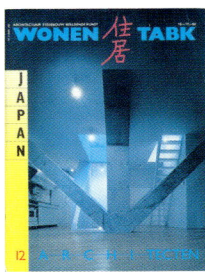

1984: Japan-AIR

This event saw the first presentation in the Netherlands of work by the likes of Arata Isozaki, Itsuko Hasegawa, Shoei Yoh and Toyo Ito. During the event, which included exhibitions, design workshops given by Japanese architects, publications and lectures, the City of Rotterdam made the former city library available to the State to accommodate the newly founded Netherlands Architecture Institute.

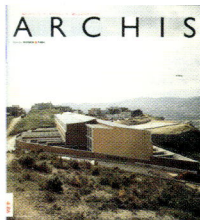

1986:
Iberia-AIR
This event introduced the Netherlands to the work of young Spanish architects who had been realizing innovative projects since the end of the Franco era. It included an exhibition, lectures and publications about built work by Jaume Bach and Gabriel Mora, José Rafael Moneo and Josep Mateo. The event stimulated debate on the quality of public space design in Rotterdam.

1988:
The Railway Tunnel Site: Nine Concepts
AIR invited a number of architects – Wiel Arets & Wim van den Bergh (the Netherlands), Peter Wilson (United Kingdom), Bernard Tschumi (Switzerland/USA), Joan Busquets (Spain), Henri Ciriani (France), Andreas Brandt (Germany), Cecil Balmond (United Kingdom), Rem Koolhaas/OMA (the Netherlands) and Pierluigi Nicolin (Italy) – to make designs for the rail-tunnel track that was to fall vacant in 1994. They were asked to comment on the cohesion of the city districts adjoining the three-kilometre-long ribbon extending from the city centre north of the river, across Noordereiland and Feijenoord to the so-called railway triangle in the south. The designs served as catalysts in the discussions about the masterplan for the area along Binnenrotte, the cross-river connections between north and south, and the railway lifting bridge 'de Hef', which was threatened with demolition at the time.

1988:
Three Squares: Six Designs
John Körmeling (the Netherlands) and Arduino Cantàfora (Italy), Hans Warnau (NL) and Helio Piñon/Albert Viaplana (Spain), and Paul Robbrecht/Hilde Daem (Belgium) and Jaume Bach/Gabriel Mora (Spain) were invited to enter competing designs for three urban squares, Eendrachtsplein, Zuidplein and Bospolderplein respectively.
The intention was to realize the winning designs by Körmeling, Piñon/Viaplana and Bach/Mora as examples of how to improve the spatial quality of public squares in the city, but this plan was ultimately abandoned.

1993,
AIR-Alexander: New Urban Frontiers
This event focused attention on the position and meaning of the post-war residential districts in the city of Rotterdam and the social and cultural changes taking place there. Designs for Alexanderpolder were commissioned from Rem Koolhaas/OMA (the Netherlands), Robert Geddes (USA), Manuel de Solà-Morales (Spain), Endry van Velzen (the Netherlands), Adriaan Geuze (the Netherlands) and Wolfgang Engel & Klaus Zillich (Germany).

The event illustrated the consequences of planning decisions for construction projects which straddle municipal borders, with a key role allotted to the medium-scale urban project. New concepts were introduced for the urbanization process in response to the creeping urban pollution of the Randstad's 'Green Heart'.

These insights were influenced by the national debate. In addition, the culture of the districts was brought into relationship with the inner city's cultural infrastructure. As an independent outsider, AIR triggered the discussion about the spatial development of Rotterdam and the region. On the basis of this discussion, designs were commissioned from architects, landscape architects and urban designers. The designs revealed the spatial potentials of these areas: the old docklands, the public realm, the city periphery. The adopted strategy proved applicable at the scale of city and region, and even provided insights that are useful on a national level. The event introduced new ways and forms of presenting urban designs, making them more insightful for policy-makers and the public. Since 1993 AIR has enjoyed an interdisciplinary approach. The exchange of perspectives and ideas between different art forms has given added depth to the designs. It has also interested a wider public in the components and eventual results of the event.

1998-1999:
AIR-Zuidwaarts/Southbound: New Landscape Frontiers

In 1998 the Rotterdam Arts Council established the AIR Foundation, an independent body, to initiate and organize the AIR events. The AIR Foundation's director is Anne-Mie Devolder.

AIR-Southbound was held from September 1998 to August 1999 at various locations in Rotterdam and on the isle of Hoeksche Waard to the south of the city. The theme was to design the southern flank of the Randstad urban agglomeration and the delta between Rotterdam and Antwerp. The event focused especially on Hoeksche Waard, a predominantly agricultural area where the pressure of urbanization is tangible. This island forms the link between the urbanized landscape of the island of IJsselmonde and the open landscape of Zeeland province with its wide expanses of water, panoramic polders and low horizons. The design research commissioned from artists, photographers, designers and scientists and the design brief within the framework of AIR-Zuidwaarts/Southbound, were prompted by the current debate on the steadily swelling city, the shrinking countryside and the radical changes in agriculture, recreation, nature conservation and water management, traffic and transport.
The urban designers and landscape architects who participated were: Frits Palmboom and Jaap van den Bout (the Netherlands) & Stefano Boeri (Italy); Dirk Sijmons and Yttje Feddes (the Netherlands) & Jörg Dettmar, Ulrike Beuter and Harald Fritz (Germany); Marieke Timmermans (the Netherlands) & François Roche (France); and Edzo Bindels, Henk Hartzema, Ruud Gietema and Arjan Klok (the Netherlands) & Peter Calthorpe, Matthew Taecker and David Katz (USA). These developed perspectives, concepts and strategies for planning the area between Rotterdam and Antwerp, the southern flank of the Randstad and the isle of Hoeksche Waard in particular. AIR-Zuidwaarts/Southbound provided a forum for research, design, debate and new concepts, focusing on a synthesis of new urban functions and the cultural-historical values and landscape qualities of rural areas. AIR-Southbound sought to inspire international solutions for the current city-countryside dilemma in Europe, solutions that would establish a new synthesis of urbanization, mobility, agriculture, nature conservation and water management.

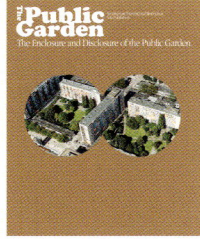

2001:
Breeze of AIR: Innovative Concepts for Urban Gardens in Rotterdam

Breeze of AIR explored the meaning of the hortus conclusus, the enclosed garden, for the modern city. The initial inspiration was the essay 'Hortus Conclusus', written by Adriaan van der Staay in the autumn of 1999. In it van der Staay describes how Erasmus viewed the enclosed garden as a place for finding the inner self and for contemplation. These values play an increasingly prominent role in contemporary urban development, which strives for more places of repose and nature within the urban vortex. AIR asked designers from Western and non-Western gardening traditions to create ground-breaking designs for public urban gardens for nine sites in Rotterdam. These sites and the invited designers were: Hofplein viaduct/Agniesebuurt – Gross.Max. (United Kingdom); Central Station area – Atelier Quadrat (the Netherlands); Arboretum Trompenburg – West 8 (the Netherlands); the Lijnbaanhoven – Hargreaves Associates (USA); Boijmans Van Beuningen Museum – Charles Correa (India); Museum Park/Het Park – Georges Descombes (Switzerland); Las Palmas – Kazuyo Sejima & Ryue Nishizawa (Japan); Valkeniersweide in Vreewijk – Kamel Louafi (Algeria); Spinoza park in Lombardijen – Piet Oudolf (the Netherlands). The Witte de With centre for contemporary art invited international artists to create works inspired by the Erasmian view of the hortus conclusus. The artists were: Maura Biava (the Netherlands/Italy), Anthony Dunne & Fiona Raby (United Kingdom), Elmgreen & Dragset (Denmark), Zeger Reyers (the Netherlands), Teresita Fernández (USA), Cristina Iglesias (Spain), Dennis Adams (USA) and Cildo Meireles (Brazil).

The Breeze of AIR exhibition and symposium was complemented by a whole range of activities open to the public including, for the first time, television programmes. The Breeze of AIR magazine provided information about the sites for the design proposals, a programme of events, walking tours, and a guide to the Weekends of Garden Design. Rotterdam galleries presented works by Dutch artists around the theme 'Hortus Ludi'. Breeze of AIR sought to inspire new ideas for the urban development of Rotterdam post 2001 in which public gardens can play a major role.

PERSONALIA

Dennis Adams (USA) is an artist living and working in New York. His work has been the subject of more than 40 solo exhibitions in museums, galleries and urban spaces in North America and Europe. In 1994 there were two separate retrospectives of his work: one in the Museum of Contemporary Art (MUHKA) in Antwerp, the other in the Contemporary Arts Museum in Houston. His work has been shown at such events as the Whitney Biennial 2000 and Panorama 2000 (Utrecht, the Netherlands). Alongside his work as a practising artist, Dennis Adams teaches art at various academies and is also the Director of the Visual Arts Program at the School of Architecture, Massachusetts Institute of Technology (MIT) in Cambridge, USA.

Maura Biava (Italy/the Netherlands) is an artist who lives and works in Rotterdam. In 1997 she completed her second-phase professional training at the State Academy of Fine Arts in Amsterdam. Elaborately detailed, fictitious female characters are a recurring theme in her interactive installations. Biava has had solo exhibitions in Galerien der Stadt Esslingen, Esslingen (2001), Stedelijk Museum Het Domein, Sittard (1999), Galerie Van Gelder, Amsterdam (1999) and Galleri Nicolaï Wallner, Copenhagen (1996). Her work has also been included in a number of group exhibitions, including 'Traces of Science in Art', Amsterdam (1998) and 'Chronos & Kairos', Museum Fridericianum, Kassel (1999).

Turgut Cansever (Turkey) is an architect. In 1951 he established his own practice in Istanbul. From 1957 to 1961 he was a consultant to the City of Istanbul. After a period working as an independent architect, he was appointed director of Istanbul Metropolitan Planning and continued to work in an advisory capacity for the City Council. In 1983 he became a consultant to the University of Mecca and won the prestigious Aga Khan Award for Architecture for a holiday village in Bodrum. At present he is examining ways of rehousing the inhabitants of Istanbul, as in the likely event of an earthquake half of that city's existing housing stock would probably be destroyed.

Charles Correa (India) is an architect. Since 1958 he has worked in private practice in Bombay. His work ranges from a commission for the Mahatma Gandhi Memorial at the Sabarmati Ashram to urban planning projects in Delhi, Bombay, Bangalore and other cities in India. Correa is a pioneer in the design of low-cost housing in developing countries.
A prolific writer on architecture, he also teaches at various universities in India, Europe and America. Correa has been awarded numerous prizes, including the Padma Shri from the President of India in 1972 and the Gold Medal of the International Union of Architects (UIA) in 1990.

Georges Descombes (Switzerland) is an architect and landscape architect. His designs focus on public space, and include a public park in Lancy, close to Geneva, as well as a square for the Westwijk residential complex in Amstelveen, the Netherlands. Descombes teaches at the Institute of Architecture and the University of Geneva, as well as in Versailles. From 1990 to 1995 he taught at the Berlage Institute in Amsterdam.

Anne-Mie Devolder (Belgium) trained as an architect and urban designer. After a period working as an urban designer for the City of Rotterdam, she programmed the architectural debate at the Rotterdam Arts Council. She also organized the following AIR events: the Railway Tunnel Site and Three Squares (1988), 'AIR-Alexander' (1993), 'AIR-Zuidwaarts/Southbound' (1998-1999) and 'Breeze of AIR' (2001). She has curated various exhibitions on architecture and urbanism. Devolder was also the initiator of Architecture Day (Dag van de Architectuur) and ArchiCenter Rotterdam. She has numerous publications to her name, particularly about architecture and urban design in Rotterdam. Since 1998 she has been the director of the AIR Foundation.

Anthony Dunne & Fiona Raby (UK) are partners in a design practice. In their work (a combination of designing and doing academic research) they explore the border area between industrial design, design and electronic media. They are attached to the Postgraduate Art & Design Department of the Royal College of Art in London as senior researchers. Recently they published **Design Noir. The Secret Life of Electronic Objects.**

Michael Elmgreen (Germany) & Ingar Dragset (Norway) live and work in Berlin where they have been an artist duo since 1995. They have a special interest in architectonic structures and in the planned and eventual functions of spaces. Their 'Powerless Structures' have been exhibited at various venues, including Portikus, 'Fig. 111', Frankfurt (2001); The Project, 'Figs. 57-60', New York (1999); Galleri Ingólfsstraeti & Reykjavik Art Museum, 'Fig. 45' (1998); and Gallery Campbells Occasionally, Copenhagen (1997). Their work has also featured at prestigious events, including the Istanbul Biennial (2001); Manifesta 3, Ljubljana (2000); 'What if...', Moderna Museet, Stockholm (2000); the Melbourne Biennial (1999); the Berlin Biennial (1998); and 'Junge Szene', Wiener Secession, Vienna (1998).

Tanja Elstgeest (the Netherlands) is an art historian. She is currently Assistant Curator at the Witte de With centre for contemporary art in Rotterdam. In 1997-1998 she followed the Curatorial Training Programme of De Appel Foundation, Amsterdam. She has previously worked for the International Association of Curators of Contemporary Art (IKT), and for De Appel Foundation in Amsterdam. Exhibitions she has helped organize include 'Seamless' in De Appel, Amsterdam (1998) and 'Wild Zone' in Witte de With, Rotterdam (2001).

Teresita Fernández (USA) is a New York-based artist. She has had solo exhibitions at, among other venues, Castello di Rivoli, Turin (2001); Site Santa Fe, Santa Fe (2000); Berkeley Art Museum, Berkeley (1999); Deitch Projects, New York (1996 and 1999); ArtPace, San Antonio, Texas (1999); and Masataka Hayakawa Gallery, Tokyo (1998 and 1999). Her work has also featured in many group exhibitions in Europe, America and Japan. In 1997 she was selected for the ARUCS project in Japan, and in 1998 she took part in the ArtPace International Artist-in-Residence Program, San Antonio, Texas.

Adriaan Geuze (the Netherlands) is a landscape architect. In 1987 he co-founded with Paul van Beek the Rotterdam-based firm of WEST 8 landscape architects & urban planners, where he is still director and principal designer. Over the years he has taught at numerous schools of architecture in Europe and the United States. He has also won various prizes, including the Dutch Maaskant Prize for Young Architects in 1995 and the Danish Green Pin in 2000.

Gross.Max. (UK) is a landscape architecture office based in Edinburgh. It was founded by Bridget Baines and the Dutchman Eelco Hooftman. The office's first project was a prize-winning design for two parks on Potsdamer Platz in Berlin, swiftly followed by a winning entry for the landscape masterplan for Expo 2000 in Hanover. Baines and Hooftman both lecture at the Edinburgh College of Art, and enjoy an international reputation as educators in the field of landscape architecture.

George Hargreaves (USA) is a landscape architect. His firm has two branches, one in San Francisco and one in Boston. His work acknowledges the fact that most landscapes are not natural, and designed and redesigned landscapes play a prominent role in his designs. Since 1986 Hargreaves has been teaching at Harvard University, where he is now a tenured professor of Landscape Architecture and chairman of the Department of Landscape Architecture. His recent important projects include event spaces for the Sydney Olympics 2000, Australia; Parque do Tejo e Trancao for Expo '98 in Lisbon, Portugal; and Guadalupe River Park in San Jose, California.

Cristina Iglesias (Spain) is an artist who lives and works in Madrid. Since 1983 she has been exhibiting her sculptural work in galleries, museums and public spaces. She has held solo exhibitions at venues that include the Carré d'Art, Musée d'Art Contemporain, Nîmes (2000); Guggenheim Museum, Bilbao (1998); Solomon R. Guggenheim Museum, New York (1997); Stedelijk Van Abbemuseum, Eindhoven (1994); Kunsthalle Bern (1991); and De Appel Foundation, Amsterdam (1990). More recently her work has been shown at 'Exposición Universal de Hannover 2000', Spanish Pavilion, Hanover (2000); 'Enclosed and Enchanted', Museum of Modern Art, Oxford (2000); and 'Año Mil. Año dos Mil. Dos milenios en la Historia de España', Centro cultural de la Villa, Madrid (2000).

Erik de Jong (the Netherlands) is an architectural historian. He works at the Vrije Universiteit in Amsterdam, where he is a specialist in the history of garden and landscape architecture. He gives lectures, works as a consultant and contributes to seminars in Europe and North America. In addition, he has organized various exhibitions about architecture, and garden and landscape architecture. De Jong is on the board of both the Clusius Foundation, Leiden and the Amsterdam Canal Gardens Foundation. He publishes regularly and is the editor of **Tuinkunst. Nederlands jaarboek voor Tuin- en Landschapsarchitectuur**, an annual publication on Dutch garden and landscape architecture.

Frank de Josselin de Jong (the Netherlands) is a landscape architect. He is primarily concerned with projects for urban areas. As senior landscape architect at the Kop van Zuid project office in Rotterdam he was responsible for the design of the outdoor area around the Entrepot building and Wilhelminaplein. He is currently working for H+N+S Landschapsarchitecten on projects for various sites for the government's VINEX housing programme. For the Leidsche Rijn site his designs include a 'Great Archaeology Park' and an avenue (Rijnkennemerlaan). In 2002 he took up the post of lecturer in landscape architecture for urban areas at the University of Wageningen.

Kamel Louafi (Germany/Algeria) is a landscape architect. In 1980 he moved to Berlin and studied landscape planning at the Technische Universität. In 1993, after a period fulfilling numerous freelance commissions, he set up his own practice in Berlin. He became well-known through his work on the Gärten im Wandel and the Parc Agricole for Expo 2000 in Hanover, where he was responsible for the design, planning, development and construction.

Eric Luiten (the Netherlands) is a landscape architect. After a number of years running a practice in Barcelona he is now primarily active in the Netherlands. Luiten publishes regularly in professional journals and is, among other things, consultant to the state and locals councils on issues of regional planning and the restructuring of parks and landscape. He is also education coordinator for the Landscape Department of the Academy of Architecture in Amsterdam.

Cildo Meireles (Brazil) is an artist based in Rio de Janeiro, Brazil. Since 1967 he has given solo exhibitions all around the world, including a number of prestigious retrospectives in São Paulo and Rio de Janeiro (2000); New Museum, New York (1999); Institute of Contemporary Art, Boston (1997); Museo de Arte do Porto, Portugal (1996); and the IVAM Centre de Carme, Valencia, Spain (1995). His work has also been presented at solo exhibitions in Galerie Lelong, New York (1999), Kiasma, Helsinki (1999), Galeria Luisa Strina, São Paulo (1998) and Centre d'art Contemporain, Thiers (1996). It was also included in Documenta IX at Kassel in 1992 and at the Korea Biennial in 2000. Another version of the work **Two Trees,** included in **Breeze of AIR/Hortus Conclusus,** was installed in the Laumeirer Sculpture Park, Saint Louis, USA, in 1995.

Ivan Nio (the Netherlands) is a social geographer. Since 1999 he has worked as an independent researcher at the cutting edge of planning/urban design and socio-cultural developments. He teaches urban sociology at the Academy of Architecture, Rotterdam, and is editor of the periodical **Stedebouw & Ruimtelijke Ordening** (Urbanism and Spatial Planning). Nio's books include **Buitenwijk. Stedelijkheid op afstand** (Suburbia. Urbanity at arm's length) co-written with Arnold Reijndorp (1998), and **De Strook. Ruimtelijke ordening in een cultuur van pluralisme** (The Strip. Spatial planning in a culture of pluralism), published in association with H+N+S Landschapsarchitecten and MUST (2001).

Piet Oudolf (the Netherlands) is a garden designer. His distinctive designs, for clients in and out of the Netherlands, are both capricious and monumental, and are particularly noteworthy for the plants he uses. He only uses plants from his own nursery, which he and his wife Anja have been cultivating in Hummelo since 1981. In May 2000 he won a Gold Medal at Chelsea, London, with the garden he designed together with Arne Maynard. Oudolf has co-authored a number of garden books, including the recently published **Méér droomplanten** (More dream plants) co-written with Henk Gerritsen, and **Ontwerpen met Planten** (Designing with plants) co-written with Noël Kingsburg.

Quadrat, studio for urban design, landscape and architecture (the Netherlands) was established in Rotterdam in 1992 by landscape architect Paul Achterberg and the urban designers/architects Roy Bijhouwer and Stefan Gall. The studio becomes involved in planning processes in a variety of ways: sometimes briefly, for example in the form of commissioned studies, workshops or consultancy work, and sometimes for the longer term, as the creators of site layout plans, as project managers or as supervisors. They always closely integrate the disciplines of urban design, landscape and architecture. Quadrat's key strategy is to design the public space in close connection with the architecture, as exemplified by the studio's plans for the new centre of Amstelveen, and the Veldhuizen housing development in Vleuten-De Meern.

Zeger Reyers (the Netherlands) is a visual artist who is fascinated by overgrowth, accumulation and bricolage. Soon after completing his studies at the Art Academy in Rotterdam (1990-1995), he created **De Aardappeleters** ('The Potato Eaters', 1995) and **Goede Voornemens** ('Good Intentions', 1997). In the first work, he poured out 300 kilos of paprika-flavoured crisps on a simple dining table; in the latter, it was an enormous mountain of crockery. Since then he has primarily focused his attention on organic materials (mushrooms and mosses). Some of the exhibitions in which he has participated are: 'WSSOHTE', TENT, Rotterdam/Galleri F15, Moss (Norway) (2001); Begane Grond, Utrecht (2001); 'Kamerschatten', 's-Hertogenbosch (1999); 'Terugblik', Kunsthal, Rotterdam (1999); Living Art Museum, Reykjavik (1999); 'Boven de Bank', Archipel, Apeldoorn (1999).

Kazuyo Sejima (Japan) is an architect. After completing her studies at the Japan Women's University in 1981 she worked at Toyo Ito's office. In 1987 she set up her own practice, Kazuyo Sejima & Associates. Her work has won various prizes in the fields of industrial and domestic design. Since 1995 she has worked together with Ryue Nishizawa on many projects under the name SANAA Sejima teaches at the Japan Women's University and at the Technical Institute in Tokyo.

Adriaan van der Staay (the Netherlands) is a sociologist. From 1968 to 1979 he was the director of the Rotterdam Arts Council. He then became director of the Social and Cultural Planning Office (SCP), a post he occupied until 1998. Van der Staay still holds a range of executive positions in the cultural sector, including vice-chairman of the Prince Claus Fund, chairman of Witte de With centre for contemporary art, Rotterdam, and chairman of the AIR Foundation. He has in addition written numerous publications on cultural politics. He is also Professor of Cultural Politics and Cultural Criticism at Rotterdam's Erasmus University.

Marc Treib (USA) is a Professor in Architecture, at both the University of Berkeley and the University of Florida. He is also the author, co-author or editor-in-chief of various publications, including **Space Calculated in Seconds: The Philips Pavilion, An Everyday Modernism: The Houses of William Wurster** and **Regional Garden Design in the United States.** Treib has received various honours, including the Best Exhibition Publication Award.

Ken Worpole (UK) is an influential author on urban and social policy in Britain. He contributes to various newspapers, including **The Guardian** and **The Independent.** The author of many books, his latest publication is **Here Comes the Sun: Architecture and Public Space in 20th Century European Culture.** He is particularly interested in the quality of contemporary urban life, new forms of civil society, planning and urban landscapes, and institutions that support a more celebratory form of democracy. In 1999 he was awarded an honorary doctorate by Middlesex University.

CREDITS

EDITOR
Anne-Mie Devolder
with thanks to Nicolette Enke,
Willemien Ippel, Chantal van der Zijl

COPY EDITOR
John Kirkpatrick

TRANSLATIONS
Robyn de Jong-Dalziel (Hortus Conclusus: the law of the garden), Victor Joseph (Four Shades of Green), Andrew May (all other translations)

DESIGN
Studio SD, Rotterdam

PRODUCTION
Véronique Patteeuw

LITHOGRAPHY AND PRINTING
Drukkerij Die Keure, Bruges, Belgium

PUBLISHER
Simon Franke

© NAi Publishers, Rotterdam, 2002
© AIR Foundation, Rotterdam, 2002
© the authors, the photographers, the artists, the architects

All rights reserved.
No part of this publication may be reproduced, stored in a retrieval system, or transmitted in any form or by any means, electronic, mechanical, photocopying, recording or otherwise, without the prior written permission of the publisher.

For works of visual artists affiliated with a CISAC-organization the copyrights have been settled with Beeldrecht in Amsterdam. © 2002, c/o Beeldrecht Amsterdam

It was not possible to find all the copyright holders of the illustrations used. Interested parties are requested to contact NAi Publishers, Mauritsweg 23, 3012 JR Rotterdam, The Netherlands.

This publication has been made possible through the generous support of: Gemeente Rotterdam, Ministerie VROM, Ministerie van BUZA and OC&W (HGIS-cultuurmiddelen), Netherlands Funds for Architecture, Stichting ter bevordering van Volkskracht.

Available in North, South and Central America through D.A.P./Distributed Art Publishers Inc, 155 Sixth Avenue 2nd Floor, New York, NY 10013-1507, Tel. 212 6271999, Fax 212 6279484.

Available in the United Kingdom and Ireland through Art Data, 12 Bell Industrial Estate, 50 Cunnington Street, London W4 5HB, Tel. 0208 7471061, Fax. 0208 7422319.

NAi Publishers is an internationally orientated publisher specialized in developing, producing and distributing books on architecture, visual arts and related disciplines.

www.naipublishers.nl
www.archined.nl/AIR

Printed and bound in Belgium
ISBN 90-5662-255-2

IMAGE CREDITS

Breeze of AIR: Innovative concepts for urban gardens in Rotterdam, Anne-Mie Devolder
figs 1, 2, 3, 4, 5, 6, 7, 8, 9, 10, 19, 20, 21, 22, 23 collectie stichting AIR;
figs 11, 12 Bob Goedewagen;
figs 13, 14, 24, 25, 26, 27, 28, 29, 30, 31, 32, 33 Hans Tak;
figs 16, 17, 18 Roy Bijhouwer

The Enclosed Garden, Adriaan van der Staay
figs 1, 2, 3, 8 Wengel, l'Art des Jardins, edition Leipzig;
fig. 4 Daniels, Humphry Repton, Yale University Press New Haven and London;
fig. 5 Van Rooijen, De groene stad, 's-Gravenhage;
figs 9, 17 Geoffey and Susan Jellicoe, The Landscape of Man, Thames and Hudson;
fig. 15 Oud Hollandsche Tuinen, 's Gravenhage;
fig. 14 Fariello, Architettura dei giardini, Roma;
figs 7, 16 Hattstein & Delius, Islam, Kunst en architectuur, Könemann;
figs 7, 16; 19, 22, 23 Bob Goedewagen;
figs 10, 12, 13 Anne-Mie Devolder

Hortus Conclusus: the law of the garden, Erik de Jong
fig. 1 Openbare Bibliotheek Haarlem;
fig. 3 Utrecht, Catharijneconvent;
fig. 4 D.Hennebo, Gärten des Mittelalters, Munich and Zürich, 1989;
fig. 5 Rotterdam, Stichting Atlas van Stolk;
fig. 6 UB Amsterdam;
fig. 7 Dumbarton Oaks Research Library and Collection, Trustees for Harvard University, Washington D.C.;
fig. 8 Amsterdam, Rijksmuseum Rijksprentenkabinet;
fig. 9 Udo Weilacher, Between Landscape Architecture and Land Art, Basle, Berlin, London, 1996;
figs 10, 11 Terence Conran and Dan Pearson, The Essential Garden Book. Getting back to basics, New York, Three Rivers Press, 1998; fig. 12 D. Imbert, The Modernist Garden in France, New Haven, London, 1993;
fig. 13 Sven-Ingvar Anderson and Steen Høyer, C.Th. Sørensen - en havekunstner, Arkitektens Forlag 1993;
fig. 15 Gemeente Archief, Amsterdam;
fig. 18 Gemeente Archief Leiden;
fig. 20 Tuinen in Detentie 1993-96. Tuin- en landschapsontwerpen bij penentiaire inrichtingen, 's-Gravenhage, VROM;
fig. 21 Den Bosch, Bureau Buys & Van der Vliet Landschapsarchitecten;
fig. 26 Michael Jacobs, Francesco Hernandez, Alhambra, New York 2000;
fig. 31 Washington, Arthur Sackler Gallery;
fig. 32 Catherine Benoît, Corps, Jardins, Mémoires. Anthropologie du corps et de l'espace à la Guadeloupe Paris, CNRS Editions/Editions de la Maison des Sciences de l'Homme, 2000;
figs 33, 34 Richard Westmacott, African-American Gardens and Yards in the Rural South, Knoxville, The University of Tennessee Press, 1998;
figs 35, 36, 37 Maggie Keswick, The Chinese Garden. History, Art & Architecture, London, Academy Editions, 1980;
figs 2, 14, 19, 21, 22, 25, 27, 28, 29 Erik de Jong;
figs 15, 16 Pandion;
fig. 23 Walter Herfst;
fig. 24 Tamar de Kemp

Weak Boundaries, Ivan Nio
all photos: Ivan Nio and Marloes Wevers

Four Shades of Green, Eric Luiten and Frank de Josselin de Jong
all photos: Eric Luiten

Nature, Art and the City, Tanja Elstgeest
figs 1, 2 Stichting AIR;
figs 3, 5, 6, 8, 10, 11, 13 Bob Goedewagen;
fig. 4 Roy Bijhouwer;
figs 7, 9, 12 Hans Tak

Park, Garden, Rotterdam, Marc Treib
all photos: Marc Treib

Afterthoughts from Istanbul, Turgut Cansever
all photos: collection Stichting AIR

Urban Parks in Europe: topology and geometry, economics and aesthetics, Ken Worpole
figs 3, 6 Walter Herfst;
figs 1, 2, 4, 7 Ken Worpole

The Urban Garden as Public Space, Ivan Nio
figs 1, 2, 3, 4, 5, 6 Ivan Nio and Marloes Wevers;
figs 7, 8, 9 Rob Ponsen;
fig. 10 Annet Delgaauw;
figs 11, 12 Walter Herfst

AIR - A Brief Chronology
all photos: collection Stichting AIR